'This book brings a broader and deeper understanding of the psychological, philosophical and spiritual aspects of Charles Berner's work and is a significant contribution to the further development of practice and for the professional recognition of Mind Clearing. I give my compliments to and have full respect for Alice's work.'

– Desimir D. Ivanović, 'Dijada' Clearing Training Center, Belgrade, Serbia, Former President of the Training Standard Committee of the European Clearing Association

'Alice's ambitious undertaking in her book *Mind Clearing* has clearly made the complex simple. Writing with insight and eloquence, she has successfully integrated the intentions of both Berner's and Noyes' lives' work. She sets the stage for clarity and transformation to free the minds who read this book.'

– Meranda Squires, Mind Clearer trained by Lawrence Noyes

MIND CLEARING

The Key to Mindfulness Mastery

ALICE WHIELDON

FOREWORD BY LAWRENCE NOYES

Jessica Kingsley *Publishers*
London and Philadelphia

First published in 2016
by Jessica Kingsley Publishers
73 Collier Street
London N1 9BE, UK
and
400 Market Street, Suite 400
Philadelphia, PA 19106, USA

www.jkp.com

Library of Congress Cataloging in Publication Data
Whieldon, Alice, author.
  Mind clearing : the key to mindfulness mastery / Alice
Whieldon ; foreword by Lawrence Noyes.
    pages cm
  Includes bibliographical references and index.
  ISBN 978-1-84905-307-5 (alk. paper)
  1. Meditation--Therapeutic use. 2. Mindfulness
(Psychology) 3. Mental health. I. Title.
  RC489.M43W495 2016
  615.8'52--dc23
                    2015023483

British Library Cataloguing in Publication Data
A CIP catalogue record for this book is available from the British Library.

ISBN 978 1 84905 307 5
eISBN 978 0 85700 637 0

Printed and bound in Great Britain

For Tom

CONTENTS

FOREWORD

For many years I have wanted to see a book about Mind Clearing come out, so I am delighted to write this foreword. Mind Clearing, informally called 'Clearing', was developed in the late 1960s by an American named Charles Berner. He drew from the work of a lot of people before him and added his own insights, which give it something special. I first heard about it in 1975 when I met Charles. To this day it is one of the truest, most honorable methods I have found for helping regular, modern people get free from mental suffering and have their lives go better. I devoted a good portion of my working life to training Clearers for this reason.

Mind Clearing is not magic, a quick fix or something that is done to you. It is not based on moving ideas around in the mind or looking at things more positively. Clearing is based on fulfilled relating. You work together with a Clearer in one-to-one sessions, in person or over the Internet. Using processes refined over decades, the two of you set out to find and clear the problem areas in your life that have been darkened by mix-ups in relating.

Clearing rests on old and new discoveries of what clears the mind of its upsets, depressions, fears, guilt and negative attitudes. A good Clearing session brings you home to who you really are and to a place of choice and self-responsibility. From this place, you can really live.

For those in the helping fields, Clearing adds something completely new to the methods that are popular now and enjoy some measure of success, such as coaching, cognitive therapy, and mindfulness training. Many aspects of Clearing are compatible with these approaches and deepen their effectiveness. I am convinced by what I have seen over the years that Clearing offers whole new levels of understanding and methodology for anyone working in any of the helping professions.

These assertions will take some explaining. Alice Whieldon has done a heroic job of it in this first book on Mind Clearing written for the public. Of course, the real power of Mind Clearing lies in the sessions themselves. From the pages of this book you will be able to see if you would like to try Clearing sessions. In the meantime, you have in your hands the place to start in learning how the mind's torments can be cleared at their source.

Lawrence Noyes
Palm Beach Gardens, Florida
May 2015

ACKNOWLEDGEMENTS

Particular and extraordinary thanks to Lawrence Noyes. Without him this book would not have been possible. He has continued to bring the work of Charles Berner to the world with clarity and compassion. He generously gave his time and several workshops to help with this project. He did not flinch when I, a virtual stranger at the time, announced I was going to write a book about Berner's life's work.

Thanks to Tony and Jean who have supported and helped me with steadiness and generosity. Tony, my father, is a Mind Clearing practitioner of many years standing. Through numerous exchanges, he has helped me develop my understanding of the work, pulled me up where I got things wrong, pointed out inconsistencies and repetitions and given me huge moral support at all stages. Jean has always been there; *really* there.

Thanks to Tom who put up with my bad moods when the writing did not go well and offered me the wealth of his experience in writing and thinking and, moreover, fed me. Thanks to all my other friends and family, particularly Jane, Bernard, Sooty, Tina, Frankie, Stevie, Dominique and Tara. Thanks also to my clients and students who have asked me difficult questions and stayed enthusiastic and not seemed to mind or notice my own struggles to understand and explain. Finally, thanks to Juanita and Charlee.

Will not a tiny speck very close to our vision blot out the glory of the world, and leave only a margin by which we see the blot? I know no speck so troublesome as self.[1]

GEORGE ELLIOT

The mind is a papier-mâché dragon that appears to be terrifying but is actually nothing at all. It's a fake. It ought to be ashamed of itself for acting like that. It's really a whimpering little thing that tries to act big in order to survive. But most people are convinced that this papier-mâché dragon is a firebreathing monster that is going to annihilate them at any second.[2]

CHARLES BERNER

INTRODUCTION

All of us have mind chatter. All of us suffer, to some extent, from ideas that get in the way of fulfilled relating. All of us resort at times to behaviour patterns, mostly learned in childhood, that disrupt easy contact with others. We want to find meaning and peace and stability, but as long as we search for them in the over-stuffed maelstrom of our thoughts and ideas, we will find only unreliable substitutes for real satisfaction. This is the human condition; life, as the Buddha said, is defined by suffering.[1]

Many people, over millennia, have tried to find ways to cure us of this condition. Some methods work for some people, some of the time. Mind Clearing offers a fresh perspective and approach for the times in which we live. A counselling-style practice, it aims to reduce the suffering caused by mental, emotional, relationship and spiritual distress. It is based on the *observation that most inner conflicts and states of unhappiness come about as a result of unexpressed communications*.[2]

In the model presented here, the *mind* of Mind Clearing is the sum total of those things unsaid. It is the outer layer of the human condition; the ideas or meaning aspect of it. Dealing with our minds is vital if we wish to improve our health and happiness at a fundamental level.

Mind Clearing builds on the vital work being done with mindfulness and takes it to the next step. It brings together the techniques of mindfulness that teach a new way of being with the insight that further progress requires more concerted help to dissolve the stuff of mind. It takes apart what material help and progress actually are and puts this into a one-to-one approach with mindfulness in a powerful dynamic. It completes the mindfulness project by giving it both a solid theoretical model with which it can progress on its own terms as well as techniques that pinpoint the key elements of help in the moment.

Defining the word 'mind' for the purposes of Mind Clearing might be confusing at the start. In common usage, we use *mind* to mean lots of different things. We tend to think that we *are*, in some crucial way, our minds. Consequently we might be uncomfortable at any suggestion that we would be better off without a mind. Even if we are prepared to countenance that possibility, perhaps through insights gained in mindfulness meditation, we almost certainly view the mind as linked to our capacity to think and operate in the world. So the desirability, as suggested in this book, of having less or even *no* mind may sound like encouraging people to be zombies.

But that is not how the situation is understood here. Mind Clearing rests on a very particular definition of the mind as fundamentally a problem. This problem is not like having a broken leg that will be fine once healed. The very existence of mind is a mistake and the mind itself inherently troublesome. Certainly it can be made somewhat neater and more efficient, but it cannot be fixed.

If we wish to make progress along the path that mindfulness and other methods of self-examination start us on, then our first task is to deal with the mind. It is the gatekeeper to becoming more ourselves. To a small extent that means improving the organisation of the mind, but finally it means going beyond our need for it altogether.

Mind Clearing is a very good tool for doing this. It literally clears the mind away through helping us raise our ability at communicating with others. As we get better at communicating how things are for us, this in turn reduces the actual quantity and complexity of unhelpful ideas we have put between us and others that prevent us from relating easily and well. It is based on the insight that our most basic drive and purpose in life is to connect with each other; so the better we are at this, the more fulfilled we become and the less we need substitutes.

The better we are at relating, the clearer we also become in ourselves about who we actually are and what we want. The better we become at presenting who we are and what we want, so the clearer about life we become and the more likely we are to live in harmony with who we are; this includes our relationships, which will be deeper and more real.

Charles Berner (1927–2007), the founder of Mind Clearing, was always interested in what progress looked like and spent his life in pursuit of that understanding. As he worked on the project that became Mind Clearing, he gained an increasingly clear appreciation of what we are up against; the situation is both better and worse than most of us suppose. It is worse because we are in more of a mess with our minds than we suppose; it is better because we can do something about it, at its very root. As he developed his work, Berner put together a map that explains how the mind operates and why it is a problem. This book explores that map and the conclusions Berner drew about what real help and progress look like and how to achieve them in practical ways.

Intended audience for this book

Mind Clearing offers a fresh perspective for practitioners in the field of mental and physical health. In addition, for those interested in self-help, Mind Clearing offers insight into the nature of our minds and in how to address its problems.

Description of the content

Part I of this book, 'Background', comprises two chapters. Chapter 1 ('The Search for a Resolution to Human Suffering') traces Berner's journey from New Age seeker to a teacher in the Indian traditions. It maps out his work through Mind Clearing to Surrender Meditation with Swami Kripalu. It introduces Lawrence Noyes as Berner's student, and latterly the architect of Mind Clearing in its current and comprehensive form. Chapter 2 ('Berner's Formula for Change') outlines the keys to help that Berner identified. It looks at his development of the Mind Clearing model and the formula he crafted for helping people dissolve the mind through communication work.

Part II, 'The Mind', also contains two chapters. Chapter 3 ('The Problem That Is the Mind') discusses how the mind can seem like an overwhelming mass, whereas in fact it has a clear beginning and can have a clear end. This chapter looks at how the mind comes into being and why. Chapter 4 ('The Structure and Content of the Mind') builds on the previous chapter: this section maps the mind from its less fixed outer layers through ever more fixed layers to the core. It discusses how we can deal with these layers in practical terms.

Part III, 'Dealing with the Mind: Mind Clearing', contains seven chapters. Chapter 5 ('Why We Must Do Something About the Mind') discusses taking control of the mind and how reducing its influence is not only a recipe for greater happiness and fulfilment for ourselves, it is a moral imperative. Chapter 6 ('The Clearing Communication Cycle') deals with the practical matter of how we can dissolve the mind. It gives an account of the principles of Mind Clearing and how the mind is dealt with through a gain in the ability to communicate directly through clearing communication cycles. Chapter 7 ('Working with Attitudes') discusses how the fixed attitudes that make up the mind are distorted communications. This part of the book discusses the Mind Clearing formula for working with people in dealing directly with fixed attitudes through focusing on what people are really saying in distorted ways and helping them communicate more directly. Chapter 8 ('Guilt and Karma') examines the common stumbling block of guilt along with how to help people release themselves from it and progress. Chapter 9 ('Dos and Don'ts of Mind Clearing') covers a few things to always do and never do in sessions. Chapter 10 ('The Mind Clearing Project') gives a brief overview of Mind Clearing results and training. It briefly introduces some of the other methods Berner developed for dealing with the body emotions and for deeper spiritual progress. It also looks at how we can work on do-it-yourself projects using Mind Clearing principles. Chapter 11 ('Mind Clearing and Mindfulness') discusses how Mind Clearing is the next step in the mindfulness revolution that has taken the world of health, well-being and personal development by storm since the start of the new millennium. Mind Clearing is mindfulness mastery; taking the practice into the dynamic of one-to-one relating, it marries the insight that help happens within the therapeutic relationship with the practice of being in the moment. Chapter 11 looks at mindfulness training as an important development within psychological health and well-being and how Mind Clearing brings it more usefully into one-to-one help with a confluent theoretical model and concrete techniques.

Part I
BACKGROUND

1
THE SEARCH FOR A RESOLUTION TO HUMAN SUFFERING

Charles Berner (1929-2007)

Charles Berner was born and raised in California, USA, and like many people of his generation became interested and involved in mysticism, esotericism and psychotherapy as a young man. It was an interest that blossomed into a lifelong mission. Fired by a desire to master for himself the mind and emotions and reach the highest levels of understanding, he studied under many teachers and read voraciously with the intention of personally experiencing the truths about which he read.

Alongside his passion for self-understanding, Berner worked to translate what he learned into practical processes others could benefit from and developed stepped methods for dealing with the mind, emotions, body and spiritual problems. He broke these aspects of the person down into components and into a map that could explain the whole.

In many respects, his body of work is a quintessential product of the USA of the mid-twentieth century, being a quilt composed of pieces valued for utility over provenance. It was a time and place bursting with new ideas and techniques. Religious movements and therapeutic methods, and combinations of the two, were springing up like mushrooms around every corner, both inside and outside of the more established health industries.

The psychological health industry, during the late 1950s to early 1970s, saw rapid growth, initially to meet the needs shown up by universal conscription and made worse by war on a huge scale. Many of the therapeutic systems current today came out of methods developed at the time, such as humanistic psychotherapy, behaviourism, cognitive therapy and developments of psychoanalysis.[1] The advances in this industry were matched by huge social change; also, in many ways, they were by-products of international conflict and the concomitant growth in the economy.

For the first time, ordinary people had appreciable leisure time and more disposable income. It was this very boom and consumerism that allowed for the exploration of psychological ideas and practices on a mass scale. Those who identified with the counterculture[2] questioned the goals of the mainstream and looked for deeper meaning. At the same time they tended to leave unquestioned the assumptions of that culture which promoted growth and gain as unquestionably good, and applied them vigorously to self-exploration and psychological health.[3]

Berner's quest, like that of so many around him, was fixed just as much on this world as the numinous.[4] Self-help and therapy developed in line with the zeitgeist, away from exploration and education for its own sake towards methods that could be commodified for the customer and which offered measurable gain. Berner trod a fine line between this industrial, medicalised approach to health and his more metaphysical interests.

None of this mid-century change came out of a void, however. Since at least as early as the mid-nineteenth century, Eastern religions had been embraced and plundered for their powerful practices. Home-grown movements, such as mind-cure, American Harmonial Religion[5] and methods based on Mesmerism,[6] drew on these and developed hybrid beliefs and approaches of their own. By the 1950s, these were considered outmoded. Yet some of the less prosaic ways of thinking they espoused, such as a mind/body approach to health and positive thinking, were firmly entrenched in the public imagination and had found their way into some of the more respectable and mainstream psychological health professions. This was not least because they had proved so popular with the general public. Movements such as the short-lived but influential Emmanuel Movement had taught the medical profession that it could ill afford to ignore the psyche as an important aspect of the health of the nation.[7]

The medical profession, recognising an important market and role for itself had, since the first decade of the twentieth century, been seeking ways to bring mental health care exclusively into its orbit. The Second World War acted as a catalyst for rapid expansion and professionalisation.

Berner was in the eye of this storm, barely distinguishable from his cultural landscape and yet also dedicated to a rigorously contemplative approach. A non-professional in a rapidly self-regulating industry, he remained outside the professions that were now under pressure to define their methods and training to serve a sudden recognition of the need for expansion and funding.

He was also starting to do something a little different from most classic psychotherapeutic approaches in reconceptualising what the person and personal progress actually are. In making an explicit distinction between the mind and the essential individual, as Eastern philosophies do, he was taking a step away from the medical model of health and, especially, the somatic or material explanation for all ailments, including those of the mind.

This is not entirely foreign to psychotherapy; for instance, the work of Roberto Assagioli and psychosynthesis and some transpersonal psychotherapies drew similar distinctions. But whether it was his philosophical model or a natural inclination to remain on the fringes, he neither sought nor was given formal recognition for his work, except from individual therapists who worked with him over the years. But his interests were also not confined to establishing one method of working towards psychological health. That was only part of a whole system of understanding. He may have been influenced in this through his early contact with the Church of Scientology.

Among the many teachers he came across in his years of exploration was the eccentric founder of Scientology, L. Ron Hubbard (1911–1986). These days, even the name signals to many people a dangerous cult to be avoided. But this was not yet the case when the young Charles Berner came across Dianetics, the forerunner of what became Scientology, although Hubbard was already a controversial figure who had, even by then, alienated many of his early followers and brought scorn upon himself from many, though not all, in the psychological health industry.

Hubbard is rarely described in neutral terms. He was loved, loathed, dismissed and admired in turn by people who came into contact with him. *Dianetics: The Modern Science of Mental Health*[8] was first published in 1948 to extraordinary success and rapidly spawned an international movement of group and partnered self-help that has had an influence on some more mainstream approaches over the years. The book seems to owe more to Hubbard's experience as a writer of science fiction than to psychology. But flawed as he and his work undoubtedly were, he, like Berner, was a sponge for all modern America had to offer and, whatever the professionals thought, put together a mind/body/spirit method of help that appealed to millions, and even, at the start, to some medics and psychotherapists.[9]

Many of the accounts of people who have left the movement and subsequently been highly critical of it and its leaders often also credit some of the psychotherapy-style work[10] they experienced within it as having been beneficial.[11] In some of its key elements, the early psychological work developed by Hubbard had its roots in Freudian theory and the work of Korzybski in particular.[12] The florid language and bold claims obscure some fairly well-established theories and methods.

The movement was also good at recognising a useful member when it saw one and, in Berner, found a young man willing and able to work on the in-house psychotherapy project and an able leader. He, in turn, found Scientology an interesting and supportive environment for addressing his own questions about life and meaning.

Though he spent about 10 years in the organisation, the differences between its approach and his own finally became too great to sustain. As Scientology sought to control its members more and more strictly, and lay down officially sanctioned methods and beliefs, Berner was in an increasingly untenable position. In contrast to Hubbard's emphasis on survival as the primary human drive, his own experiences and research drew him more and more into the belief that our fundamental purpose in life is to connect and communicate with one another.

Berner was asked to leave the organisation in 1965 when he fell out of favour with the movement's hierarchy. But rather than seeing this as a setback, he forged ahead on his own, released to pursue new lines of thought from which came the Enlightenment Intensive workshops, Mind Clearing, Emotion Clearing and, after a few years, Surrender Meditation through his Indian teacher, Swami Kripalvananda (1913–1981), or Kripalu as he was generally known.

The Indian connection

In 1974, like so many of his generation, Berner made the journey to India in search of a teacher he could commit to, recognising a need in himself for guidance. Going on the usual hot and dusty circuit of gurus along with hundreds of other hippie seekers, he finally found that for which he was searching. Accounts of this meeting suggest Berner was somewhat surprised to have found a teacher of great enough wisdom to satisfy him and to whom he could submit. But as he heard what Swami Kripalu was saying in his dharma[13] session, he described an experience of his heart expanding and opening and tears streaming down his cheeks. From that point on he dedicated himself to learning at the feet of this humble teacher in the Kundalini Yoga tradition.[14]

As a result of this Indian connection,[15] his work shifted. Although the techniques he had used and taught remained much the same, their philosophical underpinning gained the sharper focus and the direction we now see in it. Mind Clearing, already basically in line with Indian philosophy, was reorientated in step with Swami Kripalu's teaching and also Patanjali's famous *Yoga Sutras*.[16] It is to that tradition that it swiftly became anchored and through which it can be read.

Following Kripalu, Berner devoted the rest of his life to the project of liberation or enlightenment. But Mind Clearing remained a clearly defined project limited to dealing with the mind and of which he was proud. Cognition and the mind, as he saw it, belong primarily to the world of concrete things and language, and can be dealt with to a large extent within that arena.[17] Yet it rests on a description of what the person is that is in step with yogic philosophy and, in Berner's modernised map of the journey to freedom, represents the first step on the yogi's path. Patanjali, too, describes yoga not as physical exercises, as it is often thought of, but as primarily concerned with controlling the mind, because it is the mind in particular that hides us from who and what we really are.

Lawrence Noyes (born 1951)

Lawrence Noyes met Berner in December 1975, and found in this work and the teacher an approach that promised to answer the questions he had been asking himself by then for some years. He subsequently joined Berner's group of students and worked with him, first in California, then Hawaii and, for the final years of their association, in South Australia.

Berner's work on the mind had more or less ground to a halt by the time Noyes came on the scene. Those who had originally trained in Mind Clearing had followed him into yoga or had gone their own way, and Berner himself was deeply involved in Surrender Meditation. Noyes, however, in looking through the centre's archives, found a box of old cassette tapes with hours of talks on Mind Clearing, and the material he heard immediately fired his imagination. Berner, though no longer interested in working with offering sessions himself, was happy for Noyes to compile the lectures and notes into manuals and instructed him as he did so. Those manuals have formed the textbooks of Mind Clearing training ever since and are the theoretical basis for this book.

Noyes left Berner's community in 1993 and returned to America, but he has continued to work with Berner's methods. He has been rigorously faithful to Berner's principles and added greatly to the utility of all the methods, taking Mind Clearing in particular from a sketchy growth-movement experiment to a fully developed practice with explicit ethics and stepped processes. Noyes has been responsible for teaching hundreds, if not thousands, of newcomers as well as continuing to refine and lead Enlightenment Intensives and teaching others to do so. He has extended the original manuals into techniques and guides of his own, dealing with common issues such as depression, boundaries and trauma.[18] He continues to teach Clearing and related practices, in America and Europe.

Conclusion

The work Berner did on the mind reflects its American roots, calling on a long history of influences variously in tension with one another but all pushing towards exploration and development. His core legacy asserts personal agency and responsibility in self-authorship as fundamental. This is a reworking of a familiar theme; dissenters who established the ideological underpinning of the USA saw their move across the Atlantic as a journey to the 'Promised Land'. As the land itself was swiftly fenced and swallowed up by hungry immigrants, it soon became a metaphorical space, an *idea* of space – enough that, by the early twentieth century, it could be mined by doctors of the psyche working from Freud's map of the unconscious territories.[19] American psychotherapy, and later Berner, were more than ready to explore this space, remodelling the interior territory and tapping its infinite resources.

This goes hand in hand with an attitude of determined optimism. No doubt born originally of necessity, it can give American psychological explorations and the principles of self-help a different tone from their relatively conservative European counterparts. In the Old Countries,[20] the unconscious tended to be seen as a dark continent of uncomfortable suppressions. Exploring it was something to be done for its own sake, for moral and personal growth. In America it was seen rather as a land of opportunity and promise and a journey embarked on for the purpose of arriving at a better destination.[21] Rather than self-knowledge for its own good, Berner and his compatriots, partly driven by the implicit demands of the market and accountability, saw mental exploration as having a definite and positive outcome as its basic justification.[22]

Another characteristic of Berner's work is found in the Calvinist underpinning implying that, while a person cannot strictly earn her or his place in heaven through good works, worldly success and prosperity can be interpreted as proof of God's grace in personal salvation. This thinking can be seen in the dictum of worldly progress achieved through right thinking that remains a strong feature of American self-help and therapy. Mysticism and worldly aspiration may seem like strange bedfellows, but Berner's model of the mind clarifies and normalises the relationship.

Furthermore, in setting direct communication and relationship above tendencies towards narcissistic individualism as the overarching purpose of human existence, Berner's work promotes another national ideal, though one in tension with the individualism of the post-industrial age. Since Berner suggests that our very existence is a consequence of our drive to fulfil relationship, it adopts a basic code of ethics as insurance against harm.[23] As such, it prioritises community over the solipsistic desires of the individual and is thus fundamentally a political project.

His body of work is economical in brushing aside all that is extraneous in order to focus on the main game; it is utilitarian in using techniques designed to meet specific purposes; it is technically precise; it is thorough in its mapping of the entire journey of the individual; it is about human connection and empathy as its means *and* end; and finally, it identifies the individual as the author of her or his own destiny within a greater meta-narrative of meaning. In these features and despite its grand project, it calls to an innate humility that recognises our duty to our neighbours above all.

Razor sharp and comprehensive, Mind Clearing is founded on a philosophy and practice that has emerged from the crowded melting pot where therapies, the new spiritualities, philosophies of East and West and self-help meet and merge. Both at home in this mix and standing as a question mark to the often under-defined assumptions that have made it possible, it emerges crystal clear: an integrated diagnosis of the human condition with a prescription for sanity that bucks some of the trends that gave it life.

While for practical purposes it might be classified as psychotherapy, it is a cuckoo in the nest since it aims not so much to mend the troubled mind as to obviate our need for it through re-learning the normalcy of simple human contact.

The practice sits on the edge of spirituality, resisting that categorisation by remaining solidly practical and secular; it is strictly business. Yet, paradoxically, the stripped-bare clarity of its purpose allows it to signpost the numinous by the very same virtue of being *precisely and properly* practical and secular.

Today, the Eastern practice of mindfulness meditation is being welcomed by the psychological health profession as a valuable tool. It has been shown to work in all kinds of circumstances to add to the general health and well-being of those who learn it. Researchers know it works, even if they do not know why. Berner's work rests on mindfulness between individuals and takes it further. He knew how and why it worked and had the rare ability to explain this.

2
BERNER'S FORMULA FOR CHANGE

Berner took many years to work out the precise formula for Mind Clearing. In the early days of his research, in the 1950s and early 1960s, he did not have such a well-developed model of the mind and what to do about it but, like most people in the business, based his work broadly on Freud's map of the psychological universe and its behavioural outcomes. The work he did during these years gradually built up to the model presented in the next chapter and departs from the Freudian model, finding its final form in mapping onto Patanjali's account of our real nature and purpose.

As he developed his abilities, working on himself and with others, he noticed that, in rare instances, they and he would have significant breakthroughs that changed the structure of the psyche and removed the motivation for associated neurotic behaviours such that they did not return. In such cases, help took people beyond managing their minds to a place where part of the neurotic structure simply ceased to be there. So it became his personal ambition to work out what particular combination of events and ideas were necessary in order to spark this kind of fundamental progress.

One of the processes for which he had great hopes was the method of recalling the past. The idea of this was in line with the model of the mind Berner was gradually putting together himself, but also confluent with many Freudian-based psychoanalytic approaches. Since, it is posited, we are motivated by subconscious agendas based on events in our pasts that we have suppressed, it makes good sense to suppose that bringing these memories to consciousness would mean the person would no longer avoid them and no longer be subject to their power in present time.

Freud and others had already recognised that recall could bring with it insight and understanding. But he never claimed people would be cured of their neuroses in this way. In better understanding themselves, the best most people could hope for was to find a measure of peace and personal development. He knew that even being conscious of previously suppressed events did not necessarily mean people were no longer influenced by them.

Berner, seeing the value of the approach in principle, mused on whether the problem of limited effectiveness was down to not having *total* recall. Freud had not necessarily seen this as a problem, but Berner's goal was different.[1] If nothing at all was suppressed, we would, he hoped, be free from the power of the subconscious entirely.

However, the first stumbling block in this method is that most people are unable to recall everything that has happened to them because they have done a good job of suppression. As Freud also thought, the greatest skill in this approach is in finding the most effective way of helping people to remember. Freud had first tried using hypnosis and then the use of actual physical pressure to the forehead combined with a verbal instruction to remember. He finally decided on free association as the best way to access the subconscious and this became a core technique of classical psychoanalysis.[2]

Using his own methods, Berner confirmed that recall helps people gain some freedom from the reactivity of the mind. But recall itself remained problematic and Freud's methods unsatisfactory. Even if total recall can be achieved, it is inefficient as a global method since he realised that it would take longer to remember all these events than it had to actually live through them in the first place, so it was not practicable. Furthermore, in the process of remembering there was also the very real danger of inadvertently creating yet more narratives about these events in the attempt to defuse them.

The next thing Berner worked on was mental charge. This came about because he wondered why people could not make something happen by having a clear enough idea that it *should* happen. Not unlike mind cure[3] and its offshoots, he thought it plausible that if a person could conceive of something clearly enough, then they could surely bring it about in concrete form. For instance, if they could conceive of being successful clearly enough, they would become successful.

This was somewhat different from magical thinking because it posited a positive, causal link between conceptualising a thing and it coming into being; the link was not mysterious. But people often cannot do this because they cannot in fact conceive of ideas clearly enough. The reason for this is that they have mental charge around those ideas. So Berner worked with people on their ideation to try to clear that charge. As people communicated about the area they were working on, the mental charge would dissipate and they would be able to clearly conceptualise.

For some time, Berner thought this was the part of the jigsaw of help he was looking for and developed ways to help people remove the mental charge more and more efficiently. But in the end, useful though it was, it did not take away the whole of the problem.

Even when the work seemed thorough, the charge either was not entirely gone and it was unclear what more could be done with it, or it appeared to be gone but people were nevertheless acting from these past events, though generally less so. He had not found the key ingredient for the type of change for which he was looking.

So he continued to try out different methods. Following on from reducing the charge around problematic areas of life, he tried a variation on aversion therapy in line with the behaviourism that was popular at the time and based initially on the work of Ivan Pavlov (1849–1936).[4] By getting people familiar with something they had been avoiding, they could in principle stop suppressing or avoiding it. They would build up a tolerance. Once more, this was useful, but it did not result in change at the root of the issue. He noticed that people in fact seemed to be stuck at least partly at the level of meaning or cognition, and this needed to be linked more clearly to behaviour. So he, along with others in the field,[5] went back to cognition and meaning assignment as an important locus of the psychological problems we experience.

Each time Berner took a method as far as he could, and each time another way of approaching the mind was suggested. He confirmed that there are many ways in which people can become more aware and less neurotic, but in all cases the person would come up against a block to fundamental change. In all this time working with a wide spectrum of people, he had begun to appreciate, however, that guilt was an important factor in why many of his clients remained locked in their difficulties even when they had worked on them extensively. They felt bad about the way they had behaved to other people and would not *let* themselves progress as a result. He thought he might be able to get them over this if they took full responsibility for what they had done.

If people chose to accept what they had done to the extent that they knew they would choose to do the right thing in future, then they would be satisfied that the harm they did to others would stop then and there. This was something he could achieve with people in the context of a session, but he found that people did not continue with the changed behaviour out of session. Although he made good use of this insight later, there was still something missing as a stand-alone method.

Continuing to chase clues in all the techniques he tried, Berner caught the scent of an answer when, in 1959–1960, he understood that a big part of the trouble we are in is that our ideas about ourselves and others are fixed. Because of this, we cannot see past those ideas to how things really are. This was not new; people had been looking at variations of this notion for some years; ideas such as projection and transference include the notion that we have erroneous views about the world that cause us problems.[6] Moreover, Eastern ideas about life as varying degrees of illusion was a take on the issue that was, by this time, commonly known if not widely used in therapies.

Berner put his energy into developing techniques for helping people undo that fixidity. This came closer to the ideas of Albert Ellis who developed rational emotive therapy, greatly informing the development of cognitive behavioural therapy,[7] and has some echoes in other areas of psychotherapy such as psychosynthesis.[8] The descendants of Berner's early experiments in undoing fixed ideas are still used in Mind Clearing, particularly, and formally, in *attitude clearing*.[9]

Berner developed a way that helped people improve their ability in getting in and out of fixed ideas by choice. He argued that if a person could develop their ability to get into and out of their fixed ideas, then they would be increasingly conscious and in charge of the process rather than at the mercy of their own unconscious automaticity.

By this time he was very experienced and the results of this new approach were pretty impressive. People functioned in their lives considerably better with fewer fixed ideas around their assumptions about how things are. They found they had greater freedom to choose how to be in all sorts of ways. It was looking good and his sessions with clients went well. But then he made an important error: thinking he could reach more people with this innovative series of steps to unfix ideas, he made a recording of himself running through the technique in clear stages. Handing this over to his clients and students, he hoped the work could be continued without his physical presence. This had the added bonus of being cheaper than one-to-one work, so clients could do as much of the work, or as little, as they wished, and it could potentially reach far greater numbers. He was an impressive therapist and leader, so he did not have a shortage of people willing to test out his new method. However, he found that the tapes alone simply, and bewilderingly, did not work. There was virtually no long-term gain for people who tried it and nothing like the gains of the same work done face to face.

Since the beginnings of psychotherapy, the idea had been mooted that it was not just the techniques and theories that mattered in helping people get over their neurotic ideas and behaviours; the relationship with the therapist also mattered. This view had gradually been gaining ground over the previous 50 years or so, and by the 1950s, many therapists believed it mattered a great deal. Carl Rogers (1902–1987), for instance, established the need for what he called *unconditional positive regard*[10] on the part of the therapist with respect to their clients. Others recognised the relationship in different ways, such as Harry Stack Sullivan (1892–1949) who believed people were driven primarily by a desire to connect with others and that true relating in therapy was consequently vital. Also the transference, so important in psychoanalysis, is something that can only happen within and about relationship and, in the 1950s, increasing numbers of analysts were emphasising the therapeutic relationship at least as much as insight and interpretation for effective work.

In one way or another, most therapeutic models increasingly pointed to the relationship itself as a factor in development and change.

In the twenty-first century, this is more or less taken as read. But quite *what* factor that was, was harder to pin down.

As Berner tried to home in on what it was about the connection with the client that was so important, he experimented with what would happen when he really listened to someone and when he did not. Sure enough, if he gave the person his full attention, they made progress. If he went through the same techniques in the same face-to-face situation with the same eye contact and posture but was not really listening, they did not make progress. But being a good listener alone, while clearly helpful, still did not get people over their cases in a way he could reliably replicate. It was narrowing down the area in which help took place, but not the specific factor.

Finally, in 1963, right in the middle of a session, he saw in an instant what the key to conclusive change is. The relationship *is* what matters, but what went on within it had to be very specific for there to be actual progress. As he worked with his client, he saw with sudden clarity the mechanics of what was going on between them and why it was working at that point. There was *explicit understanding between the parties*. In the terms in which he described it,[11] when there was explicit understanding, the result was a reduction in the actual quantity of the mind and so less interference with the relationship:

> To get a person to improve takes two or more live individuals understanding each other. If you do not have that taking place, you do not get a result. It has nothing to do with removing charge or getting the person to do anything, because you can't get anyone to be more able at anything unless that factor is fulfilled.[12]

The apparent obviousness of this point makes it easy to miss and dismiss. Surely any helper worth their salt makes it their business to understand their clients. So, if this is the key, why are people the world over not making more progress?

The reason progress is not more common can be seen when communication is broken down and looked at step by step. It is then apparent that very little actual, mutual, understanding goes on; understanding is fundamentally compromised. This should be no surprise since it is in line with why we have minds in the first place, as will become apparent in looking at how the mind comes into being.[13]

The mind is a *substitute for direct communication*. Consequently, the solution is doomed to be overlooked for the very reason we need it so badly. We think we are communicating when in fact many of our attempts to do so are partial and mediated substitutes for relating. This happens even in situations where people are explicitly setting out to help. It is a truism that we cannot easily get past our ideas about each other *because* we have ideas about each other. This is the problem of the mind. Alongside this, the focus of a great deal of psychological help is on the *content* of the mind, the ideas themselves. This is hardly surprising since this is what people bring to their sessions and present as the source of their troubles. That content is a distraction, however, which skilled helpers learn to see through.

Even when we think we are doing a good job, we may not be fostering actual progress. Berner realised that real progress is measurable by the *gain in skill* in communicating directly. The communication is not confined to language either. Cleaned-up language will probably help, but it is not the key. Communicating is a complex series of events, each one of which has to be complete for it to work. Without this as the focus rather than the by-product of the helping relationship, that help will be hit and miss. For greater efficiency and economy, help must focus on the ability gain in *conscious communication*. Story will be a vehicle for contact, especially at first, but sorting out the story is not the primary element of effective help.

Berner refocused one-to-one sessions and cut to the heart of what constitutes help in the light of this insight. His contribution may seem like a small thing, easily overlooked. It is perhaps something like the Chinese story of Ting the butcher whose knife was never blunted in 19 years of use: his great skill in knowing precisely where to cut meant that the meat fell away at the lightest touch and his knife stayed sharp.[14] The butcher's skill looks like other butchering, but it is fundamentally different in precision and effect because this butcher is interested in and sees the Way.[15] Berner's technique has similarities to others, but the precision and understanding of the aim changes everything. The other thing that makes it different is the model of the mind that underpins it. It shows us where we have come from and where we are going, so we do not just have to perform the actions and hope it works, we know why these actions work.

The principle of raising the ability to communicate is hidden in plain view. Not knowing it is how we keep ourselves in a state of non-relating. It is how we anaesthetise ourselves against the reality of other people. It is also how we keep people on the hook and ourselves locked in the repetitive victim dramas of our lives.

It is easy to miss because we think we know what understanding another person is; after all, we are attempting it for much of our waking lives, whether in a session, chatting with a friend over a cup of tea, buying a pint of milk or writing an article about butterflies. But however well functioning and pleasant those communications are, people are not usually *gaining in their practical ability to communicate with others.*

The individual is always already perfect. Berner's model is not medicalised because there is nothing there to cure. The only thing we can get better at is our relationships with others.

Fundamental change comes about through a small but seismic shift in consciousness. This results in acting more from who we are and not from the false notions of the mind. It is only to be found in returning to the root of the problem and transforming relationship through increasing capacity and skill in communication and then *communicating what was not communicated up to the point we broke from others and gained a mind.* At the precise point of recognising the message and then expressing it, the compensatory ideas and behaviours become irrelevant and fall away.

> Our approach is 1) to get the person to become conscious of the fact that he is involved in the formation of his mind, and 2) to get him to become conscious of, and then get over, his reason for having a mind in the first place. At that time he is ready to give up being involved in the formation of his mind because he has discovered that he no longer has any use for it. Therefore, he operates without a subconscious mind.[16]

For change to take place, the message must also connect with the emotional charge it signifies and be expressed directly from the true person. This is a connection with the body and emotions. It is why cleaned-up language alone is not enough.

Putting communication, rather than content, at the heart of help puts the individual centre stage. Once the individual can communicate directly, then content is a matter of choice.

The person helping must address the individual as a reality. As this happens, the individual comes to the fore as a reality. The individual is not based on any ideas of what the person is or any bringing together of hitherto disparate or unrecognised characteristics. The individual is a different kind of thing from the ideas of the mind.[17] For this reason, Mind Clearing clarifies and puts into action exactly what helps people get over their minds and come more from themselves. It takes the principle of mindfulness meditation right into the heart of relationship and animates the real person behind the ideas. This is an economical and precise approach to help.

Part II
THE MIND

3
THE PROBLEM THAT
IS THE MIND

So what is the mind? To answer that, it makes sense to first say something about what the mind is *not*. The mind is not who we are. The mind and our true identity are fundamentally different types of thing. In fact, it does not make much sense to talk in terms of who we are as a *thing* at all. Things are in the realm of the dualistic world and what we can talk about and where we assign meaning. The mind is this realm. Our real self belongs to a dimension that language does not touch; it is not about thinking and assigning meaning.

So this model puts the real individual outside the remit and reach of science, which can only properly work with what can be seen and measured. The mind, however, does operate in the realm of the measurable, so we can know and speak about it.

> Ben: I was going to the meditation class because my girlfriend and then my mother had got into it. They kept going on at me to join them and said it would help with my stress. I don't think I'd have continued had my girlfriend not been going to the class. But it was always the same. I'd sit there and try to focus on my breath, but I just found myself thinking about anything and everything except my breath. My back would ache and my nose would itch. It was like torture. I just couldn't stay fixed on anything for more than a few seconds at a time. It felt like everything in me was protesting.
>
> Then, one time, it was the same as usual, and then something else happened. It's a bit hard to explain. It only happened for a second or two. It was like, suddenly, there was all this thinking and a bit of a headache behind my eyes, and that was all still happening but I was just observing it. It wasn't me, all that stuff going on. I was just sitting there and I could get into it or not. It was a huge relief. Just for those few seconds I could choose whether

to listen to all that stuff in my head or not and I simply chose not to. It's not like the noise stopped, but I wasn't in it, it wasn't me. I was in a calm place where I could see clearly and I really felt like 'me'. Wonderful! It didn't last long but that's what's kept me going with the meditation. That few seconds changed things. I know that all that stuff in my head isn't the only thing there.

The individual

Who we are was there before we had a mind. We might call this pre-mind state 'us', that is, the real or *original* self. But that term has been much used in religions and psychotherapy and may not be especially helpful here. Patanjali used the term *purusa*, which is often translated as 'person'.[1] Berner preferred the word *individual* because it emphasises that the true individual is unique and indivisible. The individual transcends gender, ethnicity, sexuality and all other random qualities. Berner said:

> When I use the term 'individual', I do not mean body, a brain, a mind or a personality. I just mean someone. I can't say 'soul' because the soul is really the basic personality. I am talking here about an individual, that which is individable [sic], that which is not a body and that which, if it is involved with a mind or body, can become conscious of the body and the mind.[2]

Only the individual can deal with the problems of being a human being because only the individual can become a conscious actor. The mind does not have independent existence apart from the individual. The mind is created by the individual. It is something like a fog through which we are looking. Because of that fog, we are confused about what we see. We become out of touch with which experiences are actually 'us' and confused between the ideas of the mind and who we really are.[3] We also get confused about where and what we are for the same reason. The mind is in fact just part of what keeps us from being our true selves but it is the part we need to deal with first if we want to progress.

The individual has consciousness; the mind does not. As a result, when we act on the supposition that we are our minds, we are actually stepping into the shifting world of interwoven stories, the instability of which is a significant source of our suffering. The mind can never be sure of anything. So identifying with the mind and not the individual is a real problem for us, fraught as the mind is with the anxieties and insecurity of perpetual change.

When we engage with other people with the assumption that they are their minds, it is mostly an exercise in colluding with the changeable story of their lives. People know this, if only in a vague way. On the other hand, people also know implicitly when they are being addressed directly. They feel they are being taken seriously; the contact has a different quality. Addressing the individual is proper contact, and that is what we particularly want.

> John: I remember meeting Robert for the first time. This was years ago and I was going on an Enlightenment Intensive[4] he was running, down in Dorset. I wasn't doing the Intensive because I felt terrible about life but actually because I felt pretty good about things and wanted more. I was in my twenties and I was drifting a bit but not badly, and experimenting with different therapies. But meeting Rob was something I'll never forget. I was having a cup of tea and wondering what I'd got myself into when I was called upstairs to meet him for a chat before we began. He had an interview with everyone, so it was no big deal. I went into the room and there was just this ordinary bloke there. I remember he was wearing an old Aran jumper and some pretty dreadful slippers and sitting cross-legged on a sofa. I was hoping for someone who fitted my idea of a guru a bit more, so I was mildly disappointed. But when he looked at me it was different from being looked at by other people. There was nothing weird about it, but I just felt like he was seeing me. I guess maybe I'd felt that before in my life. My grandma gave me a bit of the same feeling when I was young. But this was interesting. I felt kind of 'met' like I didn't remember feeling for a long time. And on that Enlightenment Intensive, whenever I spoke to him I just felt that he was taking everything I said really seriously. He wasn't putting up with any shit. I must admit,

I probably wasn't the easiest person to deal with back then. But he just seemed to look through all that and see 'me' and I had to respond. I was a bit embarrassed at first and made jokes, but it made me grow up and take myself more seriously. I'm really grateful to him for that.

Patanjali addresses his entire philosophy explicitly to the individual and not the mind. Like Berner, this is because individuals are the only ones able to receive the message and act on it. There is no one at home where the mind is concerned; it is like a big computer that only works because individuals write the software for it. Or maybe it is best described as being like a play or drama; it has no life of its own, it cannot create itself. It is the author in which we are interested.

A big mistake we invariably make as human beings is putting the mind in charge of the individual. It is like leaving a child in charge of an adult; all the wrong way round. Patanjali says, 'The immutability of the person consists in being the master of the character of the mind, which it always knows.'⁵ The reality is that it is the individual who is in charge.

The core characteristic of the individual is being the one who can have real knowledge. When the individual is not put in charge, we do not grow up, we do not take responsibility for ourselves in life and we are out of touch with ourselves. We have no real wisdom or only partial understanding. We base our actions, to some extent or other, on stories that make piecemeal sense of the world.

Berner talked a lot about how to reach out and contact people who had no sense of themselves apart from their minds. This was a significant part of his work; it is why he devised the Enlightenment Intensive. He put together various techniques for working with people at different levels of awareness, but all of them focused on contacting the real individual and enhancing it. This was because he, like Patanjali, was absolutely clear that it is only possible to make real progress when the individual is addressed and invoked. Even when someone is confused about who they really are, being addressed directly, from one individual to another, is powerful and, above all, actively helpful for progress.

Another thing that differentiates mind from individual is that while the mind's structure can be mapped out and dealt with, that of the individual cannot; it has no structure. The individual is beyond description or any notion such as 'conscious' and 'subconscious' that can be used with reference to the mind.[6]

The individual is also the source of our uniqueness. The mind by itself is not unique and does not account for why we are all essentially different. It reflects the individual but it is *borrowed* individuality. As Patanjali says, 'mind…is the most rarefied aspect of Nature,[7] and the closest in quality to *purusa-s* [individuals] themselves'.[8] But each mind is still not unique because, while it reflects the individual most closely, it comes into existence as the result of a mistake we *all* make, that is, misidentification of our true self as the mind. The fact that all of us make the same mistake in the same way and with more or less the same results means there is nothing really different about any particular mind. They are all the same sort of thing.

The real difference between people comes down to differences between individuals. The important properties of the individual that makes each one different are the will and the ability to act. This is the same in the Judaeo-Christian tradition, where it was essential that God created people with free will and choice, for otherwise they could not choose to know the divine.[9]

If we suppose, as many of us implicitly do, that the individual and the mind are the same thing, then the only useful job of psychological help is to get the mind into better shape and order, since that is what and who we are. This is a plausible model. But Berner offers an alternative. In his model of psychological health and help, since the individual is obscured by the mind, the only logical goal is to work towards *dissolving the mind* and strengthening the individual. If we believe the mind and individual are identical, then this goal would not only be undesirable, it would be impossible to achieve. The idea that they are the same is why the Eastern idea of no-mind can seem so challenging and absurd from the mainstream modern view.

Following Berner, as soon as we allow that the mind and individual might be different and separable, and once the mind's structure and purpose is understood, then it makes excellent sense to de-emphasise mind in favour of uncovering the individual. Moreover, it becomes apparent that we do not have to untangle the entire mind in order to be in a better condition. There is a different platform from which the true individual operates that does not even involve the mind. The work then is in identifying and strengthening the individual. When we do that, the mind simply ceases to be a problem.

For Patanjali, and for Berner, the individual is also divine. But this should not be confused with God. God, for Patanjali, equates with *Isvara*, which is the perfect individual, though not a creator god in the Judaeo-Christian mould.[10] Isvara is an individual that has never been troubled by memories or past action.[11] So, while not God, individuals are all unique in the same way Isvara/God is.[12] This uniqueness is our divinity; one does not have to call it God.

There is something of us, our individuality, which transcends the mundane world. It is beyond language and measurement and can be alluded to only through poetry and art, though it is experienced by all of us whatever we prefer to call it, because it is at the very heart of our being. Talking about the divine is not necessary for understanding the mind, though. To understand the mind, we have only to understand relationship.[13]

Before the mind

We did not start out with a mind. We started out in life as unconscious and untroubled,[14] relating to other people easily and naturally. As will be obvious to anyone who has ever been in close contact with an infant, we certainly were not zombies but conscious, though not self-conscious. We had no ideas about existence, we just got on with it; after all, there really was no other possibility.

What marks this stage of development is that the infant experiences no sense of separation, either between themselves and other people or between themselves and the world around them. No separation means that there is no sense of self, no idea of others and no viewpoint on the world.

In many religions there are stories that illustrate this early phase of human development; religions are, if nothing else, attempts to explain human experience. In the Biblical tradition, this phase is represented in the story of the first couple, Adam and Eve.[15] They exist in perfect harmony with each other in the safe world of the Garden of Eden. They are fulfilled and unselfconscious for they are simply being themselves without thought of self. It has never occurred to them to be any different, and this is innocently joyful. But they and we were created with inherent choice. Choice means there *is* another possibility; we *could* choose to think and act differently.

Being in Eden is similar to the enlightened[16] state, discussed particularly in Eastern religious contexts as the ultimate goal of this life. The enlightened state is, like the consciousness of Eve and Adam, unified; the individual does not have divided perception of 'me' and 'other'. It is like the consciousness of a baby. But the consciousness of a baby is also different from the unity of enlightened consciousness, because the enlightened state is self-conscious, while this state of unity is not.

Being in Eden, or life as an infant, is a kind of heaven, but we do not give it any meaning while we are in it; it is not special. We are bonded with others in a kind of bliss. But we only think this in retrospect, when we long to return to its warm embrace. The memory, being largely or wholly pre-verbal, is a felt kind of knowing.

Some romantic relationships give us a body memory and connection to this place of love and easy relating, which is why they can be so intoxicating and touch our unconscious yearning so forcefully. It is also partly why they can be so devastating when they go wrong.

We do not need to mythologise the infant state in order to understand it, but the fact that it is worked into myths and stories that are embedded in our collective myths and unconscious reinforces the point that it is a primary and universal experience. Yet it is also the common, mundane story of the happy enough child who has love and comfort sufficient to experience the world as part of themselves.

The child experiences hurts and discomforts, of course, but, for a period of time, infants are able to tolerate a certain amount of dissonance. Especially if carers are sensitive to a child's distress, threats are smoothed over and the reassured child can stay in their unselfconscious bubble longer. Even if they teeter on the brink of not tolerating it from time to time, the strength of the unconscious state is strong enough to pull them back from the edge many times before the final break. Even a very distressed child does not become self-conscious immediately. It takes a bit of time, though it will likely occur earlier in this case.

But all children inevitably develop and change, and self-consciousness is unavoidable. Like Adam and Eve in the Garden of Eden, we start to test the known world and question the assumed authorities. When we do not get what we want, we resist.

The mind comes into being

There is a certain point when the emotional charge becomes so great that the person can't take it anymore and they start acting the way they think people want them to act. This could happen at any point from conception on, but it usually happens around 2–5 years old. This is the split between you and your personality, between the real feeling self and a personality.[17]

When we fall from our original state of unselfconsciousness we gain a mind. The event that finally prompts the mind to come into being is the culmination of a number of incremental steps. Even the happiest childhood has its threats: a bee sting, a tired and unresponsive mother, too bright a light, too rough a game. At these points, the child starts to have some inkling of the world as potentially hostile and outside their control. The point where enough is finally enough could of course be actual and deliberate abuse and neglect but can equally and more commonly be something that appears benign and minor in retrospect.

In any case, a point of no return is reached when the pain of disrupted relationship becomes intolerable. While we might imagine this distress must logically come with too *little* contact, it is in fact the full force of the *reality* of others and their threat to our existence that is so troubling. *Too much* contact is the threat.

The mind, in the beginning, was the solution to an intolerable feeling or sensation that you couldn't understand or were simply unwilling to experience. It was something physical that constituted too much contact with others. You didn't trust it and couldn't stand it. You wanted contact but not that much that soon. So in trying not to altogether break contact with others, you tried to tell them that it was too much for you, or you weren't ready yet, or you weren't yet willing to have that much intensity of contact. And in the attempt to try to get that message across to others, you became willing to adopt certain mental attitudes, and did so.[18]

The emotional distress is not just a mental event. Emotions are physical events; so it is an actual body sensation we do not want to experience. We think the feeling might kill us because we are too small and vulnerable to bear the intensity. So we block it from consciousness, at least to an extent. Consequently, our break from others manifests physically as well as in the mind. In fact, the mind is actually a false solution to the problem of the body; it was the body where all those nasty sensations of emotion were happening.

There is no going back from self-consciousness. In most cases it does not trigger any dramatic change, at least not from the outside, it is just part of growing up. But it *is* a dramatic change nonetheless. We tend not to remember it clearly, but, like Gillian's case below, we may be able to identify some sense of it when we understand the principle. What she relates here has a mixture of things going on, but what she broadly identifies is a felt sense of change that marked a new attitude to the world around her.

Gillian: I do remember being happy as a very young child. I don't recall much detail. But it was as if it was sunny all the time, like a summer afternoon. I know people were there, but the memory is really about me. Me playing and being happy. There are two or three less golden memories I have. Like my little brother being born. I remember a kind of anxiety when my mum showed him to me. And I've got a vague memory of being shouted at by my dad. I don't remember why. But then I have a distinct sense of it all changing. I'm not sure if there was one point, I don't remember. But yes, when I think back it's like the sun went in a bit. I don't remember anything much, although going to school pops into my head as a 'bad' thing. And I do remember other people and not liking a teacher and crying about things. It has a really different atmosphere in my head to when I was really small. I was still happy, but I was more wary of people. So I do sort of see that there was a change. There was this time when everything was warm and sunny and friendly and sort of soft. Even puddles were friendly, puddles and insects. Then it was darker and there were people who were not so nice and insects were horrible. My childhood was fine really, actually lovely in many ways. But I do have a sense of this shift. It wasn't that I became unhappy, but I became aware that the world was out there and I had to be more careful and calculate how to deal with people.

If Gillian were to work more on this, she might be able to sort out the different thoughts and strands to find the crucial incident that marked the point when she stepped back from others conclusively. This break could in principle be mended, not to return to the child state, but to work towards unified self-consciousness. This is more like Christ's injunction that we must become (again) as little children.[19]

The context of this separation is always the child's relationship with others. We would not have minds were we not relational. If we did not want to relate we would not end up with minds. What we commonly think of as the 'human condition' is dependent, in every respect, on our wanting to be in relationship with others.

Eating the apple: knowledge of good and bad

In the moment of separation from others we become irretrievably self-conscious. As this happens, we also become conscious of others as separate from us. This is the nature of duality. As soon as some*thing* or some*one* exists, there has to be something or someone to which it exists in opposition.

With the split from others we took on fixed ideas about life rather than just being in the flux of in-the-moment existing. In the story of Adam and Eve, this happens when Eve eats the fruit from the tree of knowledge of good and evil.[20] It is the moment when we become self-conscious and gain a dualistic mind.

In the dualistic mind, for the first time, there is 'me' and 'you'. These ideas are distinct from the reality of two individuals actually existing. Two individuals existed all along and still exist. But now there are additions to that simple fact. These are the *ideas* of me and you. These ideas of 'me' and 'you' are the foundations of the mind.

This shift from a unified consciousness to dualistic self-consciousness is characterised in myths the world over as a fall into darkness. In the Judaeo-Christian tradition it is represented by the Fall from Eden into the darkness and suffering of the human condition, alienation from God.[21] When the first humans eat from the tree of knowledge, they instantly become aware of self as object. This is starkly described as instantly becoming aware and ashamed of their nakedness. They become aware of themselves from the outside. They equally become aware of others as separate. Now that there are 'two', the seed of discord is sown; now we have to *think* about how to relate to this other. This realisation is a banishment from bliss, from the Garden.

The mind is a substitute for direct communication

The difficulties in relating that caused us to break from others were fundamentally failures of understanding and communication. The contact was too much, too soon. But we could not say that. Had we been skilled in communication when these things happened, we would have been able to sort it out then and there. In that case we would have had no need to develop distorted ways to get ourselves across. We would not have needed the mind at all. But we did not have those skills, as we were infants. In our fear we did what came naturally and recoiled; the consequence was the mind. The mind is our substitute for the communication we could not fulfil.

But even though it became difficult, we never actually gave up trying to get understood. We might have felt like we did, but deep down we are all still trying to communicate with all our might; otherwise we would not have taken on the mind to try to achieve this.

The communication, however, became distorted and indirect with the mind. It became wrapped up in ideas about life and others that manifested in aberrant behaviours; these ideas are necessarily false. So the message we originally wanted to communicate, but could not, becomes a drama in which the message is always implicit but never direct. This drama is the mind.

The mind is self-defensive in origin, but as a drama it is not a straightforward rejection of others. It performs a neat double action, brilliant in its way. The key to the mind is that it not only puts up a barrier that keeps others at a safe distance, it is also a movement of reaching out to others to relate to them. In this respect it is a communication. Backing away from others is a manifest desire to relate to them *and a communication in and of itself.*

If we were simply fed up of others and decided we had had enough of them altogether, then we might have decided to cut off and go on alone. But we do not do this. It might *seem* like we do sometimes, because this is our narrative, the one we tell ourselves and others. Some people certainly do their best to *look* as though they are doing this and believe it themselves. But we do not *know* of anyone who has really opted out. If someone did so, we would not know about it because they would not be interacting with any of the rest of us. The rest of us, those we know about, demonstrably did not cut off from others. All of that seeming to turn their back on the world is just another form of relating.

Boris: I've had a tendency to sulk as long as I remember. I stop speaking sometimes but I also used to leave the room occasionally. I never thought it was a particularly intelligent reaction, but I still thought it was just me wanting to get some distance from something I didn't like. I also believed it was actually a pretty manly way of getting a grip too and avoiding conflict and thought of myself as restrained and good at dealing with difficult stuff. Typically, what brought it up was an argument of some kind, or the threat of one, but I even did it at work a bit, and that really made me stop and think. So I brought this incident up in a session.

There was a particular time at work when, for some reason, everyone ended up at the tea point at the same time one morning. We were a small company but it was still funny and we were laughing. And then we started to have this conversation out loud about something we'd been talking about on email all week. The boss was there too, and everyone was chipping in. I said my bit but I remember feeling angry because no one agreed with my idea. In fact, someone said it was crazy, and there was a bit of debate and it got dismissed. Looking back, it was all perfectly reasonable and good humoured, but I was furious at the time. The reason for that is another story. But anyway, instead of carrying on with the discussion with everyone else, I just left and pretended I was going to the toilet. It was easy enough to do because we were all standing there by the exit. But I didn't go to the toilet. I went off for a walk and was really angry. Like usual, I thought I was doing the sensible thing, going off for a bit to gather my thoughts and calm down in a civilised way. But it kept going round and round in my head and I went home and talked about it until my girlfriend got fed up.

When I got honest with myself in the session, I knew that the story I was telling myself wasn't really true. Well, it was true a bit, but most of it was an excuse. When I walked out I was gone for much longer than I needed to calm down. Deep down I knew I was doing something else. I wasn't just removing myself from a difficult situation in an adult way, I was sending a message. I worked on it in the session for ages and finally realised the message was something like, *You fuckers, how dare you laugh at me! I'll show you what fuckers you are!* It reminded me of things that used to go on in my primary school. Anyway, I didn't say that, of course. That wouldn't have been good either.

Of course, I can see now that sulking was not an effective way of getting my message across, and I've understood much more about the whole thing. But the point was – and this was the real revelation for me in the session – that I wasn't really going away from them. In my mind, walking away was the same thing to me as being right in those peoples' faces, screaming at them. I wasn't even going away to stop myself saying it, not really and truly. The message was right there in my going off. But it was all messed up and even I didn't get it. How on earth I expected them to understand I really don't know. But I did; I thought they should understand me and it made me even more furious when I came back and no one even seemed to have noticed I'd left the room; they hadn't got it at all. When I really and truly saw what I'd done, I saw how funny it was, and how sad.

Our connections with other people might be pretty tenuous sometimes but, with the mind, we created a mechanism through which we made sure we also maintained contact but in a reduced, mushy and tolerable way. This mechanism *is* the mind. The mind is not our capacity to think; it is not our consciousness; it is not the seat of our intelligence or soul. The mind is the body of ideas and their combinations that we use to stay at a safe distance from others yet stay in touch.

The mind controls relating

At an unconscious level we have an idea that, if we can control our relationships with others, then we can all go back to being happy. To our way of (unconscious) thinking, we do a deal with others and life in general. A large part of our subsequent difficulties with people is that they are unaware of this contract we think we have with them. We find this bewildering and frustrating because we buy our own propaganda that our distorted communications are clear and obvious. Then we blame people for not understanding us.

With the mind established, we believe we have a grip on the situation and are in control of all the relating. We think this will mean we will not be hurt again if it goes wrong. In other words, the mind is a way of relating with others that seems survivable.

What a good solution it seemed to be too. We did not plan it; it happened when we backed off. But it looks neat; we have a buffer zone of ideas set up to protect us from others, but we can also stay in relationship with them, mediated safely through these ideas.

We now see others and the world through this screen of ideas we have about them. It is a distorted lens, though, so the world we see through it is not quite the world as it is. The more mind we have – we tend to accumulate mind as we age – the more distorted the lens. Sometimes we really do not see anything much of reality at all, but operate on the basis of this ongoing inner movie. Berner did not use the term 'projection' to describe this situation, but it easily maps on to the idea of projection commonly used in psychotherapy.[22]

Our solution to the problem turned out to be a mistake because we believe it is true. Rather than being in control of it, it dominates and is in control of *us*. We are pulling the strings in there somewhere, but we have lost ourselves and believe our own stories.

We attempt to control relating by not allowing others to be the way they are. Of course, we cannot actually stop them being the way they are. But we can construct ideas about ourselves and others that *appear* to control the world and have actual consequences in the world that look a lot like proof that we are right in our ideas. So we persist in believing our own propaganda. Underlying this is the desire to be in control. It is 'achieved' in the mind not just by pushing others away, which we might expect to be the case, but also by pulling them *closer*. Pushing away and pulling close are the same thing psychologically. In one of his lectures, Berner described this pulling closer in the following way:

> We want the others…we love the others, but we can't tolerate the way they are. So we bring them right to where we are and they can't do anything to us. And we had no consciousness of it… But we still want to relate so much, and the only way to get to relating *and* the tolerability is to mush yourself together and lessen the relationship, lessen the polarity, or lessen the energy.[23]

Ideas seem like such a good solution because they act as cushions against others and tone down relating to a level of intensity we think we can handle. We have got other people neatly packaged up and controllable in this ideal world. Reality is on *our* terms now, our rules.

Forcing and resisting reality

> …you cannot create a mind. The only thing you can do is either accept what another is or not. When you do accept what another is, there is no mind; when you do not accept the other, the mind comes into being. This is the origin of the mind… The mind **is** one's forcing or resisting others.[24]

Another way of understanding how the mind happens is to see it as a result of our resisting and trying to force life and others. We resist the part(s) of reality that seems to be causing the pain. It is instinctive to resist pain and our survival depends upon it in some rare situations. Our survival does not depend on resisting most of the things we actually resist, however. We get it wrong because we do not understand. Resisting reality is the same as trying to force reality. We are under the illusion we can modify others by resisting and forcing them.

For example, you might deny a bit of reality that seems to be causing you acute emotional pain, such as your mother shouting at you. You might not deny and suppress all of the memory, just the part of it that seemed really intolerable. You might blank out the sound and what she was saying, or 'forget' the precise words and meaning. Or you might recall the whole event, as far as you are aware, but could not stand the emotional feeling and therefore resisted and blanked out that experience such that the memory is running in your mind but with no feeling or affect; this is hidden away in the subconscious. You might believe you are perfectly reconciled to the past event and only discover a resisted emotion when you are looking at something else or because the memory is oddly persistent and you finally look closely enough at it to discover what is missing.

The bit you resisted was intolerable so, in your mind, it seems like a monster that will jump out if you let it into your conscious reality. What we do not realise is that nothing is actually intolerable. Some things might actually kill us, but nothing is intolerable. Yet we are still frozen in place by the monsters of our childhood until we turn and face them squarely. Facing them with equanimity is partly how mindfulness meditation can help us. But sometimes we need to metaphorically hold someone's hand to give us the courage. We go to great lengths to avoid the thing we have resisted and anything that reminds us of it. We resist so hard that if, under stress perhaps, parts of those resisted bits of reality start intruding into our conscious mind, we can become paranoid and believe that people or 'things' are out to get us.

Unless we find a way to receive resisted experiences, we will always deny those pieces of reality. That seemingly little denial of reality, usually but not always originally done in childhood, affects how everything looks; it is a blank spot in the field of vision. It becomes a fixed idea about how things are that acts as a filter for other experiences. At a conceptual level, that fixed idea might be identified as 'It's bad when people shout' or 'Others can't be trusted not to hurt me.' Filtered by this idea, other experiences accumulate around the original denial and reinforce it. Another person shouting makes you flinch again and resist parts of the new situation. It looks like proof you were right. It all makes perfect sense.

With trying to force and resist reality, relationship now appears to have something in it that gets in the way of relating. This is the blank spot or the thing being kept away from the conscious mind. It can be felt in the body as a tension, particularly around people who may remind you in some way of the original cause. This 'something' is part of the mind. It is the aspect(s) of the other you do not want to experience, suspended in the space between you.

The parts of experience you were willing to accept do not get suspended in the mind and do not stand in the way of relationship. They were accepted in the moment and became part of history. We can remember these things, if we wish to, but they do not affect behaviour. The bits of reality that were resisted, however, have a huge and continuing effect on our functionality in the world. As they accumulate, there are increasingly large chunks of reality we are not open to experiencing. We are, with the same mechanism, trying to force reality to be the way we want it to be, by behaving in certain ways.

Siobhan: I realised I had a bit of a problem because I used to get upset when my boyfriend got annoyed about things. It would have made sense if he was angry with me, which he hardly ever was, but this was just generally grumpy with things round the house in particular. He's really nice to me usually and we get on well, but he has a real thing about inanimate objects. If they don't work, he starts swearing at them and seems really angry; no doubt he has his own demons under there somewhere. He thinks it's funny and I know it's about him and not me, but I would get really upset. I would get a horrible lump in the pit of my stomach and felt really quite scared. I started noticing that my heart rate would go up when he was like that and I'd be on edge and snappy.

It had just happened again when I went for a session, so I brought it up. We did some stuff around our relationship and then finally Jackie [her Clearer] asked me when the anxiety around my boyfriend's temper began. To my surprise I remembered incidents that had the same sort of feel to them that had nothing to do with my boyfriend. We went back over about three incidents until I came up with this one about my dad. And then we went over that quite a few times. I'd never told anyone about it because it just didn't seem to mean anything, even though it often popped into my mind as something about my childhood. But when I started to tell the story, we could both see there was something important there; there was this little twang of emotion around it and I now know it was really affecting my life, at 34 years of age!

In my memory I was about seven and really happy, and skipping down the hallway of our house and into the kitchen, and my dad was there, sitting at the table. I asked him something and he looked up at me but like he wasn't really seeing me, his little girl. He looked furious. I remember him shouting something at me; I think it was 'Get out!' It scared the life out of me.

I went through the incident and at first there was just this general feeling that I'd really prefer not to go there. But then, as I went back over it the third time, I got to the bit where dad looked up and suddenly I had this feeling of fear and upset, and it all flooded back. I had no idea it was all still there, but I sat there crying like I was a little girl.

When I looked at the memory again it was amazing. It had changed. I didn't think memories could change like that. But it was really different. My dad looked different this time. When he looked up at me he looked frightened. Not so much angry but frightened, and that was what terrified me more than being shouted at. I couldn't bear it that my dad was scared and upset himself, so I completely blanked it out. But when I saw that, everything shifted. Jackie got me to speak to my dad as if he was there.[25] It took me a few goes but all this stuff came out about how scared I was that he was worried and depressed all the time and unpredictable. I was often not sure what kind of reception I would get when I spoke to him.

It was a relief, but it was only in the following weeks that I noticed a change in myself. When my boyfriend got annoyed with things, I just didn't feel tense. I might feel a bit worried, but there was a definite gap between him being grumpy and me feeling any tension at all. In that gap I had time to do something different; I had more choice. One time I even found myself laughing at him and he joined in. I was amazed. It wasn't what I thought it was all this time. And life seemed a bit more colourful.

The effort of keeping all this resistance going is exhausting, although we do not notice this most of the time. Were we able to stop resisting others and accept them completely, as they really are, the mind would vanish and whole structures of tension and effort would fall away. But even if we understand and agree with this in theory, most of us are too closely identified with our minds simply to drop the structure just like that.[26] There is a lot more to the mind, keeping it in place. Intellectual understanding only goes some way towards letting it go. Even getting the emotion of the situation, as Siobhan did, is not enough usually. We have to really understand what we did not understand the first time round and then get it across to someone if we want to really change the pattern. Siobhan did this and it changed a whole aspect of how she was.

No one sets out to create a mind; were we actively to try to create a mind we would fail. Its creation is only and always an unintended consequence of the choices we make; unintended, but still chosen.[27] But the point of those choices is buried very deeply in the subconscious by the time we become conscious enough to contemplate what we have done. The choices themselves are buried so deeply that few of us really appreciate our potential freedom and experience our lives as being in the grip of drives we have no control over, at least some of the time.

Even if we try to undo the choices, this is immensely difficult once we have a mind. It is certainly impossible to achieve *using* the mind. We can consciously try other ways to behave when we are adults and can figure out what is going on, and we can find some success in this. For instance, we can do our best to let others be who they are and not try to change them. But even when we know enough to attempt this, it is tremendously hard to achieve in practice. The energetics of what we believe underneath are still active in our behaviour, though perhaps more subtle.

The thing about having made choices, however, is that we can choose something different.[28] The problem is relational; we need to approach the problem within relationship.

Others are unknown

Ultimately, the reason we struggle so much with others is because we do not really know what they are.[29] Yet at first glance, this might sound like a ludicrous statement. We relate to other people all the time and assume they are much like we are. But others have a scary way of doing things we do not understand and do not expect, and that causes us distress. We do not fully know what others are and this problem is very real for us. We love others but are afraid of them. Not being sure what others really are results in not trusting them completely, even the ones to whom we are especially close. It might be better with those ones, but we still do not know what they are. So, however much we want the contact, we put up barriers.

The mind is a bad thing

The mind represents our best efforts to remain in relationship with others, despite the distress of things having gone wrong. But as a substitute for real relating it is a false solution. It is clumsy and ends up getting in the way. It feeds us misinformation and therefore cannot be trusted. The mind is a stuck position of backing away from others at the same time as reaching out to them. It is an attempt to manipulate others to get ourselves loved. The mind is a problem by definition and thus a *bad* thing we would be better off without.

As shall be clear, this book advocates working towards no-mind. But this is not a zombie manifesto. On the contrary, it is a manifesto for seeing reality clearly and without a fog of fixed ideas. Without the mind we act from the sure platform of our true self. We relate, we react, we love, we may even hate. But we do not get stuck in any of these ideas about things and people. We exercise our choice and gain freedom. We act from our adult self and not on the basis of decisions made as young children. Without minds we are simply free to be ourselves.

The mind is a good thing

The mind is also a *good* thing because it keeps us in relationship; we did not walk away and not look back. Relationship is fundamentally what we want in life. This is what brings fulfilment.

It is also a good thing because, without the mind, we would not be able to move *beyond* the mind. Without the self-consciousness we gain when we assume the mind, we would not be able to examine ourselves and make progress towards dissolving the mind. We would never become conscious, acting adults.

The mind is neither good nor bad

Finally, the mind is neither good nor bad. We are fulfilled when we get to a place beyond designations of 'good' and 'bad'. That is not the same as a nihilistic message of 'anything goes'. When duality is transcended and we act from who we are, we discover our innate conscience and care for others and the world. At that point, this is no longer based on ideas of good and bad. It is simply in harmony with reality.

Conclusion

The mind, this neat solution to the problem of relating, is not as helpful as we have believed. It turns out that it gets in the way of our contact with others instead of putting us back into easy relating. When we really want to reach out and have good contact, the mind throws up all sorts of problems for us and we often find ourselves getting further away from others. We put it there, between us and them, and now it is in the way. What can we do?

Some people have more mind than others. But we are all in its grip to some extent and struggle to know what to do. So most of us continue to work with the first solution we came up with: the mind.

We keep on digging deeper into it. We do not actually know we have a mind because we are so identified with it and there seems to be no reality outside it. So we do not appreciate that carrying on digging only makes the problem worse and takes us further from real relationship. We think we need to fix the mind and make it work better for us. Also we think much of the problem is *them*, others. But it is all the mind.

The mind looks like a big thing. But really it only looks big because it is right in front of our noses, obscuring our vision. Really it is very small. Health comes when we start to put it back in its place. Peace comes when we can establish relationships without fear, when we can contact others, or not, with reality and love. Then we no longer need all the ideas that go to make up the mind and it simply falls away.

How to work towards no-mind is what Charles Berner bent his whole life to finding out and teaching. To appreciate his approach, we need to understand how the mind is structured and works.

Key points

◉ You are not your mind.

◉ The mind is a substitute for direct communication.

◉ The mind is all the ideas and their combinations an individual has made up from a fixed attitude.

◉ The mind is one's resisting and trying to force others.

◉ We start out with a unified experience of life, but this is unconscious. This is the child state.

◉ The mind comes about through a break in relationship, usually in the first 5 years of life. This break results in dual consciousness.

◉ The mind cannot resolve itself. Only the individual can resolve the mind.

4
THE STRUCTURE AND CONTENT OF THE MIND

We accumulate withholds due to our failures in relating to others. What we withhold is what we really thought or felt but which we did not say and think we should have said, according to our own inner standard. This is especially true of things we feel bad about and really want to confess. But there are so many injunctions on doing so that we do not say those things and they become little lumps inside us, held back.

The mind is made up of these withholds; a stuck-together lump of upset, misunderstandings and false conclusions as well as a great deal of confusion about what we actually think and what is actually true. The result of this confusion is yet more difficulties and failures in relating because our continuing attempts at relating are based on increasing layers of uncertainty and things unsaid. Not expressing these things makes us increasingly inauthentic and we dramatise more and more. Mind Clearing could have a subtitle: *What are you really trying to say?* Because that is what it mostly boils down to.

If we could ask this question and the person in front of us really said all the things they had been withholding, there would be no need for further method and technique. But most people would not get far with this approach because they are too confused and distressed to know where to begin. To understand a way forward, it is useful not just to have an idea of how the mind comes about, but also to see how it is structured and what is in it. We need to take it apart in the way it was put together, and for that, we need to see that structure clearly.

The dualistic structure of the mind

Why is this world this way? Why is there duality? Why are there two? Why is the world relative? ...[the] answer is shown in [our trying to communicate with each other]. Communication would not be necessary if you already knew that other totally; and if that other knew you totally... But the fact is that you don't. You are not totally understood, you are not totally experienced, you are not totally appreciated and totally loved, although the potential is there and it is what we are striving for. As a result there is some separation between you and the other. That is the basic duality of the universe.[1]

Reality is not divided, but the mind is. When the mind comes into being, we enter a world of dualism. The mind only exists and creates meaning through opposites. The very fabric of the mind is dualistic.

Unity is sometimes considered superior to duality because Eastern traditions in particular promote the non-dual state as our ultimate goal. This can be spoken of in Christian terms as well; we might speak of being reunited with God after the Fall from Eden. Salvation is when we allow the unified reality (in the Christian case, God) back into our consciousness. It is greatly to be preferred to the state we find ourselves in, stuck in a world of this *or* that, up *or* down, black *or* white, with no certainty. But as with so many things, it is actually more tricky to achieve than we may hope.

Unity and dualism are not real opposites. They are different categories of existence. Like the mind and the individual, they cannot really be compared to one another because they are in fact not opposite to one another. We only think they are opposites when we are in a state of duality. To prefer one to the other is to misunderstand the situation.

Unity cannot be consciously attained *without* there first being duality. To be consciously attained there must be another person or viewpoint from which it can be seen and worked towards. But these metaphors of time and space also do not work here because the difficulty is our perception. With minds we see things in the wrong perspective. But we are not actually in the wrong place. The individual is already a unity but it needs the mind in order to begin the process of knowing itself consciously as that unity. This is the dynamic paradox at the heart of the matter.

In a way, enlightenment is superior to the state of duality because, in the state of enlightenment, reality is seen clearly and this is what ends our suffering. But this cannot be achieved without being in the state of duality first. The difference is one of perception, so although we often talk about a path or journey to enlightenment, there is actually nowhere to go and nothing to attain.

The mind is a condition of duality. We think it is reality because, for there to be meaning and narrative, there must be relativity and opposites. Nothing has meaning on its own. Everything has meaning only in relation to other things or beings.[2] Patanjali says:

> The action of the yogi goes beyond contraries like black and white (enjoyment producing and pain producing), whereas the actions of others are threefold (enjoyment producing, pain producing, or both).[3]

If we want to deal with the mind at its core, we have to deal with its dualistic substructure. The task of self-development or yoga is 'to rewrite the narrative of our lives'.[4] This is not about finding a new story, but takes the narrative right back to its inception and sets us on an entirely different path.

The nature of conflict

Duality is a state of mind which is conflictual by nature. Nothing is really in conflict with anything else, it is just itself. So duality is a kind of illusion. But there is one real duality and that is the duality of one individual and another individual. Unlike the false duality of the mind, in true duality there is no inherent conflict; it is simply a relationship between individuals.

Sarah: When I went on my last Enlightenment Intensive (EI) I was at a point in my marriage of thinking it might be over. I was doing the EI partly to find some clarity on it and get the courage to end it if I had to. It hadn't been going well for a couple of years. It wasn't anything in particular; there were lots of little things. When people asked me how James was I would feel myself slumping and I realised I had come to think of our marriage as a problem. On the EI it did come up a bit, but not that much. But on the third day I had this wonderful experience of who I am. I realised that I was 'me'. It was me doing the EI, me having thoughts. It was beautiful and obvious. I'm just me. Later that day when I was eating my dinner, James came into my mind and I suddenly saw that I'd been seeing him as this big problem to the point where the problem had been obscuring everything else. But really he was just a person and what we had was just a relationship. Not a problem, a relationship. It put everything back into perspective and, although things didn't all get sorted out instantly, the main thing was that James was a person again to me. I could talk to him and be with him and enjoy his company, or not, because it was just him and me, not this problem.

The conflict is only really within oneself. It comes about through trying to understand the other while, at the same time, pushing the other away. So we want contact but we feel the need to keep the people we want the contact with at a safe distance. We project this inner conflict onto others and the world. Conflicts do of course manifest in events and material reality and people agree they are in conflict; the world is rife with conflict. But all of this finally comes back to the inner conflict we are projecting onto the world.

Patanjali advises that when people express opposition and advocate action that causes harm to others, then they are really reacting to past trauma.[5] This is also the basis of much psychotherapy, and it is no wonder some people have suggested that Patanjali's is the first recorded psychotherapeutic model. He goes on to say that, when we react and argue with someone who is opposing us, this is also really a reaction to our own past experience. Taking such opposition seriously, to the extent we believe in the conflict, is to misunderstand the reality of the situation.

> ...the proper attitude that the yogi should have to such arguments is compassion, for without penetrating knowledge, such karmic bubbles from the depths of our psyche (that is, the fruits of past dispositions) are without end.[6]

Unless we recognise the real location of conflict and deal with that at its root, then our attempts to change things are likely to breed more conflict and our suffering will continue, together with the harm we are doing to others.

Levels of the mind from outside to core

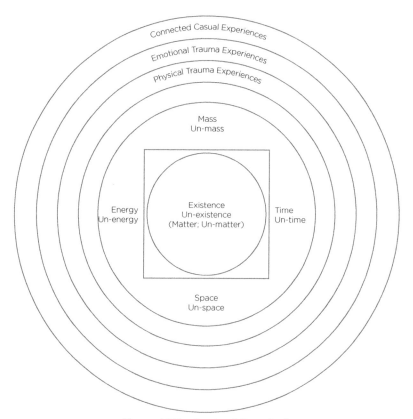

Figure 4.1 The levels of the mind[7]

The mind can seem to be an overwhelming muddle. But it actually has a structure that can be mapped (Figure 4.1). The map is useful for knowing where we are and helps us measure progress. If we want to help others deal with their minds, then it is also important to see where they are starting from in this map so the work can be done at an appropriate level.

In most cases there will only be satisfactory progress if a person starts from the outer layers of the mind, where there is less fixity, and works down through the levels. They may finally get to a point of being able to work on the inner core. Trying to work on the deeper levels first, with the idea that dealing with the core will cut through a person's case swiftly and economically, is tempting. It may be beguiling in theory, but in practice it does not work.

The core of the mind is very deeply buried and mostly unconscious. It is possible to understand at an intellectual level the principles on which it is built, but this is different from understanding it at an experiential level. It is the experiential, or embodied, level of understanding we must work towards. This is because the problem of the mind, while it might sound like a purely cognitive problem, is fully real and visceral.[8]

This can be demonstrated time and again if you work with someone at a level deeper than their experiential understanding. This is even if they have a good intellectual understanding and have requested working at that depth. Unless they have worked on the outer layers with some success, they will simply be blocked by the mass of their own subconscious mind and feel like they are in an impenetrable fog. The other, related reason, is that they need to get good at getting themselves across on the smaller stuff before they can hope to tackle the deeper, more rigid material in the deeper layers. Little progress will actually be made and they will be discouraged. That does not mean progress must be slow, but it must be methodical.

The mind is made up of *resisted* experiences. Experiences that we did not resist did not end up as the detritus of the mind but become part of the unproblematic past.[9] Further, when there is a resisted piece of experience to store away, the mind will not leave it free-floating but try to make sense of it because, as something resisted, it seems like a threat to the integrity of the personality.[10]

The mind is a system of control and meaning; it operates in order to try to make sense of life. When we have lost sight of who we really are, we crave stability and meaning and look for it in the mind, which seems like the only place there is. But since it is only ever shuffling round random bits and pieces that have no inherent meaning, it will never offer us a satisfactory account of anything much. But even knowing this does not stop it and us. So we work away, mostly at a subconscious level, but sometimes a bit consciously, to file resisted experiences into categories in such a way that we can make sense of them within a narrative.

In some ways, the mind acts like a filmmaker. It has all these scraps of film as stills or shorts and does its best to splice them together into a coherent story. The particular stories it chooses are based on deeper levels of attitudes in the mind. But what we forget is that all the bits are really, fundamentally, unrelated. They were originally stored in the mind for reasons that have little to do with the current plot. But the persuasiveness of the world of mind is such that we tend to believe in the story the mind as filmmaker has made up out of all the bits in its storeroom.

Level I: connected experiences

The most surface of the connected experiences consists of casual experiences. They are not deeply buried in the mind and not very fixed. These casual experiences are resisted because of deeper attitudes that cause blind spots, so the person is not open to some things or not in the present moment and fully aware of what is going on. Or they did not quite understand something so it hangs there, undigested. This not being in the present, or not understanding, accounts for most peoples' state a good deal of the time, so there are a lot of resisted casual experiences. They get caught in the mind as something not fully digested.

> Jane: The most obvious example for me is when I don't quite hear what someone has said or don't quite get it. I've noticed that the actual words get repeated in my mind until I take note and 'hear' them. It's actually quite useful as there have been many times when I've known I should be paying attention but haven't been, and it's my subconscious that keeps doing the work and makes sure I finally do hear. I imagine there are things that slip through the net, though.

The existing structures of the mind take these casual experiences and connect them to pre-existing ideas and memories that bear some kind of similarity to the new resisted experience. It does this through its system of basic logic. That might sound clever, but it is a stupid kind of logic, filing things according to anything that might be similar to anything else. It might be as random as being filed according to shape, or colour or name.

> Helen: I had this persistent thing with a song going round my head, Mull of Kintyre, a song I'd known from childhood. I didn't recall having heard the song for a long time, let alone thought about it, so it seemed odd that it kept going round my head. And then one day I was tired and having a lie down in the middle of the day, and I was especially still and relaxed, and the clock in the church up the road chimed the quarter hour. I knew it did that as I was vaguely aware of it having started up a couple of months before, after having been silent for a year or so, but I hadn't particularly listened to it. And I suddenly understood where the song was coming from. The first three notes of the clock chime were the first three notes of the chorus of the song. That's why it kept going round my head. I hadn't put two and two together, but my subconscious had, and it kept playing me the song. Once I'd realised the connection, it wasn't so strong any more and quickly stopped.

This is also illustrated with free association[11] as a person jumps from one thought to another according to random connections. This might go something like: chair, leg, foot, pavement, road, car... A lot of conversation is based on this sort of thing; people being reminded of one thing and then another, through random connections in the mind. These connections can form more complex webs.

> Joan broke her leg and was given a pair of metal crutches to get around on while it healed. Whenever she noticed the crutches, which was very often for a while, she automatically thought of a flute she used to play at school. Her mind connected the crutches and the flute because both are long, silvery-metallic and have holes drilled into them. Because of these properties, there is

a similarity of meaning between crutches and flutes in Joan's mind. They are consequently filed and cross-filed according to these similar features. Those similarities are actually random. Flutes and crutches are not connected in Joan's actual experience, only in her mind. Joan automatically thought of her long-gone flute every time she picked up the crutches. She didn't even know she was making this connection until she wondered why she was reminiscing about her flute so much and sat down to work it out. Up until then she thought she was having some curious and rather pleasing flashbacks to a happy time in her past, but when she found the connection and brought it fully into her consciousness, the automatic nature of the connection was broken. She was freed up to think about the crutches without thinking about the flute, unless she actually chose to do so.

Working on these random connections of casual experiences as though they had real significance is to misunderstand the nature of the mind and assign meaning where there is none. We can deal with this level of the mind by bringing the connections to consciousness. When a person can differentiate experiences and memories, one from the other, and become conscious of the mechanics of the connections that were being automatically made, then that connectivity comes out of the subconscious and is discharged. As a direct result of this work, the mind becomes correspondingly clearer.

This is the easiest level of the mind to work with because the casual experiences and connections are not very fixed. Also, it can be done alone with enough focus and discipline.[12] Once a connection is noticed, the person can focus on it until the connection is exposed and experienced. Done successfully, people can emerge with a little bit of repetitive thinking gone.

SERIES

Series are experiences that are caught in chains of repetitive thinking that link one idea to another. They are often a little more fixed and a little deeper than the casual connected experiences.

Whenever Maureen hears the word 'gate', she automatically thinks of a black car her grandmother used

MIND CLEARING

to drive, then she automatically recalls the feel and smell of the leather in the car which automatically connects to the leather jacket an old boyfriend wore with whom she had an unpleasant experience. This all happens very quickly and subconsciously and means she tenses, just a little, when she hears the word 'gate'.

This is a series of thoughts or events that are subconsciously connected in the mind. A series can be complex or simple; it is a chain of ideas that has unconscious links. Unless a person becomes conscious of what leads from one idea to the next, and the next, and so on, they will be stuck in this kind of automatic thinking.

Berner found that the way to deal with series was the same as with other connections: we need to work on what significances of meaning connect them from a trigger through a series. Then we can be in the presence of the trigger, be it a word, object, place and so forth, without making those automatic connections. The original reason is buried in the mind. But it is possible to trace it back, step by step. Only one link in the chain needs to be brought to consciousness for the series to be broken. The person will no longer need the reactivity to that word or thing. It was not just a mechanical reactivity; it was there for a purpose. They were not willing to experience all or part of an event. The trigger took them back, in unconscious steps, to the event they were resisting through other resisted experiences. The resisted experience was like a pain the person was trying to ignore, but would not really go away, and kept coming through. If the events are significant, they can then be brought into the consciousness and dealt with. It is the automaticity of the connections we are looking at dissolving here, not necessarily the events that are connected. Dealing with that automaticity is a layer of unconscious thinking without which we are clearer.

A person will only maintain their reactivity to the trigger, after the series has been broken, if it is serving some further purpose for them. For instance, the trigger might also be put into service as an excuse for not engaging with people socially. If the trigger was feeling upset by something to the point of getting a migraine, and this enabled the person to give a plausible reason not to go to parties in addition to the series it was supporting, then they may hang on to the trigger, even when the series has been made conscious. They may hang on to it because they have some other reason for not wanting to go to parties and the trigger is serving as a convenient excuse for them.

STACK-UPS

Stack-ups are a type of series but consist of a number of experiences that are all very similar to one another. Because of their close similarity, they are associated with each other very closely in the mind and difficult to tell apart. As a result, they are highly charged clumps in the mind that are hard to disentangle and discharge.

> John has, stacked together, lots of very similar experiences of his mother shouting at him in the kitchen. He blocked a good deal of the experiences at the time because being shouted at like that was intolerable to him. Now they are in an undifferentiated lump in his mind, and he is resistant to looking at it.

The key to unlocking stack-ups is that, although they shared many features in common, each experience was different in some way. In the example above, John was a different age each time, he was wearing something different, the kitchen was arranged a bit differently, some of the incidents took place in the doorway, some at the table. But his mind has them filed all in one bundle because they were all so similar in really important respects: his mum was in all of them, and she was shouting at him or otherwise admonishing him, and most of these experiences took place in the kitchen.

Stack-ups clog the mind and affect behaviour more than casual connections. A person might have whole areas of undifferentiated stack-ups around their mother that, combined, leave an area of their mind suppressed and subconscious and charged with emotion. They will resist anything that 're-minds' them of those experiences. There can be a lot of reminders in life and some people are very reactive.

To take a stack-up apart, a person does not have to go through all those experiences again; there is a more economical way of dealing with them. We have to see clearly that each experience is different from every other experience. This simple expedient dissolves the connectivity and we can deal with the resistance. The easiest difference to grasp is that each event took place at a different time. Realising this intellectually is not enough. A person has to be willing to experience the actual impact of one of these incidents as different from another in order for the stack-up to come apart. When the automatic connection that sticks them together is made conscious, then, as with other types of connected experience, it loses its power as a no-go area.

A person might suppose they could deal with a stack-up simply by deciding to experience all the unexperienced events at once; in other words, by deciding to stop resisting the events in one shot. This may be appealing, for as soon as we understand the nature of stack-ups, and see how they are the result of not being willing to experience part of reality, a reasonable solution would seem to be to let it all in and get it over with. But this is harder than it sounds. Doing so is likely to be overwhelming and we would, more than likely, re-traumatise the person. A person might resolve some of it in this way if they are experienced at dealing with their mind, but the best, easiest, most economical way to approach a stack-up is to start small and tell one incident apart from the rest.

Being willing to experience one event is a willingness to experience all things like that in the mind. On a simple level, if I am willing to stop resisting one instance of 'spider', and let it in fully, then all spider-instance triggers will be disarmed. In more complex situations, a person might still need to go back and look at some of the experiences in more detail to clear all the trauma around it, but it will not have the same charge and power it had before. Berner says of connections like this one:

> All…connections in the mind are based on undifferentiated similarities of significance. If you've understood that, you've got the whole key to connections in the mind. And it is easy to see, then, that to discharge a stack up you have to become better at differentiating.[13]

CIRCLES

Another kind of connected experience can be called 'circles'. These are much like series but instead of being linear, they go round and round, going back to the beginning and starting up again. They can be repetitive and obsessional. A circle is stuck, going round, because some part of it is being resisted.

> Jim feels lonely, and when he feels lonely he thinks of his empty house, which reminds him of the costs of keeping such a big house going, and this in turn reminds him he has less money than he had. This leads him to recall that this is partly because he gave a substantial amount of money to someone he hoped would be his companion but has now left him. This reminds him of his loneliness. He goes back to the beginning of the circle and keeps going round.

Berner offers another illustration:

> 'What am I going to do with my husband? What I'd like to do is get a better relationship going; a better relationship means that we've got to talk things out; talking things out means work; work means I've got to struggle; struggle means pain; pain means a hard time, and a hard time means unknowing.' Round and round goes the mind. And suppose you felt unknowing whenever you were sick as a child, and whenever you were sick as a child you also felt connected to your mother, and so your mother connected to a nice feeling, and a nice feeling makes you think of your husband, and the nice feeling with your husband makes you think that you've got to get things worked out with him. You are back where you started.[14]

The connections that keep the circle going can only be stopped by the person becoming aware of one of the connections and disarming one of them. They are being made automatically, so taking away the automatic thinking stops it. The circle is broken and will not start again except by conscious choice.

Saying that all one has to do is to become conscious of a previously automatic connection sounds as though it might be easy. Sometimes it is, especially with casual experiences, but the reason it is automatic and compulsive is because something about it is unconscious and based on resistance to some part of reality. We have to stop resisting something we are strongly keeping out and that can take work. Then we must communicate fully where we need to do so. Then the circle will be broken.

MENTAL MACHINES

Like other connections in the mind, mental machines are habitual ways of thinking that we get into and keep going because those connections are unconscious. They are usually put together in the first 5 years of life. They are mechanical, like actual machines, and go through a particular, repetitive pattern of moves in order to achieve a particular outcome.

A common form of mental machine is one for retrieving memories. We might ask someone to remember something, and finally they come up with a memory. But how did they actually go about doing that? Few of us pause to consider this. If they are asked how they did it, they might draw a blank at first. It can seem like a stupid question. So it can take some work to really see. But eventually, if they do have a mental machine for bringing up memories, they will start to be able to see what process they are going through to recall things.

For instance, they might have an image of poking around in their memory with a stick and finally poking the right thing. Berner noted one person who had something that looked like a windscreen wiper in their mind; they would have an image of it wiping one way and then the other. Searching for the right memory one would come up and, if it was the wrong one, the wiper would 'wipe' it out going one way and, going the other, would present another memory for consideration until the right memory appeared.[15]

Mental machines can be used for anything, such as solving mathematical problems or working out logical arguments. A common one for this is to imagine writing up sums on a board in order to do the arithmetic. This is a simple mental machine.

Many mental machines are made up of images that reflect what happens in our physical reality, like the writing out of sums or a filing system one has to leaf through to find something. Some machines are made up of images that do not reflect reality but work in some mechanical way nonetheless.

Many mental machines perform some kind of task for working things out and retrieving data, but others work to help us forget things. These can be more difficult to identify because they are specifically designed to make us forget. Plenty of people simply blank out memories, but others have a mental machine; one person had a machine that rubbed out memories like a cloth wiping out writing on a blackboard.

People use other mechanical ways of avoiding unwanted thoughts that have a physical mechanical element, such as someone tugging at their jacket unconsciously or angling a shoulder to achieve some purpose for themselves.

> Julia had a particular way of suggesting that what she was saying was really of no importance. If she was not happy about something but thought it would be unacceptable to say so, she withheld the importance of what she said with a mechanical action of shrugging her shoulder in such a way that it withdrew the impact of her communication. Her listeners generally, though usually subconsciously, picked up her withdrawal of impact and tended to disregard what she was saying. This reinforced Julia's idea that no one took her seriously in life and no one really heard her.

To deal with a mental machine a person needs to see it clearly: what they are doing and what the purpose and effect is. They will probably need help to see it. When they see its purpose, it will instantly stop being automatic.

Without the habitual mechanism, the person might feel a bit lost at first. It might be they have had a mechanism for getting by in social situations that they had put in place at a young age. They might do this by putting on a certain persona of being haughty. When they see what they are doing, they have to choose whether to do it or not to do it. It might have been in place for 40 or 50 years. Knowing they now have the choice usually means they will choose not to do it, or it will lose its power if they attempt to use it, and feel fake to them. But even if they are not quite sure what to do in social situations for a bit, they will begin to behave more from themselves instead of through an automatic mechanism. This will eventually help them feel freer.

Mechanisms and machines are not problematic in themselves. A person can choose to use them to good advantage when they do so consciously. For instance, they might usefully construct one in order to be better at remembering things. The problem arises when mental machines are automatic. This takes up space in the mind. Finding the purpose of a mental machine is the key to stopping the automaticity, because that is what holds it together. Stopping a mental machine results in greater freedom for the individual.

MULTIPLE CONNECTIONS

The connections in the mind are often fairly straightforward and obvious, but when we dig down, many of the connections are actually highly complex. We find that ideas are used for different purposes from the original reason they were stored in the mind. The mind will use any of its content to construct narratives and convoluted mental machines into new ways of handling a perceived problem.

Berner gave an example of a complicated group of connections as follows: it involved a mental machine, the purpose of which was primarily to block the sound of actual music. He did not want to hear the music for reasons that will become clear. To do this, he unconsciously used an image or idea of cotton wool that he had in his mind. This was connected to an idea that cotton wool could muffle unwanted sound. He already had an emotionally charged impression of cotton wool lodged in his mind because he hated the feel of it as a child (it was attached to a traumatic emotional event) and resisted the idea of the physical feeling of cotton wool. So there was a pre-existing, emotionally charged experience of cotton wool lodged in Robert's mind along with resistance to it and an idea of dislike. He also had an emotional feeling of dislike about the music. So he resisted the experience of particular music too.

Now, subconsciously, this pre-existing impression of cotton wool was put to work for a new purpose: to resist the music. He connected them, though previously there was no connection. He subconsciously made a connection from the way things work in reality between unwanted noise and the fact that cotton wool can muffle sounds plus a feeling of dislike. So a mental machine came into being, through subconscious decisions and incomplete understandings, which consisted of the impression of cotton wool and the idea of putting it between himself and the music in order not to hear it.

The dislike of music is a different narrative from the dislike of cotton wool, but they were associated because the cotton wool narrative was being used to deal with the music narrative and because there were some similarities of significance between them.

This person experiences some music, the kind of music that triggers the mental machine, as beautiful. In his internal narrative, only good people can make beautiful music. So accepting the music and really experiencing it would mean also accepting that other people are 'good'. Allowing that to be true would, according to his existing ideas about the world and himself, mean that he, himself, was 'bad', because he was *not* making the beautiful music. He resisted the emotion/feeling in his body that this idea of him being bad brought up. In consequence of this complex, automatic, subconscious connectivity of ideas and experiences, he resisted the idea that he was bad by resisting the music.[16] He achieved this by unconsciously constructing a mental machine that toned down the experience of the music to a level he could tolerate, where his idea and feeling of being bad were at a level at which he could operate.

This degree of complexity will take time to unpick, but the complicated mental machine will yield as soon as this person understands the purpose of his construction. He can then go on and unpack the attitude that he is bad, but the point here is that he will no longer have a mental machine running in his mind about it. He will have taken off a layer of unconscious reactivity in his mind and this particular aspect of his mind will be easier to deal with as a result.

In a lot of cases the degree of complexity is at least as tortuous as the example above. We have got ourselves very buried under layers of resisted and randomly connected ideas and experiences. We are so deeply mired that it can seem impossible to find a way out. But taken slowly and methodically, it starts to clear and we can find relief from our reactivity and greater clarity as randomly associated ideas come apart.

ATTITUDE CONNECTIONS IN THE MIND

Connections in the mind are all ideas, but Berner calls some kinds of the ideas *attitudes* because of the way they work. In brief, if you have an attitude that 'life is bad' wired in at a deep level from a young age, as most deep attitudes are, and when you have a *bad* experience, such as your parents splitting up, the mind connects the new bad experience with the existing attitude that 'life is bad'. The new experience actually had nothing at all to do with the original experience that led to the 'life is bad' attitude. However, it gets stuck firmly to the deep attitude because of the similarity it has to the original experience in some important ways.[17] (For a detailed discussion on attitudes, see Chapter 7.)

Attitude connections are at every level of the mind. They are ideas and all the connections are, at base, ideas that are also connected to body sensations that are emotions.

Level II: emotional trauma experiences

The connections in the mind at level I are fairly easily dealt with, though the more cross-connected they are, the harder it can be to differentiate between the parts and discharge the automatic connections. However, once a person can see what they are doing, and why, they gain freedom from those particular automatic connections.

The next level down is the emotional trauma experience. This is more difficult to deal with. Many people get stuck at this level because of the big investment they have in keeping it going. They are using the idea of it, unconsciously, to control others.

In an emotional trauma experience there is a trauma that was not dealt with at the time. A trauma that was understood and accepted at the time does not in fact become a trauma at all as the effects are dealt with and dissipate. Where it becomes a problem is where some or all of an emotionally traumatic experience was intolerable and resisted.[18] As a result, it stayed in the mind and affects current behaviour.

In an emotionally traumatic experience, there is a connection in the individual's mind between the idea of an experience and some particular emotional sensation in the body. Consequently, when a person remembers the emotional trauma experience, it will often go along with that unpleasant sensation or emotion, or the person has suppressed it so thoroughly that they do not even get as far as the body feeling but steer away from it by using some kind of unconscious distraction, perhaps a mental machine. So the memory is shut out and so is the feeling in the body. It will usually manifest as physical tension and increasing distortion. The person goes into a state of physical resistance to the body-based emotion when the life experience is evoked by something. Neither can be fully experienced without the other, even if this 'knowing' is deeply suppressed.

The thing that makes it a trauma, and not just an emotional experience, is the resistance to some or all of it. This resistance is caused by a non-understanding that took place with another person or persons about part or all of the traumatic experience.

When an emotional trauma has to do with someone else, and in some way they all do since we associate bad experiences with others whether others were in any way responsible for the events or not, then the person will often deal with it by acting in some way like the person with whom they had the non-understanding. This happens, once more, unconsciously. Were it conscious, it would not happen. As a result of traumas, a person may start behaving like their father or mother or whoever else they perceive they had that emotional trauma with.

This is because, since the non-understanding was not satisfactorily dealt with, with that person, they *became that person* in their own mind in order to control the process of understanding. Fundamentally we fervently *want* that understanding and will do what we can to achieve it, even if that means becoming the other person.

The person wanted to bring about resolution with the individual(s) with whom the trauma took place, but they could not find a way to do this with the person themselves, directly; they were not skilled enough. So they unconsciously got an image of the person in their minds and related to that image instead of to the actual person.

Some of that might have been perfectly conscious. They may replay some part of what happened over and over in their minds and rehearse various conversations with key people in order to try to resolve what happened. But the reason they are doing it is mostly unconscious and the behaviour they take on will almost certainly be unconscious. They effectively become an actor in the ongoing dramatisation of the trauma and take on the role of the other person, as well as their own, in the trauma drama. In doing so, they will take on mannerisms of the person in question. Some of our likenesses to our parents are benign and maybe genetic, but other aspects are learned mirroring as an attempt at communication to resolve non-understanding. This is an attempt to take control of the trauma by acting their own part and acting the other person's part as well, in order to mend the non-understanding. But of course, this does not work because they are not dealing with the real person, they are dealing with themselves; it is a closed circuit.

To tackle this internal situation, the person has to find that non-understanding in the trauma and bring it into the conscious mind.

Usually, with help, the person can recall what happened and find the non-understanding at the level of the mind. They may also have to experience the discomfort in the body in order to get through it, and, done consciously and with support, this will come with insights about what they did and why they did it. But this should not be done in such a way that the person is re-traumatised. Successfully achieved, a person would be released from acting like the person with whom the non-understanding took place.

For instance, if the non-understanding is with a person's mother, they may find themselves acting like her, talking like her, being critical like her, maybe even moving a bit like her. Some of this may be genetic, but if they release the non-understanding they have had with her, they may find these behaviours vanish. In this case, they will start to act more from themselves and less from an idea of *her*.

Emotional trauma experiences are more difficult to deal with than casual resisted experiences because they come with huge charge and resistance. But they can be handled because there is almost always some conscious memory attached to them, so there is something with which to start. When they come apart and non-understandings are cleared up, then a great deal of emotional freedom and capacity can be regained.

Level III: physical trauma experiences

Deeper still than emotional trauma experiences are physical trauma experiences. These get locked into the body when an experience of an intolerable physical sensation forces a change in the person's consciousness. The reason a physical trauma experience becomes traumatic is because the person is unwilling to continue to experience it and shifts their state of being to avoid it, unconsciously. They choose to become unconscious.

Emotional traumas are also experienced as unwanted sensations in the body, but they come about through *emotional* distress. Physical trauma experiences are different as they are not sourced in the emotions but usually as direct trauma to the body.

This kind of trauma is difficult to deal with because it originally involved a change in consciousness. The person chose to make themselves effectively absent. For this reason, the effect on the person's life will be considerable because the trauma is wholly unconscious. It will have effects on behaviour that seem inexplicable to the person, and probably to those around them, because they are not associated with remembered events.

The effect is described by post-traumatic stress disorder (PTSD), but PTSD is usually understood as relating to remembered traumas while physical trauma experiences are specifically about physical traumas without conscious memories. The person may have no idea what the root of their symptoms is and may consequently feel crazy in particular respects. This is because the change in consciousness they went into originally is, by definition, not accessible to the person in their usual state of consciousness.

> In the mind, a physical trauma results in an enforced change of state of being because of intolerable pain. The pain became so bad that you couldn't stand being what it is you were being, and you are forced into another state in which you won't feel the pain. That pain is almost always in the body.[19]

Since the person goes into another state and dissociates from the body, they do not know what is going on with the body; this is the desired effect at the time. When the actual experience of pain goes away, then the person comes back to the original state of consciousness but does not recall what happened. As a result, the experience is buried in the mind as something completely resisted. Of course, the individual is the agent of change; they are choosing these changes in state or they would not know when to return to the normal conscious state. But the decisions made are not at a conscious level.

Not having a memory attached to the physical trauma makes it harder to uncover and deal with. The effects will often be greater than that of other traumatic experiences, because the cause is not known by the conscious mind and cannot be negotiated with by the person because there is no cognitive understanding of it.

More than with emotional trauma, the person with the physical trauma will unconsciously act like the person who, in their view, caused the pain. If they have been bullied, they will tend to act like the bully. Or maybe the person acts like a doctor because a doctor was the one doing the things that caused so much pain, or like his mother, because his mother was the one he regards as responsible for the pain caused by the doctor, since she sent him to the hospital in the first place.

To deal with physical trauma, the person has to get into the original viewpoint they were in at the start of the trauma and experience everything they avoided when they changed their state of being. This means the person has to develop the ability to consciously change their state from one to another. When they recognise that it was actually they, themselves, making the changes of state, then the whole problem of physical trauma dissolves. When you really get the 'I did it', then the problem goes.

The whole experience is suppressed and unconscious, so the person only has the effects to go on at first. They have to look around in the dark for hints and fragments. This can seem like dealing with shadows, but there is no other way than to start looking and see what a person discovers. It is only when there is a substantial breakthrough that the value of it can really be appreciated.

Level IV: implants

Implants are attitudes that have been taken on from outside. They are not lodged in the mind as a direct result of decisions made due to some kind of trauma, or from an existing attitude. They are whole concepts that arrived in the mind from outside it. In a sense they are a kind of brainwashing, but it is not as simple as that. While some messages are aimed at people with the intention that they take them to heart, others are conveyed completely inadvertently. Even the ones deliberately given may have been understood differently by the receiver. For instance, some parents deliberately give their children repeated messages that they are, perhaps, ungrateful or bad, or that they are wonderful and good, in the hope of imprinting these messages on their minds, and they have their own, probably unconscious, reasons for doing this. The child may or may not take on these attitudes whole; they may well take them on in a very idiosyncratic way, based on their experiences with their parents and other factors.

Other instances of implants are more random. One example might be that a child is taken to the doctor and the doctor remarks in the child's hearing that there is something wrong with her. Perhaps the message is repeated by others. Even worse, the child might be under the influence of anaesthetic, so the message goes in subliminally. The intention is actually to help the child rather than burden her with some message about something being wrong with her. But the particular circumstances in which the child heard and understood that there was something wrong with her got stuck at a deep level and became a behaviour-altering attitude. As an adult she believes there is something wrong with her and this causes her to behave in particular ways, unless and until she can uncover the implant and release herself from its spell.

In this case, the child, going around with the attitude that there is something wrong with her, becoming the adult, latches on to anything that can be interpreted as evidence that there is indeed something wrong with her. She might be somewhat hypochondriac, exaggerating pains and identifying easily with symptoms she reads about. On the other hand, she might be quick to hear disapproval in what others say to her and become resentful, blaming others for seeing her as having something 'wrong' with her. The one attitude spawns a variety of other attitudes and behaviours.

There is no trauma attached to these beliefs from any original event. There may be later traumas that come as a result of having the implant, but the implant itself may not be attached to any trauma. When a person acts on an implant in later life it can look random and we struggle to see how a person's history could have led to that kind of behaviour.

> Lucy had a perfectly happy childhood and no memory of major trauma. However, she had a deep idea that she was bad and this caused her to block out good things that happened to her and go round in a state of belief that she was a *bad* person to whom nothing good could happen. It is true that this might be a physical trauma experience since she has no memory of it. But implants have a different feel to them. They are not lodged in the body in the same way and do not have the feel of trauma about them. They are more cognitive yet still powerful. Feelings of betrayal are common indicators of implants because a person feels betrayed at having been, effectively, tricked into taking on the idea of 'I'm bad' or 'I don't deserve a good life.'

The implant is not caught in the body but lodged at a conceptual level. They are hard to root out because, like physical trauma, they originally came from outside and the origins are buried in the subconscious. The key to release from them is to understand that, at some point, in order to take on any attitude, including implants, a choice was made to do so. No one can ever make someone think anything against their will or *make* someone take on an idea without their consent. So at some point, even if it is buried under layers and layers of other ideas and deeply lodged in the unconscious mind, we chose to take the idea on. We agreed to it. By the same token we also have the capacity to make the decision not to have that idea.

This point of choice will often be hard to find, and it can be difficult to believe that we have played a part in taking on an implant. It is our investment in keeping them that makes them so hard to locate and remove. We have to find out how we are using them and for what purpose in order to clear them. When we let go of the investment in having an implant, we can choose not to have it. In other words, the implant, when fixed, becomes something we use. We have blamed people for it and we are now using it as a way to try to control people. It is only when we see what we are actually doing with it and mark our own behaviour and reasons clearly that we can get the 'it was *me* all along; *I* am doing this' and can work our way through to dropping it.

Level V: the basic states of being

The basic states of being are at the centre of the mind and form the foundation for all the outer layers. These are basic attitudes we took on willingly in order to stay in contact with others. They are buried so deep in the subconscious that they do not look like they could have been voluntarily taken on or that they are ideas at all. All attitudes are voluntarily adopted. But these are such fundamental attitudes that it is more accurate to call them basic states of being. We think of ourselves as that thing and find it hard to see them as attitudes.

We give our power to these ideas and act from them rather than from who we are. From the start, we did this in ignorance; it was an attempt to get closer to others and we still have this as our goal. Understanding that there is a better way to get closer to others is key to our recovery. Once we can contact others directly, we do not need these ways of being.

> ...the individual does not get involved with any of these things except as a means of trying to get closer to others. When you have gotten people so that they can be closer to others without the use of these parts of the mind, then they don't need the mind at all. The use of the mind no longer has value and it will cease to exist. The individual will withdraw his involvement in the mind's formation, in the absence of any need for it in relating. So, although all these mechanical aspects of the mind are true, the basics behind all recovery is improvement in your relationships with others.[20]

Due to the dualistic structure of mind, each of the four attitudes at the centre comes automatically with its opposite. Each of the four attitudes below, and their opposites, come about through identification with our bodies. Likewise, when we increasingly de-identify from our attitudes and ideas, we also identify less and less with the body.[21]

Time is an idea. It is the case that everything changes: we are young, we age, we die; the seasons cycle; the day comes to a close. But this is not time; time itself is actually an idea. We take on this idea when we become self-conscious and identify with a body that is subject to change. That is not to say that things do not change if we do not become self-conscious, but that we do not take on the *idea* of being in time and so the concept of change is not there, nor are we attached to things staying the same.[22] Because of the dualistic structure of the mind, where there is the idea of time, there is always also the idea of un-time.[23]

Most people are more closely identified with one side of the pair than the other. Degrees of identification dictate behaviour and their combinations form the basis of particular personalities. For example, a person might be identified with un-time and this could manifest in feeling like they never have enough time. They might feel at the mercy of their schedule; it is a problem that has turned into an ongoing drama and seems to be running them, despite the fact that they are the ones making the schedule.

This is different from someone just being busy and needing to reorganise their schedule. Being identified with un-time is more charged. Time may seem like an enemy, malignant and out of control. If you are dramatising a lack of time on a regular basis and are feeling victimised by it, then you are probably identified with un-time. Yet what is described here is an extreme; un-time is often manifested in more subtle anxieties and ideas around time.

If you are identified with time, rather than un-time, it might manifest in a feeling that you have all the time in the world. You may never get much done because time seems to stretch out ahead and nothing is urgent. It could be driving people around you crazy with your laid-back attitude. You might be late for appointments or never get around to things until it is too late. It is as much of a dramatisation as the identification with un-time, and both are ideas, not reality.

The basic attitude of time/un-time gives rise to more surface attitudes in layers on top of it affecting the most casual behaviour as well as deep, fixed patterns or personality traits.

SPACE AND UN-SPACE

Like time, space, and its opposite, un-space, is taken on as soon as there is resistance to reality. It is also an idea. When you deny the physical sensation of emotion it becomes fixed in the body and so you become identified with the body as a result.

With identification with a body, inevitably we also have the idea of being located in *space* with its corollary, *un-space*. Again, this manifests in concrete ways in peoples' lives. Someone who is identified with space might literally take up a lot of space or it may be they give the impression of doing so. They are dramatising space in order to convey a message. A person acting out 'space' may be saying with this attitude something like, *listen to me* or *here I am* or *don't push me away*.

Someone identified with un-space, on the other hand, might dramatise this with an idea that they take up no space and do not really exist. They could have a floaty feel about them and give the impression of being hard to pin down. They might seem rather disembodied and ethereal and try not to take up much space and behave in a way that tends to erase themselves spatially from situations. They might have trouble taking up an appropriate amount of space in life. This behaviour is actually a message to others that they are acting out with spaciness or un-spaciness. Maybe it is based on an idea that if they do not take up any space, if no one can really see them, then they cannot be wrong and cannot be admonished.

MASS AND UN-MASS

This is the idea of *mass*; it is not the same as matter. The two are easily confused. Matter is the reality of stuff; it is the actual hard stuff itself that can be touched and has heft. Mass or weight, on the other hand, is the *idea* of matter or stuff. We took on this idea when we became identified with a body. There was a body anyway, but then we became identified with it; we thought we actually *were* the body. We go around thinking that this, *my body*, is 'me'. So we identified with mass, which is the idea of matter. When we took on mass we simultaneously took on its opposite, *un-mass*.

If you identify with mass, you might have a rather heavy presence and be physical in your approach to life. You might prefer to sort arguments out physically or show affection physically. It could look something like identification with space but has a different, more gross feel to it.

Identification with un-mass may look like un-groundedness, such as a dislike of the body manifesting in preferring to engage in non-physical activities and body-denying practices. It could look a lot like un-space. Identification with un-mass, with not being a body, might be manifesting in the idea that you cannot be pushed around because you have no mass, no weight. If a person could not be pushed around, at least in their own idea of how things are, by virtue of the fact that they are identified with un-mass or un-weight, then they may have an idea that they cannot be controlled by others who might want to push them around.

All dramatisations have a purpose and tell a story. In this dramatisation, it means they cannot be abandoned; it is a way of controlling relationship. They could also attach themselves to people with the idea that they could not be pushed away, because they have no mass to push. How can something that has no heft be pushed around or away? It is a neat idea. While it is *only* an idea, it is powerful, and people act on such stories. If you asked most people if they believed this, they would be adamant that they thought no such thing. However, at base people are identified with these ideas, but they are so basic that this is almost impossible to appreciate without considerable mindful concentration. A person might really act like they cannot be pushed away because that is how their idea of how things work is set up. These are examples of how someone might be using the idea of mass or un-mass to control relationships but stay in contact with others.

ENERGY AND UN-ENERGY

Energy and *un-energy* is the fourth pair. If you are identified with un-energy, you may be limp, listless, not have much get-up-and-go and feel tired all the time. This will have physical manifestations but is primarily, and certainly at first, a state of mind. That is not to say that all tiredness and listlessness are initially states of mind, though Berner was certain that most are.[24]

On the other side of the pair, someone identified with energy is likely to appear full of energy, bubbling with ideas and forcefulness, but this, too, is a mental construct. It is energy that is not coming directly from who they really are. The true individual is not aligned with the attitude of energy because it is an idea and not real, so the energy will be forced to some extent and will not necessarily flow easily. A person may have a very real connection with their life force, but when it becomes an identity rather than a natural expression, then it will not feel quite real and may falter. It has a reality associated with it, but the mental construct, the identification with the basic state of being, is an idea and a dramatisation.

A professional soccer player may experience this, for instance. They may have had a natural alignment with their energy early in life and this was harnessed into playing football so successfully that they became a star player. But then they increasingly experienced themselves objectified, in the media, in the reactions of people they meet and in their own sense of themselves. They may stop coming from just who they are and come instead from the idea of this star player with flair and energy, and it stops being quite real.

LEVEL V SUMMARY

On the whole, these basic states of being will run alongside each other and intersect at points. Un-energy might work with un-mass and both manifest in listlessness, but they have slightly different characteristics. These ideas and their associated behaviours might seem too convoluted to be operating us, but they do. People engage in them for a reason. They get themselves hooked up in complex ways of thinking and behaving because it was all they could do in order to stay in contact but feel safe. It appeared to be a matter of survival.

Level VI: the core of the mind, existence/un-existence

At the very core of the mind is the first decision, the decision to be *someone*. This is the basic state of 'I am' or existence, together with its opposite. It is also the beginning of being socialised.

'Existence' could hardly look less like an attitude, but it is nevertheless an idea and operates in the way any other idea does. It is the individual made manifest in ideas. This idea is so deep-seated that it is more properly described, alongside the others, as a basic state of being.

This may seem absurd since it is self-evident to most of us that we do exist and that this is not just an idea. But the problem is that we confuse the *fact* of our existence with the *idea* of our existence. At the point when the mind comes into being, we misunderstand what happens and start to identify with the *idea* of ourselves as existing. We cannot identify with the fact of our existence since we simply exist. We identify with its idea. This is the 'I' or 'I am' and marks the first moment of mind.

In flinching from the other we simultaneously become aware of ourselves from a new perspective. We become 'I' or 'me' for the first time, existing in relation to others. Of course we already existed, so it is not our existence that begins at that point, but the *idea of ourselves*. In a sense, we do start existing at that point since we come into time and space. Outside time and space it makes no sense to talk of something existing or not. We award meaning to ourselves and the world around us from this point. This is part of the process of learning to conform to the pressures of social living.

The theologian, Bishop Berkeley (1685–1753), asked the conundrum that was expanded into the now famous question: if a tree falls in a forest and no one hears it, does it make a sound? The implication is that sound does not happen in any meaningful way unless it is heard.

Once this level, of existence and un-existence, is worked on successfully, a person will have gained freedom from the mind. They will no longer be held captive by their own mechanisms for making sense of, and categorising, the world around them, but will be free to think consciously as they choose.

The four functions of the mind

Like any organisation, the mind has a kind of bureaucracy that keeps it going as an integrated system. It has content that acts as filters and organisers of other content. Deeper attitudes act as organising points for other, less fixed ideas. In terms of these actions or functions, the mind can be divided into four areas of activity: memory, analysis, decision-making and personality/ego.

1. Memory

> Your memory is a monster; *you* forget – it doesn't. It simply files things away; it keeps things for you, or hides things from you. Your memory summons things to your recall with a will of its own. You imagine you have a memory, but your memory has you![25]

The memory can certainly seem to us like a monster with a will of its own, holding on to unwelcome recollections and nagging us with them. But, in fact, a specific and useful function is actually being served.

Memory consists of 1) all the memories a person has accumulated together with 2) the mechanism with which they are remembered, which is itself, made up of memories.

Memories are held in the brain and also in the mind. But they are held in each place for different reasons and in different ways.

Memories held in the brain fade after a while; they are held in the circuits of the physical brain and have no real significance. They are subject to disintegration along with the rest of the body.

The brain interacts with the mind in that information from the senses goes to the brain and then to the mind, which sorts the data. The mind then informs the brain which in turn informs the sense organs. So the content of memories held in the brain and mind are the same, up to a point, since the brain is feeding information to the mind. But those in the brain are like after-effects of the event; they stay for a while but gradually degrade. So the brain does not hold as many memories as are usually held in the mind.

There is a third type of memory. These are ordinary, unproblematic memories that the individual can access if they wish to do so. They might be in the brain but they are not held in the mind. They are simply part of what has happened and the individual can draw upon them at will.

Memories held in the mind, however, carry meaning and do not fade. These are made up of experiences we have resisted and are held as emotion/body/meaning packages. This book is concerned with the meaning element that is specifically part of the fabric of the mind. The emotion/body elements are more energetic and physical but are locked together at the surface level by meanings or stories in the mind. They may be buried so deeply we cannot readily connect to them, but they are still there until such time as they are consciously accepted by the individual. Memories are not merely stored like a film of one's life. They are the energetic flow of an event that has been resisted and held out and away from the person who is resisting them.

It might be useful to imagine experiences we have resisted as trickles of water. We did not want to experience them because we thought we could not tolerate the experience. So we metaphorically held them out. If they were trickles of water, we built a little dam to stop one, then another. Before we know it, we have lots of dams holding back lots of water. It takes physical, emotional and mental effort to keep those dams serviced. The water being held back is the mind, made up of these memory events. The mechanisms for holding them back, the dams, are also mind constructs. It is no wonder we slow down and become tired. We have all this unfinished relating and unexperienced life being held at bay. We are rarely conscious of this until we make a practice of looking inside with disciplined concentration. Then we discover layers of tension and unprocessed material just at the corners and underneath our normal conscious mind.[26]

These memory events serve a function for us; they are stored because they are connected to significances of meaning we refuse to accept. The persistent presence of resisted experiences prompts us, if we are willing, to become more conscious of reality. They keep tapping on our shoulder, as it were, until we are willing to receive the experience fully and open to more of life. People as whole beings tend towards resolution. We want and strive to be whole, to stop resisting others and life and connect. So we prompt ourselves to become aware of what we are holding out; we have this tendency innate within us.

Memories held in the mind are easily identified as being in the mind, rather than just the brain or real memories that are done with, because they are charged by the mental state the person was in at the time it was made. They are time capsules containing the event and its intolerableness. For instance, if a person was angry when something happened, that anger will be part of the memory. And it goes deeper than this, for not only is emotion stored, but the ideas that prevented the event from being fully experienced are also suspended until they can be released consciously.

Graham: This memory was from when I was about ten. I'd just joined a new school because we'd moved to the area, so I didn't know anyone. So one day I was playing with these boys and it all seemed fine until a bigger boy called over to us to come and join some game they were playing. I don't know exactly what happened; maybe they only needed a certain number. These days I doubt it was especially sinister. Anyway, the three or four boys I was playing with all moved off to join this other game and I went to follow them. But one of them turned back and said, 'No, not you.' And I was left standing there feeling bad, really terrible. This memory stayed with me and came up loads of times in the therapy I've done and I thought I must be done with it; I didn't think there was anything else I could possibly say about it even though I had this sort of grey feeling around it. When it came up again in a Clearing session I almost didn't mention it. But I did and I tried to say it didn't matter and that I'd dealt with it, but Keith [his Clearer] encouraged me to stay with it and express myself more thoroughly, including to the other boys, which I hadn't done before. Suddenly I became aware of all this pain in my chest. I had felt so rejected and alone; it was horrible. I was just standing there, all alone, and it felt like no one wanted me. There was this big lump of emotion I'd never known was there, I'd avoided feeling it all these years. When I'd looked at the memory before, it was more like an intellectual exercise. I'd worked out what I must have felt and what effect it had had, but I'd never actually experienced it. And when I did, I really felt how sad I was as a little boy, moved around the country so often, with no real friends, because of my dad's job. It was interesting. I understood myself a bit better and really felt a bit kinder about that little boy I'd been. My memories kind of rearranged themselves and this one stopped coming up and lost that grey feeling.

For Patanjali, whose *Yoga Sutras* are so closely woven with Berner's later lectures on Mind Clearing, memory is also far from passive. He says, 'Memory is the prevention of loss of experienced content.'[27] Memory is an attempt, on our part, to understand ourselves through holding on to past events. By doing this we construct a picture of who we are for ourselves. We use memory to create this picture and present it back to ourselves, like the mind as filmmaker. With this picture made out of memories, we think we understand who we are as though looking at a photograph can tell us something true about ourselves.

Through memory we do our best to define ourselves. But by doing this we effectively define ourselves through our past traumas. This is because we have forgotten who we really are and think we have no choice but to piece all the little bits of memory together to form a more or less coherent whole. It is really anything but coherent as it is full of inconsistencies and some bits are given importance because they are heavy with emotional charge, not because they are any more true than any other idea.

However, once we understand what we have done, then, through an equal effort in the other direction, of de-identifying with our memories, we can, suggest Patanjali and Berner, redefine ourselves.[28] But not through ideas. This time we do so in an entirely new way by finding ways to enhance our original self, consciously.

2. Analysis

The mind uses the capacity to analyse with the specific purpose of organising its content. Content is organised according to its self-referential criteria. These criteria are the basic ideas on which the mind is built. We have built our houses on sand.[29] The analytical function of the mind, however, tries to make sense of memories like building blocks being made into a wall. It uses basic logic. Memories are shuffled into patterns that seem to have plausible narrative in relation to the underlying fixed ideas. (An example of its basic logic can be seen in the connections the mind makes as discussed in Chapter 4.)

Memories are categorised into meaning groups as well. Memories, say, of people being nice are sorted into that category and, if the dominant attitude is that people are bad, then they will tend to be resisted and filed away in the subconscious mind. In this way we build grand narratives for ourselves with heaps of supportive evidence backing them up. We have corresponding heaps of subconscious or semi-conscious memories of things that do not fit with our dominant attitudes.

3. Decision-making

Once ideas, attitudes and memories have been shuffled into narratives by the analytical aspect of the mind, the decision-making part then chooses which of these stories are 'true' so that the person can act in a reasonably coherent and consistent manner. In Sanskrit this is the 'buddhi' part of the mind. The buddhi decides what is correct and chooses the impressions that fit with that chosen story.

The way the buddhi decides which possible stories are true depends on underlying principles that are themselves memories and ideas. These memories, however, are buried deeper in the mind than those that are being shuffled around on the surface into meaning structures. They are usually subconscious, so they feel like solid facts; often these are implants and, below that, the basic states of being. When a person has a strong inner sense about what is right, some call this their conscience or gut feeling, but in fact this is usually the decision-making part of the mind which acts like an inner judge. In reality, nothing is absolutely right or wrong; things are only right and wrong in relation to deeply held ideas.

At the heart of the decision-making part of the mind is the aspect we think of as our personality.

4. Personality/ego

The fourth action of the mind is what Freud called 'ego' and Berner preferred to call 'personality'. This is the part of the mind that thinks of us as having a particular character: 'I'm like this' or 'I'm like that,' 'I'm a nice person,' 'I'm a good person,' 'I'm the kind of person who makes an effort with others,' 'I'm the kind of person who says it like it is,' and so on.

Patanjali wrote that personality consists in erroneously putting together the power of the individual with the powers of perception into a single idea of a self.[30] In other words, personality is the failure to see the difference between the individual and transitory aspects of the mind in oneself and others. We fall into the mistake of thinking we are our personality when we confuse our true self with our contingent aspects and memories, not just with respect to ourselves but also in the case of seeing others in this way, including animals. It might even be easier sometimes to see this in the way we are with animals. How easy it is, sometimes, to attribute emotions such as spite and revenge to a cat or dog when they pee on the carpet, when all they are doing is being a normal cat or dog who has not been trained well enough. These are our own emotions and behaviours, projected onto the animal. We are confusing the creature with our own personality.

To fail to treat other people and animals in the way we expect to be treated as individuals is to fail to understand reality.[31] What is truly valuable is *only* that which is important to individuals.[32] This is not the same as what is important to the personality. The personality may be offended by a tone of voice, may find it important that others be sensitive to their anxieties, may expect others to sympathise with their victim state. The individual does not project such ideas onto others, but wants to connect and relate through and regardless of these contingencies.

Patanjali goes further to assert that the mind 'is created from egotism alone'.[33]

> The very possibility of a mind…is a function of egotism…
> Egotism thus is the error that allows features of Nature to be
> converted into minds. Egotism is like the interface between
> the *purusa* [person or individual] and Nature… It is an error
> that occurs both on the side of *purusa* and on the side of the
> natural qualities that constitute the mind.[34]

The personality is the part of the mind we often feel most identified with, so we are understandably resistant to losing it, but it is not who we actually are.[35] We will not, as some fear, become personality-free and dull by losing it. On the contrary, we will be lighter, less reactive to our inner states and freer to act from our true self if we liberate ourselves from our fixed personality states.

Consciousness

We seem to be at the mercy of our minds until we see clearly that we are not identical with them.[36] But the mind cannot know this because it cannot know itself. As Patanjali says, 'Mentality is not self-illuminating, but it is known by its knowability [to the person].'[37] Only the individual can know the mind. But the individual and the world, including the mind, are in a symbiotic relationship. Consciousness cannot know itself simply through its own mechanisms but must have a mirror. The individual cannot know itself without the mirror of the mind.

We have different degrees of consciousness of the content and workings of the mind. We are often more or less aware of the surface workings of the mind and our immediate motives. But there are other times when we might be completely unconscious, such as when we are drunk and cannot later recall what we did.

There are wide variations in how conscious we are of the content of our minds, even within the same person; they may have a deep understanding of their motivations and influences in one area but be acting unconsciously in other areas due to particular, deep attitudes.

The idea that consciousness is not part of the mind but can be applied to the mind is easy enough for most people to establish for themselves. For instance, this can be experienced in practising mindfulness meditation. In this a person can learn to observe the mind from a distance. So, although we are usually strongly identified with our minds, we can understand this distinction as long as we have developed the capacity to observe the inner landscape.

The mind is not itself conscious and does not have consciousness or awareness. But the mind can be perceived through shining consciousness onto it. This experience of observing the mind has led many people to the conclusion that consciousness must be identical with the individual. This is closer to the truth but not exactly the case either. The individual is in fact the one who has the *capacity* for consciousness, but it is not identical with consciousness.

The one who can be more or less conscious of the mind is the individual.

There is often confusion on this point because it is fairly unusual for any of us to have had the experience for ourselves of separating these elements out and seeing the differences first hand. Most people can get the difference between consciousness and the changeable stuff of the mind but, because we so rarely get beyond that stage of perception, we tend to put consciousness and the individual together and suppose that the consciousness *is* the individual. It is often said that the 'observer' is the individual. This is closer still to the truth, but the observer is, finally, an *idea* of the individual; it is not the *reality* of the individual. The individual is not an idea. An experience of who you really are[38] reveals that the individual is not an idea.

An implication of breaking down the individual, consciousness and the mind like this is that it can enable us to be more precise in understanding ourselves and giving help. Consciousness can be *applied* to the mind by the *individual*. When we know this, then we are no longer so closely identified with our minds and the individual can begin to come to the fore. A person can increasingly act from who they really are and not from the dramas of the mind. In giving help, we are also less likely to be beguiled by other people's minds; this helps others tremendously.

The conscious and subconscious mind

Consciousness, a capacity of the individual, is different from what is conscious and subconscious in the mind.[39] The conscious and subconscious in the mind is a structural distinction originally made by Freud as a way of trying to understand the way the psyche works. It was and is a hugely influential model and has allowed us to talk usefully about motivations and agendas that drive us, but of which we are not aware. It has given us language and methodologies for explaining and dealing with the effects of trauma that have seen huge strides forward in approaching psychological distress and aberrant behaviour.

The model discussed here is different, for here there is no *de facto* unconscious mind. The mind can be likened instead to one box, inside of which is a floating line that divides it into conscious and subconscious. At any given moment, some of it is easily available to the individual and some of it is not. If the dividing line goes right down to the bottom, then everything is conscious. That does not mean that everything is always in our awareness, but that it can be easily called up and be available to the individual. Many people, however, operate with the line somewhere close to the top, in a situation in which nearly everything is unconscious.

The conscious mind is that part that is easily accessible to a person and upon which an individual can readily shine consciousness. There is a grey area where, with a bit of effort, a person can bring something into the conscious mind that is usually subconscious.

In principle we could bring everything into the conscious mind and there would be no dividing line. A person with no subconscious mind would be aware of all their motives. Patanjali also asserts that bringing subconscious drives, attitudes and ideas to the conscious mind defuses them so we can observe them rather than being ruled by them.[40] This has been a large and important part of most psychotherapies and continues to be so. That does not mean, however, that such a person would necessarily be free of their aberrant behaviour or non-reactive. There are, alas, other powerful reasons why we do not let go of our distorted ideas and behaviours, even when we know about them.

The seat of reason

The mind is not the seat of reason, even though, when we use the word 'mind', we are often referring to reason in some way. The confusion comes, at least in part, because the mind makes use of the reasoning capacity to sort its contents. Our language and conceptual traditions make it difficult to appreciate this, but mind and the capacity to reason must be carefully differentiated.

Reason is an ability to perceive and differentiate between things. The better we can differentiate, the better our reasoning powers will be. The mind employs basic reasoning to sort and arrange content, but it is not the source of the ability to differentiate. We tend to think of someone as 'mindless' if they are unreasoning but, in this model, we can perceive reality and reason more clearly without the mind. For example, preconceived ideas, which are the stuff of mind, are barriers to clear perception. Ideas are like the building blocks with which reason plays. Fixed ideas are of the mind, but reason is not.

The question people tend to ask here is whether or not we need the mind in order to think. Mostly we do, because the majority of the thinking we do is engaged in rearranging ideas according to hierarchies of other ideas; most of what goes on in our minds is fundamentally neurotic. We have clear perception without the neurotic activity of mind. Ideas, however, are useful to us just as long as they do not become fixed.

Once we understand that the mind is not the seat of reason, we can afford to look at it critically, without fear we will lose our reason by doing so. Losing our mind is not the same as losing our reason; the former is desirable, the latter not so. Understanding this, dealing with the mind becomes easier and is not a threat.

The individual and thought

Thoughts and mind are not the same thing. When we talk about dealing with the mind to the point of being in a state of no-mind, this can sound, to many people, like an alarming and unattractive proposition. We might have an image of ourselves as mindless, *unable* to think. But this is not what is being proposed.

It is important here to look again at the distinction between *mind* and thinking. It is the mind we are looking for ways to dissolve. However, as long as the individual is in any way identified with time and space, that is, operating in the world as we currently see it and engaging in tasks and participating in life, then we do need tools with which to operate.

The individual makes use of ideas. Thoughts are employed to get us from A to B, to cook dinner, to do the shopping and all the other tasks and interactions of daily life. These thoughts are not a problem. They can be seen as the operation of the ordinary mind. What makes them different from 'mind' is that they are not fixed. It is the fixed ideas and attitudes that become a problem and are what make up the mind as defined here. These are the ideas we are unconscious of and which drive us.

We cannot stop ideas from coming and going, or not unless we are very advanced in dealing with the mind. But we can de-emphasise them and not be run by them. We can also choose them and use them in interacting with the world.

In summary, dissolving the mind does not mean losing our capacity to think. Having a mind gets in the way of seeing things as they really are.

Going victim

The state we go into when the mind comes into being is always, ultimately, a victim state. It is a failure to take responsibility for how we are in the world. As soon as we become 'I', we also create 'you'. To maintain this duality, I must be right and you must be wrong at a basic level of definition.

Judgement is often a victim state. Of course, not all kinds of judgement generate victimhood. I might judge this pumpkin to be better than that pumpkin for the purpose of decoration. Discernment is not a victim state, but judgement based on distorted views of reality is. This accounts for all attitudes, including those that appear to be victimising others, such as bullying. We still make others wrong and our actions, in this narrative, are their fault, as in 'Look what you've made me do.' The element of self-justification is always there; it makes us the star and victim of the drama. The opposite of the victim, the victimiser, might be easier to see in operation because it is often active and aggressive, but both are always there.

Until we fully see our agency in how we are in the world, we will be in a victim state to some extent. The victim state keeps us in illusion about others, and projects that illusion onto them. We are victimising others, which means not seeing them as they really are and not treating them well as a result. We do harm because we are not allowing others to be as they really are and treat them more or less as objects in our world.

When we are caught up in the illusions of the mind, we are constantly resisting and trying to force others into the story we have made up about them and us. The story is a myth about what others are like and how they treat us. We find it hard to allow others to be truly who they are and free, because this would mean giving up the idea we have created about them as being wrong. We think that, if we give this up, we will have lost them too.

For instance, if Malcolm withdraws from people in response to a particular set of circumstances, the withdrawal is actually a communication. But it is distorted. Malcolm probably thinks his message is loud and clear. Let us say the withdrawing actually translates into the message 'Don't leave me!' In his subconscious mind he thinks the withdrawing is getting the message across, but that the person he is communicating with just does not get it, perversely. So the other person is in the wrong in Malcolm's narrative, and that becomes the point of the attitude. The distorted message is not just an isolated fact, it has a purpose. It is designed to keep the situation going. It is a communication but it got stuck in a loop and, as long as the attitude is running, it is never being delivered or received. So it just keeps on going.

The attitude and associated behaviour sets out to recreate the situation that perpetuates it not being communicated satisfactorily, over and over. It is like saying, 'Well, I'm communicating like mad here, but you don't get me, so you are in the wrong, I am right, it's all your fault so I'm going to withdraw my love.'

However, if Malcolm, for example, realises what he is doing and gets better at direct communication instead of withdrawing, he would have to give up the narrative in which he is right and others are wrong. The communication is the key to change, but deep change is not about improving communication in general; it is about finding and making the original communication that set off the attitude in the first place. This is why empathic conversations do not usually result in deep change. They are not specific enough. If he were then to see what he was doing in its entirety, including the message, then he would have no need for his dysfunctional habits of behaviour. He would communicate and others would get it, or not, and he would not have any need for withdrawal. The only reason to keep the behaviour going is if he did not get it across completely, or had some other investment in maintaining that state or he is still invested in a person getting the communication yet that person is refusing it.

Key points

- The mind can be mapped.

- The first, outer layer is made up of casual connected experiences.

- The second, more fixed and deeper layer is made up of emotional trauma experiences.

- The third layer is made up of physical trauma experiences.

- The fourth layer is made up of implants.

- The fifth layer is made up of basic states of being.

- The core of the mind is made up of the dualism of existence and un-existence.

- The mind has four functions:

  - memory

  - analysis

  - decision-making

  - personality.

- The individual has the property of consciousness; the mind does not have its own consciousness.

- The contents of the mind can be conscious or subconscious.

- We can still think when we have no mind.

- The mind is a victim state.

Part III

DEALING WITH THE MIND

Mind Clearing

5
WHY WE MUST DO SOMETHING ABOUT THE MIND

To deal with the mind we have to directly address the original problem, or it will still be there and we will still use aberrant ideas and behaviours to address it. So working towards dismantling the edifice of the mind is achieved through relieving our problems with relationship. We do not achieve this by attacking the mind through some process of removal or by trying to overcome its effects. That approach would only serve to add to the mind. The beauty of Mind Clearing is that we do not set out to do anything at all to the mind, beyond tidying it up a bit so that we can engage in a process. What we do is strengthen the individual and get them communicating better. When an individual is more able to get across how things are for them to another live person, then their mind simply dissolves to the degree they have improved in doing so.

The will

> ...the principled exercise of the will, geared to procuring liberation...for Patanjali comes about when we can abide in our true nature.[1]

The fact that each of us is unique is down to the different will of each individual, not the personality or the mind.[2] This definition of the will is not like egotistical wilfulness that we may think of as being about wanting and getting what we want.[3] The will referred to here is a defining feature of the true individual. It is not a capacity we may or may not have. It is the essence of what an individual is.

Patanjali argues that it is the will of each person which leads us into difficulties. This is because it is due to having free will that we individuals have choice. It is in exercising that choice that we find ourselves with minds. Consequently, it is each individual alone who is responsible for their own plight.[4] We, separately, made choices that led to the mind coming into being and took us away from direct contact with others. Because each one of us made that choice, so each one of us is responsible for uncovering our true self again.[5] Moreover, it is only we as individuals who can bring about change in ourselves.

> Ray came for sessions because he had had what he described as a 'breakdown'. He was in his early sixties and at a stage in life when his career was winding down and the social life that had revolved largely around parties and holidays with similarly wealthy friends was also quieter than it ever had been, as his friends were older and increasingly looked forward to a quiet retirement with their families. An unhappy love affair and the feelings of shame and hurt this had left him with had thrown him into huge doubts about himself. Having been an apparently confident, even bullish character, well known in his local town, on numerous committees and thought of as a somewhat pompous though pleasant addition to any company, Ray found his confidence shattered and had no idea how to proceed in any direction in his life. All the old structures of personality, work and socialising, which he had always felt defined him clearly, seemed to have fallen away. His response was to retreat from the world, and his behaviour became so erratic and self-defeating that the friends who persisted in making contact with him, despite his obstinacy, had persuaded him, with the help of his doctor, to enter a psychiatric institution for treatment.
>
> But Ray was a difficult patient. He seemed to be crying out for help, sometimes literally, and declared a great fear of being left alone, but was nevertheless determined to refuse much of the help that was offered, especially where it involved looking to himself for at least some of the causes of his own distress. Yet he continued to insist that he needed help to the point where doctors, friends and family were at their wits' end, trying to work out what to do with him.

Finally, a change came when his mother, a fit but elderly woman, became seriously ill herself. She had, up to that point, done all in her power to support and sympathise with Ray, travelling regularly to visit him and helping to manage his affairs while he was unable to do so. But the strain became too much for her and she finally came down with pneumonia, which put her in hospital some miles away from Ray.

Only then, when the main pillar of his support was no longer there, did Ray reach a point where he felt forced to choose. When he heard the news about his mother, he sat on his bed in hospital feeling completely abject. He felt so low and alone that he could not even conceive of raising his hand to swat at a fly that rested on his leg. He had felt angry and depressed before, but now the sense of being alone was so enormous and so beyond his understanding that he suddenly gave in to it. Initially it seemed to him as though he had given in to it as just another step in his spiral into darkness and reflective of his inability to find a way out of his misery. But as soon as he had the clear thought that he would give in to the utter misery, it changed. As he surrendered to the depression he experienced a kind of relief. For the first time he became properly aware of the pain in his chest and the grief he had been resenting and resisting for so long. Also, for the first time since he was a child, he felt clear and focused and what he described as 'utterly normal'. As he sat there, allowing anything he thought or felt simply to wash through him, the grief was initially about his failed love affair but, no longer holding it all out, this blossomed into a wider sadness about all sorts of things throughout his life, and to his great distress and humility, as he described it, he realised that he could make a choice. The choice was that he could continue to blame everyone else for the way his life had turned out and to bully them for help which he would never accept, or he could choose to act on his own initiative and shoulder at least some of the responsibility for what was happening. At that moment, the choice came down to packing his bags, discharging himself from hospital and going to see his mother and see what help he could offer her, or curling up on the bed and continuing with dramatising his own hurt and misery.

Ray had come for sessions some time after this and had already gained greater insight than ever before. He reported that, sitting on the bed there, seeing the choices he had made and the choice he could now make, he suddenly felt more like himself than he had for many years. He still felt miserable and lonely and not at all sure he could continue with his life as it was, but he also felt peculiarly adult and clearer of the circular thinking he had been plagued by for months. When he saw the choices, he said he realised there wasn't a choice at all, and he knew that what he had to do was go and help his mother.

Choice

Free will, choice and the ability to act are what make us individuals. Choice is in itself an action with consequences. Having freedom of choice is why we have the problem of the mind and is also the possibility of a solution. No one can be made to change; nothing can be done to you that will change your mind or psyche without your consent.[6]

Wisdom, intelligence and knowledge

Intelligence and knowledge are features of the true individual. They are not part of the mind. We may talk in terms of having a 'good mind' as meaning that a person is intelligent. Indeed, if there is such a thing as a good mind, then it would be one that is flexible and not much clogged up with ideas. With such a mind, a person would more clearly differentiate between ideas.

However, intelligence as it is meant here is actually wisdom. Wisdom is not a feature of the mind. The mind cannot be wise, only the individual can be wise. Wisdom is the perception of how things really are. When a person sees how things truly are, false knowledge drops away. This is not a thought process but clear vision. The gaining of wisdom is achieved in a process that begins with wilful disciplining of the mind by the individual.[7]

What makes change a moral imperative?

> Without ethical behavior, without some kind of standards, then no matter what technique or approach you use, no matter how much truth is in it, it just won't work. It won't do any good. When you release some power into someone's hands, he has to have the ethical behavior, the standards and moral principles to go with it. Every wise person throughout the ages has taught the same thing: that people have got to be good to each other. Without that you will stay forever in the quagmire of ignorance and just being at the effect of life, because you won't let yourself have the power.[8]

In the worldview which Patanjali, and to a lesser extent, Berner, advocated, regardless of what we do, we are all moving inexorably towards consciousness. We can do nothing about it. So say the sages of Hinduism and Buddhism. Other religions generally have some endgame too, one that says we are moving towards reunion with the divine, or some kind of heaven, understanding or enlightenment. But if one agrees with one or other version of this endgame, this then begs the question as to whether we should, or even could, influence this process with our personal efforts; this was a key question of the Protestant Reformation.[9] What we, as individuals, might be able to achieve is so infinitesimally small that it is arguably pointless to try. Why not just sit back and go with the flow rather than go to all the bother of examining ourselves if we are all going to arrive at the same place eventually anyway? Whatever we do, we are following the flow in any case, by definition.

Some schools of yoga take the line that, since we are part of the process ourselves, there is nothing we can do to help it and no point trying. For these schools of Indian philosophy, ethics is empty because they do not see the individual as having will and volition separate from nature. This is true of the Sankara and Advaita Vedanta schools of philosophy, for example. They also teach that ethics is merely a means to an end. We only choose to do the right thing, in other words, in order to get ourselves further along the path to personal enlightenment. Doing the right thing is not an end in itself. Even further than this, they argue that, if we wish to progress, then we must finally work towards transcending morality completely. This is because morality is just another idea, so in the end it will hold us up, like any other idea.

Shyam Ranganathan, a philosopher and commentator on Patanjali, suggests that one reason why this kind of amorality was emphasised in Indian philosophy from the late eighteenth century was, at least in part, colonialism. It suited the British governing authorities to promote this view of Indian religion in order to help legitimise their rule by claiming that there was no indigenous morality. Colonialism could be disguised, conveniently, as the Christian gift of morality and salvation. But Ranganathan goes on to say that the failure, as he sees it, to emphasise the moral foundation of Indian – and specifically Patanjali's – philosophy is in fact a failure to appreciate that this philosophy has been taken out of its original context. The original context was Moral Philosophy. In Moral Philosophy the central debate is about how to live a good or ethical life. Amorality can be found in some schools of Indian practical philosophies, that is true, but Ranganathan argues that it was not such a large part of it as has been thought in the past 200 years.

Patanjali belongs within the international context of Moral Philosophy. The sage's project is entirely concerned with moral, rather than amoral, behaviour as many commentators and translators have claimed. Berner's understanding of the work was read through that of Kripalu, his Indian guru in Patanjali's tradition, and supports this view of progress as moral progress.

Pre-dating the colonial powers by some hundreds of years, Patanjali can be seen to be explicitly opposed to the amoral strand of Indian philosophy. For him, the embodied, lived reality of how we treat others is integral to who and what we are. Moral action is not just a nicety, but key to liberation. It is not just a ladder to get us to another level of awareness, but reflective of our own true self. In a way, it is practising to be who we actually are before we can be who we are naturally and through preference.

Berner follows Patanjali in this and both are clear that we not only can, but are obliged to, act ethically. The instant we become conscious that we *can* improve the way we treat others through exercising our free will, then we are simultaneously obliged to do so. By acting well towards others we can maybe speed up our progress towards consciousness, but personal liberation is not the main reason for acting ethically. The reason we do so is that, once we know we harm others by choosing to remain in ignorance, continuing to do so is to fall further into mind/ego.

Dealing with the mind is not a neutral preference but a moral imperative. Again, this is not solely to aid our own liberation; rather, compassion for others is reflective of our true nature. But until this becomes our personal preference as we align ourselves more and more closely with our true self, ethical behaviour must first be achieved through an act of will and we must make a personal vow to do no harm.

There is, in Patanjali's view, a moral principle according to which all things operate when they are in their true nature. As individuals resting in our true nature, we do no harm to each other. However, when we mistake ourselves for our minds, we then treat each other as means to our own ends. Others are simply there for us as pawns or actors in the narratives of our lives. We do not really experience them as real. At an unconscious level we also blame them for our suffering and so absolve ourselves of the responsibility to treat them well.[10] But when we do not treat others ethically as persons, we actually fail to understand our own true nature.[11]

The state of being a human is the state of bondage to our bodies and our minds, of not being aligned with our true nature. But Patanjali thinks that, although there is no beginning to this state, there is certainly an end to it with which we must engage.

The real purpose of the mind is to help us become our true self. So the very fact that we have a mind implies a moral injunction to deal with it, since doing so will stop us from treating others badly. The mind is actually our conscience. Until we recover our true nature, we are advised to take up a code of ethics in order to reduce the harm we do in the meantime.

Patanjali sees his philosophy as universal truth; it is not a private set of rules but valid for the protection and liberation of all. Moral precepts must be consciously chosen and taken on as personal vows. Since basic morality is rooted in our true nature, it is in our best interests to adopt it even before we have found our way back to our true nature. In Book II of his *Yoga Sutras*, Patanjali gives specific guidelines about what making such a commitment means in practice, such as 'abstaining from harm, truthfulness, abstinence from theft, sexual restraint and un-acquisitiveness'.[12] It might be supposed that these things are impossible to achieve for us ordinary people, but it is suggested that, in committing to live ethically, we commit to improving our ability to live in accordance with these rules and, in so doing, come ever closer to our true self.[13] We cannot expect to be perfect at the start; this is a path towards a goal. The implication of being on a journey is that most of the time we walk it, we are not where we hope to end up. But by taking one step at a time, we gradually get closer.

The real task of yoga is the effort of the individual to gradually take control of their life. This is the first and most important moral choice to make. Liberation is not possible without first doing so.

As Ranganathan says, Patanjali's view is balanced:

> Patanjali presents us with a balanced view of moral responsibility that ought to be seriously considered. He recognises the role of practical, material conditions in a person's betterment, our need of help from those better placed to provide assistance, and the naturally benefic nature of a person who strives to live up to their inherent virtues, but he also recognises that responsibility for our plight rests ultimately with ourselves. Thus, Patanjali avoids the excesses of paternalism, characteristic of leftwing views of responsibility, and the cold indifference characteristic or rightwing views of responsibility.[14]

Key points

- We can dissolve the mind.

- This is because we have free will, choice and wisdom.

- It is a moral imperative to dissolve the mind.

6
THE CLEARING
COMMUNICATION CYCLE

Communication, understanding and thoughts

Communication involves the transfer of a *thought* from one person to another. Where this is successful, there is *understanding*. The relationship with the other person is thus fulfilled with respect to that particular communication. There is no such thing as understanding by oneself; it only and always takes place in relationship.

A thought is not primarily driven by content, such as 'I like that colour blue' or 'It's a nice day,' but by its impetus, which is that it is *a decision to relate to another person*. What differentiates one thought from another is the specific content.

We would not have thoughts the way we do if we were not fundamentally social creatures. We are defined by our relationships and a thought is a decision to communicate in a particular way to another person. The 'particular way' is the content of a thought. A thought only comes into being *because of the desire to communicate* inherent in it. If this fails, the thought does not go away because it *is* a desire to communicate in a particular way. Thoughts have actual existence. So uncommunicated or partially communicated thoughts will accumulate in the mind as actual interference because we never stop trying to get understood, even when we think we have given up hope. This is mind chatter. The idea of 'giving up hope' of being understood is itself an attempt to communicate what was not communicated, but that attempt is now distorted into an attitude about life and others.

Pure communication

Most of what we think of as communication involves some kind of spoken language that uses the body. But in its purest form, communication does not happen via the medium of the body. In this case, a thought does not even become manifest and is not transferred through any medium, including language. That does not mean it is telepathy, for telepathy involves the formation of the thought in the first place but transferred without a body. Pure communication rarely happens, but occasionally a communication is made without a thought taking form. People who are deeply in love sometimes experience this.

At its most simple, a thought consists entirely of the decision to relate to another individual in a particular way. If the channels of communication are open between persons, then that something is received by the other person without there being a transfer. In this case the communication is pure and completely fulfilled. In order for this to happen, the communicator must not be resisting the other person or trying to force the person with whom they wish to communicate. In this case the thought will arise and the action of communication inherent in it will translate into a channel of communication opening up. If the other person is equally open, they will simply receive the communication instantly. There will be a change of state of consciousness in the parties such that both know the communication has been received.

Thought and action are identical in this situation, so the thought does not manifest in separate form from the action and dissipates as soon as the action is successfully completed. There are no consequences to pure thought; in Patanjali's terms, there is no *karma* accruing to it.

The receiver, however, may not be open to the communication and so may choose not to receive it; there is always this choice open to individuals whether conscious or unconscious. But if they do choose to relate, they are simply aware of the communicator in this particular way according to the particular character of that thought or communication.

This pure communication is not strictly a transfer of a thought because the thought never became manifest. To be transferred there has to be some*thing* to be conveyed; this only happens in time and space. A transfer must have points A and B between which the manifest thought is transferred. If the thought never becomes manifest, then the person simply becomes conscious of the other person in this particular respect.

Pure communication is at one end of the spectrum of communication. It is unlikely to be achieved with clients, but if it were, the work of Mind Clearing would be complete in those cases. Clearing mostly takes place in the realm of manifest thought transferred through language of some kind.

Mediated communication

When we attach ideas to the world and name things, we develop language. Language puts a buffer between us and our experiences and changes our relationship with the world.[1] Language is a manifestation of mind. We are so used to communicating our thoughts as manifest ideas via language and the body that we talk about them as though they were subtle things to be passed on in time and space. In fact they are; they are manifest thoughts. The communication of such thoughts to another person is achieved through language of some kind and so is never 100 per cent complete.

At worst, the wish to communicate arose but there was never an attempt to communicate the thought, so it can become suspended in the mind of the communicator as an unfulfilled communication. It remains suspended in the mind only if there is an investment in getting it across to the other person. But often a thought is transferred with modified success. A communicated thought will disappear to the precise extent to which it was successfully transferred. If a person communicates to another and the communication is refused, then this will be a problem to the extent that the person has a mind or can see through it. In other words, if there is no investment in getting the communication across, they will either realise it is not worth trying, since the person is closed to receiving it, or they will take responsibility for getting it across in another way or at another time, or they will simply recognise what has happened and not be troubled by it.

In a relationship where there is charge and attachment to being understood by the other person, then the failed communication, however clear, will create more mind because of that attachment.

Who is responsible for the communication?

For successful communication to take place, the person doing the communicating must take responsibility for getting themselves across. This is especially the case in a helping situation. It is the initiator's wish to get something across to the other person, so that particular communication cycle is entirely their responsibility. The client is being trained to take responsibility for communicating such that actual understanding takes place. The Clearer acts as the initiator in order to enable new learning. It is a dialogue both parties are engaged in so, although the Clearer is taking responsibility for the communication cycles being completed in session, they have to be completely engaged. The result is that there is a true collaboration.

It is not the job of the receiver to receive. However much you want to get something across to another person, you cannot *make* someone into a receiver and force them to get it. That is their choice alone. Indeed, the person whom you want to receive your communication may be unwilling to receive it. The difficult thing for some of us to appreciate is that this is really not their problem; it is you who wants to communicate.

However tempting it is to blame the people you want to communicate to for not receiving you, life will go much better when it is understood that it is the communicator's responsibility to get the message across *in all circumstances*. The Clearer is there to help the client learn how to do this better and, consequently, stop having problems with other people.

This does not mean we are obliged to stay in relationships that are difficult and where we are not received. But we can be more conscious about what is happening and leave if that is the step we have to take in order to be more fulfilled in relating in our lives more generally.[2]

Even though it is undeniable that communication requires there to be at least one other person to communicate to, it remains the initiator's responsibility to get the communication across to the other person. In fact, no one will ultimately refuse a communication, but they may well resist strongly and for a long time. They will not finally resist because what we are here for is to be in contact and communication with each other, so that is what they really want:

> there is no individual in this universe that will ever ultimately refuse a communication. That includes your parents, children, husband, wife or your arch enemy. They may suspend it. They make take your letter and tear it up and burn it, but they will still think, *I wonder what was in there.* They still want to know. So they may delay it, studying you over to see if it's all right. But their goal in life is to be conscious of what it is that you are sending them. That's what they want or they would not be in life. That's the essence of life. It's a definition of life. If an individual does not have the goal to relate, then that individual is not in life. So by definition, we've got them trapped. You may have to serve it on a platter. You may have to dress it up and smooth it out and grease it. You may have to relate it to a thousand other things. You may have to water it down, dilute it by one part to a billion, but nevertheless, to the degree that they are open, they will receive and will not refuse. They are all, every last one of them, pitching with everything they have got to receive every possible communication that they can receive.[3]

Moreover, if we treat people as beings who are in fact trying to communicate with every ounce of their strength, whether they appear to be doing so or not, then it will be much easier to work with them or, indeed, live with them. In fact, a person's task as a Clearer is 'to bring this awareness and ability [that the client fundamentally wants to communicate and can do so], heartily and completely, into your sessions'.[4] Without that, the going will be much harder.

Breaking communication down

In ordinary communication we might engage in pleasant conversation where there is some understanding and the parties will probably feel better because of the nice contact, but no improvement in the ability to communicate will take place so nothing will change with respect to problematic ideas and behaviours. Most conversation is in fact fairly hit and miss, littered with non-understandings and half communications. To add to this is the fear, born of repeated experiences of failure, that we will not be heard and understood. So we often have little faith that things could be any different. Something can go wrong at any stage from a thought arising to getting it across successfully. That means the mind often will be added to as attitudes are reinforced with new experiences that act as 'evidence' for us, reinforcing our ideas about how messed up things can be.

However, we can go through the learning process again, clearing up non-understandings, tying up loose ends and changing bad habits. Mind Clearing does this by slowing down the process of communication and rebuilding it step by step to establish the skill on a more solid foundation.

Basic communication cycles

A cycle is something that goes round. It need not get back to the place it started, but it has a return element. In a basic communication cycle, one person has a thought they wish to communicate and then communicates it to another person who gets it and both parties know this has happened. Each time this occurs, it counts as one communication cycle; it is the action of transferring a thought and knowing it has been received.

The return element that makes it a cycle is that the thought goes from one person to the other and both know it has been received and understood. It would not be a cycle if a person communicates a thought but then does not know if the other person has got it. More often than not, there are several of these cycles within a conversation. I might have the thought to communicate to you how beautiful the flowers in your garden are. I say that to you and you get the thought as fully as a thought can be got that is not instantaneous. And there is a change in state or some other sign such that we both know you have got it; maybe you just nod and smile at me. This is one cycle. You might then have the thought to communicate to me that you grew those flowers from seed. You get that thought across to me, I get it, we both understand that I got it, and that is another communication cycle. And so it may go on.

This is an example of a well-functioning situation for both parties. It might well feel very satisfactory but it is not *progress*. It is more like contactful chat, but although the capacity for relating is being maintained, it is not actually growing. For that to happen something extra is needed, and this is where the *clearing communication cycle* comes in and gives Mind Clearing its particular point and character.

The clearing communication cycle

Communication is not a side effect of Mind Clearing, even though we may need to break it down and turn it into a technique while we are learning. *Communication is the help itself.* Knowing *why* we behave as we do is important, and people need this self-awareness and understanding before they can begin tackling deeper patterns, but being able to communicate to another live person *what we really want to say*, rather than acting out, is the key to unlocking that action. Then the why, the who and the when of any story becomes less important. We can put these variables into perspective and focus on the actual individuals.

Becoming conscious of what communication is and how to improve our ability to communicate is what successful help with the mind is founded upon. Being a good communicator without this consciousness is not enough. A Clearer must know what they are doing and pursue that. If they can get clients to a point where they are able to communicate wholeheartedly without withholding, then the work is done. Clients will be able to take that increased ability into their lives.

The techniques explored here are tools to help achieve this and keep the communication cycles on track. They are not the work itself. The tools may change according to the personnel, the culture, experience elsewhere or any other factor. The help is the magic of person-to-person communication and active understanding.

Mind Clearing breaks 'normal' communication into steps in order to rebuild it, but that is not the essential point. Mind Clearing is about communicating to the point where no more mind is being created and then to where mind actually starts to fall away.

The clearing communication cycle is different from the basic communication cycle because it is performed for the purpose of dissolving the mind. This is a communication cycle with an added ingredient, which is that the Clearer must look for a *compliance* from the client in order to complete the communication cycle. It is an action, so it embeds the learning at a body level and improves communication skills.

This *act* of finding and articulating a compliance enables the client to engage in a communication cycle explicitly or mindfully. This is why help is relational. The compliance must be an act done *in response* to an instruction from another person. The action is double: the client has to understand and receive an instruction from another person and do something with it. So the relationship is enacted and solidified in present time, reinforcing learning of good communication. Also, as the person gains in the ability to be clear about what they think and mean, and communicate that clearly and directly to another person, then distorted communications are required less and less and the mind is deactivated.

The clearing communication cycle is artificially established for specific purposes but is real communication – more real, very often, than anything the client will have experienced before.

I was working with Caitlin on issues with her work situation. She presented at first as very critical of some of her colleagues and frustrated that she did not feel she was doing what she wanted in life. It was difficult, to begin with, to establish clear communication with her and complete communication cycles. At one point I asked her about her work to establish some facts about it. Part of her difficulty was in articulating what the problems she was experiencing actually were. A typical instance of the difficulty in achieving this in the first session was the following:

Clearer: So tell me something you do in your job on a daily basis.

Caitlin: Well, it's not that there's anything wrong with it in many ways; a job's a job. But Karen...that's my line manager...

Clearer: I'm going to stop you there. It's clearly going to be important to look at your relationship with Karen. But now, tell me something you do in your job on a daily basis so I can understand your working day.

Caitlin: OK, yeah, I know, I keep changing the subject, don't I? I do lots of stuff but nothing I really care about. That's the problem; it's not something I want to be doing with my life.

Clearer: So, Caitlin, give me one example of something you do in your job on a daily basis that you are clear is part of your job.

Caitlin: Well, I don't know what my job is; it's crazy working there. And they never stop for lunch; I'm just sitting at my computer all day because that's what everyone else does. I just don't know what to do.

Clearer: Give me one example of something you actually do in your job on a daily basis that you are clear is part of your job.

Caitlin: Yeah, right, OK, yes, well I guess I do the filing, which seems to be what I do a couple of mornings anyway.

Clearer: Is that something you understand as being part of your job?

Caitlin: Yes, filing is part of my job.

Clearer: OK, thank you.

We got there in the end but it was hard going initially to keep the communication cycles on track. I explained why I was doing this and how it helped, which was useful for her. Gradually it got easier and Caitlin started to engage more directly and cycles were increasingly straightforward to complete. As this happened, Caitlin became more interested and also more clear about what the problem actually was. She also reported noticing how often communication cycles at work were incomplete and started trying to rectify this where she could in her own relationships. There were some things she was able to get much clearer on in the work environment, but also she refocused on why she had taken the job in the first place, which was as a step towards something more in line with where she hoped to end up. As she became clearer about this, she redirected her energy into pursuing that goal. The problem that had seemed so intractable to her, and so difficult even to name, became a project she was excited about and in which she eventually saw success.

The content is important but the clearing communication cycle is essential to establish as the framework in which content can be explored. Without successful cycles, the communication is in danger of being lost in the mind and the person will not be learning in the present moment and in the actual relationship with the Clearer.

The clearing communication cycle must be made concrete in deliberate actions in order to rehabilitate low ability to receive, understand and communicate. The benefits of even simple transactions will be enormous if the person is deeply lost in the layers of the mind. Experiencing a complete communication cycle will begin the work of reducing the confusion and quantity of mind and bring increasing clarity of thought and less mind chatter. It may surprise Clearers when they start working with people what a poor state many are actually in when it comes to communication.

Communicating what has been withheld reduces the mind and increases understanding, and the individual is strengthened by the work required of them. The consequent gain in ability to communicate directly means they do not need the mind so much, so it starts to dissolve naturally as a result of what is going on. In establishing new ways of being we render the mind obsolete. So what makes the clearing communication cycle different from a good conversation, in which someone might feel better but will not progress, is the act of compliance making explicit the understanding.

You and me equals more than two

The clearing communication cycle can also be represented as a formula (Figure 6.1): the adding together of my ability in communication with your ability in communication adds up to more than either of us has on our own. So, if I have 6 units of ability in communicating and you have 2 units, then added together we have 8 units.

For the duration of a Mind Clearing session, a person will have more ability in communication than usual, maybe not as many as 8 units, but perhaps 6 units, which is double the person's usual capacity. Progress can swiftly be made in session so that, when they go out into the world, they may not carry the full 6 units away with them, but even 4 or 5 units, as opposed to the usual 2 units, makes for a real change in the way they communicate. Life will improve.

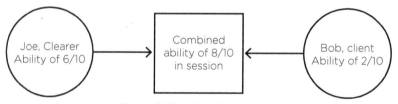

Figure 6.1 The Clearing formula

All the other techniques Berner tested out, like remembering the past, drawing off the charge and taking responsibility, are important. Even without this formula in operation, people may feel better because they may have discharged some emotion and got themselves heard. This may amount to significant improvement, but it is still in the realm of mind. There will be no actual progress because the mind has not been dealt with through the expedient of improving the ability to communicate.

Working with Denis began with quite small steps. His confidence in getting himself across and being received were low, so we worked together on various relationships and situations in his life, each time taking it slowly to develop Denis' ability to get himself across clearly. After only a few sessions, he was feeling much more cheerful and looked forward to coming along. The cycles between us were going much better and a typical example was this one, when we were looking at his sense of purpose in life:

Clearer: Tell me something you do in life that you enjoy.

Denis: Well, it may seem a bit silly, but I enjoy fishing.

Clearer: Thank you. Is there any more on that?

Denis: I don't know, it seems so silly but really, yes, the truth is I feel really good when I'm fly-fishing down in Wales where I go on holiday. It's the best thing in life. I love it.

Clearer: I got it, yes, thank you.

This may look like a small thing, but previously it had been very difficult for Denis to say anything positive about himself or his life and the cycles had taken a long time to complete. It was also hard to hear what I was saying, and even when he did, to believe I was actually interested in what he had to say. So he would give me an answer that was often not related to the instruction at all but which he believed would be more entertaining. He had an idea that he had to entertain people or they would not love him. We discussed this and that helped (later on we went back to that attitude and tackled it with great results), but what really worked for Denis at the time was to see that I wanted to know and that I cared enough to persist with him until I got a response to the instruction. Still further, acknowledging his response, when it was direct, even if it seemed mundane or ordinary to him, was astonishing to him. He said this after the session quoted from above:

> I just want to say that this has been amazing. I never really said anything about the fishing to anyone much because I thought people would think I was really boring. But it's really important to me. It's when I feel most alive. And it feels so good to tell you and for you to be interested. Thank you. It really matters.

The first step: giving the instruction

What needs to happen for a clearing communication cycle to be successful is that a clear thought must be conveyed to another person such that they have a task to perform and know what they must do to comply.

> ...get clear on what you want the person that you are helping to do and to get that thought across to him so that that person understands it. When you do this the person then knows what you want him to do.[5]

We are vague in our conversation with people much of the time; it is not OK to be vague in this situation. The thought, as an instruction ideally, but maybe a question, must be conveyed to the client fully and wholeheartedly without drama or emphasis. The Clearer must also really *want to know* what the response is going to be.

For instance, if there is the clear thought to *tell me something you regret* (about a particular situation), then that entire thought needs to be straight in the Clearer's mind before saying it. Then it should be delivered clearly and fully. It is important that the client understand and receive that thought fully, so the Clearer must do whatever it takes to achieve that end. They might first need to explain *that* they are going to give the instruction and, if necessary, *why* they have chosen that particular instruction and what it means, before giving it.

> If you don't know what you're after, what can you possibly communicate to the [client] but confusion? If you get the question off of a piece of paper and deliver it to the [client] without a full understanding of it yourself, what the [client] will receive is just that: a bunch of words with some vague idea that it says on a sheet of paper that the [Clearer] should ask. That is the thought he will receive. He will actually get that thought, because that's the thought you have.[6]

The precise expression is not what matters in getting the instruction across; the communication is what matters. Within that parameter the Clearer can use whatever it takes, as long as it is ethical, to get the thought or instruction across to the other person. The thought and the language used to convey it must be precise. Imprecision in the use of language reflects unclear understanding. Patanjali says, 'Verbal delusion arises when words do not track [real] objects.'[7] We must take care and recognise our own non-understanding reflected in our language.

Other things can also go wrong in this first step. The Clearer must be genuinely open to whatever answer the client gives. There is no right answer; there is just the answer the client gives to the instruction, just as long as it is a clear response to that particular instruction or question. Having an idea of what the response should be is an error since it is not being open to how it actually is for that client.

> Amanda was working with Matt on his relationship with his mother. Unpacking the difficulties it became clear that it could help to work with Matt's strong feelings of anger and guilt. So she gave the instruction to him to 'Tell me something you did to your mother you think you shouldn't have done.'
>
> She realised later that she had made a mistake right from the start. Something Matt had told her in a previous session, about his relationship with his mother, had stuck firmly in her mind and she had only semi-consciously thought that he must surely be carrying quite a lot of guilt around about the incident. It had been when he was a teenager and had been into drugs. On one occasion he had attacked his mother and injured her quite badly. She had had this in her mind when she gave the instruction. But this was something Matt had done wrong in her estimation. For all she knew, he did not think it was a bad thing, yet Amanda was expecting this to come up and was looking for it as a compliance. As a result, she was only half-open to what Matt was saying when it was not about this incident. She was not actually open to what was true for Matt and this became a problem until Amanda realised the restrictions she was putting on Matt's responses. She had not been willing to draw that particular technique to a close when it would have been more useful to move on, because she was waiting for Matt to come up with this one thing.

Another problem can arise if the client gives a response that the Clearer does not agree is correct. In this case, too, the cycle will not be complete. For instance, if the Clearer gives the instruction, 'Tell me something you love about life,' and the client responds, 'I love taking revenge on people at work and messing up their career prospects,' this may be something the Clearer finds difficult to accept as something that anyone could really love about life, because it does not correspond to their views about what there is to love about life. They might check out exactly why that is something the client really 'loves' and what that means for them, but if the client is sincere in their response, then the Clearer must simply accept this as a compliance.

It is the Clearer's responsibility to see that the client understands and receives the instruction. If this goes wrong, then the cycle is crashed before it begins. If it did not work the first or second time, then it is important to keep working on getting it across. That is not necessarily achieved by repeating it again and again; that may compound the problem of non-understanding and take a long time. If they do not understand, it will be necessary to find another way to get it across. This must be done until it is evident that the person has got the instruction and knows what is wanted of them. The Clearer should make this as easy for them as possible. However, the Clearer might have done what they could to get it across but not be certain whether or not it was understood. The easiest way of being sure they got it is that the client simply goes ahead and complies. But they might take a while to do this and it could be worth checking it out with them. The Clearer does what it takes to get the thought or instruction across to the client until it is certain they have got it.

Many things can go wrong, even with this relatively simple-sounding first step. There are numerous opportunities for pitfalls that will derail the cycle and mean no progress will be made. It might be the wrong instruction to begin with. This would be the case if the area being worked on is not really where the person's interest is at that time; the work is then going against the grain and it will not help much, if at all.

For example, if the client has just had a blazing row with her boss and walked out of her job and can only think about the consequences, then it may not be helpful to continue to work on her communication to her long-dead mother at that point. The Clearer would need to look at the current crisis before going back to the other area. If this mistake is made and the Clearer ploughs on in the face of minimal interest, the client will lose faith. They will probably still do their best to comply and do the work, but really the Clearer has lost them.

This happened with a client who had been coming to me for about eight sessions. The going had been increasingly sticky and, from about the fourth session, I would come away feeling heavy and confused. We would seem to be working on good, relevant material, but it felt like I was fighting something blurry. After the eighth session, I was also pretty sure she wouldn't come back because we'd ended in such a flat way and she hadn't been sure about when she'd be free next. So I got consultation and really focused on what was happening between us.

Finally, and to my relief, she did come back so, at the start of the ninth session, I asked her how things were going for her and what had helped and what hadn't so far. I was quite taken aback by her response. She told me that right back near the start, she had brought a really important issue to the session about a situation with her best friend. But instead of asking her what she wanted to work on that time, I'd assumed the ongoing trouble with her husband would be what we would look at and I just went on ahead with that. At the time I thought it was a reasonable assumption to make, as things were quite rocky between them and they had just had a confrontation. But really she had felt very troubled by the issue with her friend and wanted badly to sort that out in the session. Although we'd apparently done some good work in the subsequent five sessions, I could immediately see now that we hadn't got anywhere much at all because she'd stopped believing in the work and was sitting there being polite, going along with it all and trying her best, but really resenting me and feeling unheard.

After that talk at the start of session nine, everything changed. I really understood what effect this had had and admitted I'd made a mistake. The atmosphere between us clarified right then and we forged ahead and it really felt like we were working together. I felt very moved, in fact, humbled that she'd been honest enough to tell me and also that I'd been fool enough to think I knew best for her.

The person might not be paying attention properly when the instruction is delivered and the Clearer did not notice or went ahead anyway hoping the person would catch up. It is important to wait until the client's attention is right there.

Michaela: When Frank came to me for sessions he'd already done a lot of work, especially in Enlightenment Intensives, and was very well practised at looking inside. So he came along with a clear idea of what he wanted to work on and I saw no reason not to go ahead with that. So we plunged right in. Frank was familiar with the format, so I would go to give an instruction like, 'Tell me what was suppressed in that problem,' and he would lose eye contact with me halfway through me giving it. I was pretty sure from observing him that this was because he was so eager to get going that he was starting to look inside for a response even before I'd finished the instruction. He would quite quickly come back with a considered and sometimes powerful response. So I made a mistake and assumed all was well and allowed this to continue. But after about 30 minutes, it seemed to me that the energy had gone out of the session. I was giving instructions and he was responding, and it all looked OK but I just knew it wasn't and I had an idea it was something about that eye contact because it was bothering me a bit. I'd told myself it didn't matter, but it did. So I paused the session and spoke to Frank about the importance of receiving the instruction fully and looking at me before going inside himself for a response.

He understood and we started again. This time I gave the instruction and Frank stayed with me, holding eye contact so I knew and I could feel the difference immediately. He only looked away when he'd got the instruction and then he did something new: he paused to really take the instruction in and to consider the response. The quality of responses I then got was quite different. He had been perfectly open and clear before, but it felt like there was real work going on between us and a quality of engagement now. As a result, Frank reached a much deeper level of insight than I think he would have found had we carried on as before. At the end of the session, when I asked if he had any comments, he immediately said how grateful he was that I'd stopped it when I had and clarified what to do. He said he'd become so familiar with the style of work that it had become a bit automatic, but, when he waited to hear the instruction, he instantly felt like I wanted to know about him. This made him feel more vulnerable but also touched and he said he found himself coming up with different kinds of responses that felt like they were much more about what was really true for him.

Another error we can make is not addressing ourselves straight to the *individual* in front of us. For this reason as well, we might not notice whether they got it or not. Almost anything can go wrong; it might be beyond the client's current ability to understand or to comply. It might even be too easy for them, so they are way ahead and lose interest. There is a lot we have to get right in getting the instruction straight and getting it across to the client clearly.

The second step: the client does what they have been instructed to do

The second step, which makes [Mind Clearing] different than just communicating back and forth to each other, is that the individual you are helping now executes what it is that you told him to do and tells you what he came up with as a result of complying with your instruction.[8]

When the client has got the instruction and complies, it should be possible to see that they have gone inside and looked for a true response. They have done this, they have looked sincerely and then they find something and they communicate it.

Rachel, the Clearer: I checked it out with Lucy, in fact. I gave her the instruction to 'Tell me a time she was happy.' She seemed to really hear me and then she would look away for a few seconds before responding with something like, 'I remember when I was about four, playing in the garden with my sister and feeling really happy. The sun was shining and we were dressing up and running round laughing.'

Lucy, the client: Rachel would give me an instruction like the one here. It took me a little while to really appreciate that she wanted a straight answer to her question. Now that seems strange, but it was actually strange to start with to see that this was really what was wanted. I learned to really hear what she wanted and then go inside for a response that was really true for me. Sometimes it was difficult to say it, but I gradually learned to just say the truth for me, like that time with my sister and being happy.

Step two actually consists of two actions: 1) looking and 2) communicating what they found. It might be that they looked and could not find anything. If this happens, then more often than not, it is because they are stuck rather than there really is nothing they have done they think they should not have done. In this case, they will need to be encouraged to go back and look again until they come up with something, however big or small.

No one else can do this for the person. The learning and progress can only come from doing it themselves. The Clearer might be certain they know what the client is groping around for and it can seem like the most helpful thing to offer that insight to them. That is an error. It can be explained exactly what is wanted from them, and why, as many times and in as many ways as it takes.

Every [clearing communication cycle] must contain an action by the individual that you are helping. If it doesn't, then all you are doing is just manipulating him or chatting with him, which might be very nice and pleasant but there won't be any increase in ability. So he must carry out an action in compliance with your instruction.[9]

Just occasionally someone will look inside and do what was asked but there was nothing they could find. This is OK if they have really looked. They did what they were told to do and reported back. But mostly there will be something to relate and it is the Clearer's job to see that they do this clearly.

There is plenty that can go awry with the second step. For instance, some people easily go off on tangents and do not respond to the question or instruction. In day-to-day conversation this goes on all the time; they might get stuck in casual connected thoughts.[10] People are reminded of something by another thing that triggers a third thing, and so forth. It makes a kind of sense in that one thing is sort of related to the next; but these are chains,[11] they are related randomly in the mind. The connections are meaningless, and listening to them, while often the social norm, is unhelpful if the purpose is actually to offer real help and relief from the mind.

The instruction might be to 'Tell me something you did that you think you shouldn't have done,' and they think of something. Maybe they remember they kicked the cat one time and have always felt bad about it. They may or may not actually report this, and if they did not, then that is a problem in itself. In any case, the thought may trigger a story about the cat and then maybe a story about their neighbour's cat and so on until the Clearer has lost the thread entirely and the person is now talking about their sailing holiday in the Caribbean and the Clearer is struggling to get back to the point.

This kind of random talking should be stopped as quickly as possible. People might be a bit surprised to be interrupted initially, especially if they have had some other kinds of therapy which encourage it. Nonetheless, they must kindly, but firmly, be interrupted and the compliance must be pursued, or the cycle will be broken. *It is the compliance and cycle that helps.* The response must be expressed and understood fully, until the person is complete on it, but not more than this. It may trigger some insights and that might be positive. But this is a judgement call. If the insights are clearly something really new and valuable to the client, then it is important to hear what they have to say and possibly encourage them to say more to discharge it completely from the mind. On the other hand, what might look initially like a tangent may not be in some instances. Some people take time to work their way round to a compliance, and if they are asked to explain the relevance of what they are saying, they can do so. At least to start with, they may need to tell the whole story in order to explain the compliance; it would not be complete for them without the context. As they see it, their Clearer needs to know this background stuff in order to understand the compliance. People vary in this enormously. But if it is just jumping from one thought to another in a chain, it should be stopped. The compliance should be sought and then the Clearer must go on to the next instruction.

Another pitfall is that the Clearer did not get the thought straight before they gave the instruction and the client was consequently unclear on what was wanted of them or did not understand it for some other reason. If they have not understood the instruction, it is the Clearer's responsibility to sort it out and get it across.

> It pays to have a good instruction that's appropriate to the [client's] level, but no matter how good the instruction is, it won't work unless you know what it is you're after. Make sure the [client] has got it, make sure the [client] is satisfied that he has answered it and make sure you see exactly how the [client] sees that this is an answer or compliance to that. If you don't follow that procedure, it doesn't matter how good the question or the instruction or the technique is, it doesn't matter how appropriate it is, it won't work.[12]

Alternatively, the client might give a response the Clearer does not understand as a compliance.

> The Clearer gave the instruction to 'Tell me something they think they should not have done.' Bob's response to this was to say, 'I laughed.' The Clearer in this case had no idea what Bob was referring to and so could not judge whether or not it was a compliance. So he checked it out and, sure enough, Bob could easily explain that the instruction had immediately triggered a memory of laughing at his little brother when he fell down and cut his hand and feeling guilty about it. It was a compliance because it was something he thought he should not

have done. Once it was explained, the Clearer got it and acknowledged the compliance. The cycle was completed.

The person has come for help and the Clearer is only there to help them. While it may not seem polite to stop them in full flow, it is helping them by doing so and they will appreciate it finally, even if they find it a bit impolite or odd in the beginning. In fact, they will rapidly lose faith in the Clearer and the process if they are not kept on the straight and narrow, because allowing them to ramble will not be of any help and they will know this on some level.

The client may not be interested in the instruction given and decide to answer some alternative instruction of their own; if this is the case, it may be relevant to reassess the area currently being worked on and find something more in line with where the person is. But it may also be an avoidance, so it is vital to pursue it until either the client approaches what they are avoiding and goes on, or, occasionally, the problem area being worked on is reframed.

The most common problem as Berner describes it is that the client:

doesn't even consider or contemplate or meditate on your instruction at all, or he does it on the most superficial level. Because he hasn't learned how to execute something subjectively or from himself, he does not execute the instruction.[13]

In this case the client must be helped to understand what is wanted so they can do it. They might not know *how* to look inside. It simply might make no sense to them because they have never tried it and no one has ever asked them to do it before, so how would they know?

A client's ability to look inside and communicate might be a lot worse than one assumes it could be. They might present as a well-adjusted, aware, functioning individual with a responsible job, a house and a family all that looks normal, but when it gets down to the details of consulting themselves and reporting what is actually going on for them, they are in unknown territory.

If this is the case, they will have to be instructed, perhaps in detail, on how to look inside and comply. It will be necessary to start small and build. This may mean explaining about compliance and being precise. When it is clear they are doing their best to look inside and comply with the instruction and communicate what comes up as a result, this must be accepted for the time being. The Clearer may know the compliance is not complete, but next time it will be deeper and clearer, and they have made a start and there has been progress. The client may go home after the session and explain something to their spouse more clearly than they have ever done before. That might be revolutionary in their household.

In some cases, however, the person might not communicate what came up enough for it to be accepted as a compliance. They are coming to sessions because to some degree or another they are not that great at communicating. So, even when they have looked inside and come up with a response and attempted to get it across, they may not have got it across enough for it to be recognised as such. This is true of many people. They go around certain they have been as clear as anyone could be, but in fact no one really understands much of what they are saying and no one puts the work in to try to get clear on it. For such a person, being clearer might not be as easy as just expanding the thought; they are not really certain about what they are saying themselves. They need help.

A Clearer should never be too strict about this. As long as the communication can be understood clearly enough as a compliance and recognised that the client is doing their best, this should be accepted for the time being; it is a start. But it will be vital to help them get clearer on what they are saying and draw them out until they are making better sense to themselves and to the Clearer.

A good example of this for me was Wilson. He was very able in some areas of his life and professionally highly successful. But when it came to talking about certain areas of problem around his relationships with people around him, such as more peripheral friends and people he saw as having authority in the community, his capacity to get himself across dropped dramatically and he felt so overwhelmed and stressed by it that he even struggled to identify the problem. Finally he whittled it down to something like, 'I feel stupid and self-conscious when I have to deal with some people in my life.' We gradually worked through this until he became clearer about what was actually going on for him, and the level of charge was reduced to the point where he could relax more around it and work on it further to where he was rarely troubled by it. But to begin with, just getting to having a nameable problem to work on was extremely hard for Wilson. He came to the session knowing he wanted to work on this feeling of difficulty and stress but, when I asked him to talk more about it, he was tongue-tied and found it tremendously hard to focus on the issue, as it was so clumped up and stuck together in his mind. Eventually he said, 'Some people make me really nervous.' From that point we slowly built a picture of what happened in these situations and got clearer on it.

Withholding is another common problem. In fact, the whole problem of the mind can be described as one big problem of withholding. But there are different levels of this. There are many reasons why a person might not communicate what comes up for them when they look inside to find a compliance. They withhold the communication. They might, for instance, be ashamed of what they have thought of and assume they will not be respected or liked if they say it. Or they might not say it because they think no one could possibly understand; before, no one else ever understood, so why should the person in front of them this time be any different? Or they do not entirely understand what came up for them.

For one of these reasons they do not really communicate what came up or they say something else or only a small part of it that they think will satisfy their Clearer and get them off their back. Here is ample opportunity for going wrong because if this is ignored and the Clearer goes ahead and accepts any of these as a compliance, then the cycle will be disrupted and there will be no progress. They will lose faith if this non-compliance is accepted, even though this is what they are presenting. They will know it at some level and if it happens too often, they may not come back. In any case, the Clearer will end up having to go back later and work out what went wrong because it is a disruption in the flow between the parties and it will halt the progress – maybe not completely, but it will be clogged up.

James had a lot of withholds to begin with when he came for sessions. There was a lot of underlying shame that we gradually dealt with. But at first, he would regularly have an expression on his face suggesting something had come up when I asked him to say more about something. Then he would often shake his head, almost imperceptibly, and look around for something else to say. He always did his best to respond truthfully, but he often did not say the first thing that came into his head. The first thing was often loaded with anxiety and sometimes shame. In fact, he was so anxious about what might come up that he skirted round first thoughts just in case they were shameful and severely censored his responses, even though when he actually thought about it, it was quite difficult to come up with things of which he really felt ashamed.

When I would ask him what had come up first, he would say, 'Ah, nothing important.' I worked hard with him and gradually he began to express a part of it: 'Oh, I didn't like myself very much around that time but I'm over it now, I accept myself'; or even 'Nothing came up really, I just had a thought about what I've got to do later.' It took some skill to know which of these answers to pursue since it was clear he was doing his level best to communicate what came up and felt highly stressed by some of what he was holding back.

Then, one day, he came in and said, 'I had decided not to say this, but I'm going to anyway' and proceeded to tell me something about his past he'd been withholding, about the way he had behaved in a business deal of which he felt very ashamed. He told me also that, as far as he was concerned, he had never shown his real self to anyone. This was huge for him. But just saying these things lightened his demeanour immediately. His ability in getting himself across in sessions, and also in the rest of his life, leaped up and his business also started to flourish again.

The Clearer can derail the cycle all by themselves by not listening properly. They could have been triggered by something the client said into thinking about their own problems, with their mother, for instance, or they could simply be distracted by thinking about what they are going to cook for dinner or that they need to do their accounts. In any case, they were thinking about something else when the client was communicating and did not understand fully or missed a crucial word or phrase. In this case, the Clearer will need to ask them to say it again.

Another way a person may not have listened properly is that they were listening in a narrowed way because they were judging what the client was saying, perhaps not even consciously.

> Ginny: I realised I was hearing what Rachel was saying about how she feels she should be doing more to help her mother, but although it was going into my ears, I was all the time thinking that, as far as I was concerned, she was doing more than enough. So I made an error that nearly destroyed the whole session. I told her she was giving herself a really hard time and was doing lots for her mother already and perhaps she should work at getting some support for herself.
>
> As soon as I'd said it I could feel it was the wrong thing to say. Rachel looked at me in a strange way and I could see that I just hadn't been listening properly to what her concerns really were. Whether or not she might be wise to look at her own support systems, that was not where the session was. At that point, it was essential to Rachel that I really understand her sadness about her mother and her feelings of being inadequate. My own ideas about what was reasonable had pretty much completely blocked out the real person in front of me trying to articulate her difficult feelings. From what I understood, I was the first person she was confiding in, and I was off on some mission and not with her and getting how it was for her at all. Even if I was right, and later had thought it was clear that Rachel could do with looking at her own support systems, the error was in not getting how it all was for her and making my own judgement, which was

actually quite different in many respects from her real sense of what was appropriate for her to do.

If the Clearer thinks the client is not really giving a compliance in line with the instruction, even though the client may think they are, and the Clearer does nothing to stop this, then the Clearer will become sleepy. They must think back. Was there something that was left unchallenged that they were not convinced by?

> Clearer: Tell me how going around with the attitude that you're special affects you in life.
>
> Client: It means I treat people better.
>
> Clearer: OK, yes, thank you.
>
> In this case, the Clearer was not sure how having an attitude of being special, which is what this client identified as something he often experienced, made him treat people better. It needed to be checked out. Letting this go and acknowledging it as a compliance in the face of uncertainty would derail the cycle.

If, on the other hand, the client is responding and the Clearer is happy they are getting compliances, but the *client* is not really convinced they are giving proper compliances, then the *client* will get sleepy. If this happens, the Clearer will need to check out what is going on with the client and get them to explain their compliances more until both get that they are complete.

> Clearer: Tell me how going around with the attitude 'I'm special' affects you in life.
>
> Client: Well, I suppose I tend to be quite proactive at work and put myself forward for new projects.
>
> Clearer: Thank you. Tell me another way in which going around with the attitude 'I'm special' affects you in life.
>
> Client: Being special means I treat people better.

Clearer: OK, thank you. Tell me another way in which going around with the attitude 'I'm special' affects you in life.

Client: Um...well, I guess it probably makes me a bit mean sometimes...like when people aren't as good as I am at things, I can get impatient sometimes.

Clearer: Thank you, yes, I get that. Tell me another way in which going around with the attitude 'I'm special' affects you in life.

Client: (quite long pause) I'm not sure, really. I suppose thinking I'm special is a bit arrogant, so I probably offend people. I've mostly got it under control, but that sounds right, some people are offended by things I say.

Clearer: Thank you. Tell me another way in which going around with the attitude 'I'm special' affects you in life.

Client: (much longer pause) I don't know, really. I don't think this attitude really holds me up much in life. It seems to work pretty well for me most of the time.

In this case, it *sounds* like a clearing communication cycle, but it is not. The Clearer had had some experience of working with this sort of attitude, so she drew on this as well as her own case and filled in the gaps in the cycle herself. She understood how going around thinking you're special can make you think you're treating people better, so it could be a clear compliance and she made a mistake and elected to understand the responses in her own way. She did not check it out.

In fact, the client was feeling uneasy about his responses from the start. He was giving compliances he liked to think were true but he had already identified this as an attitude that was a problem for him, so what he was saying was out of line with that. The fact that his Clearer seemed to think it was OK was also confusing because of what they had been talking about with respect to this attitude. So his judgement felt mixed up. On the other hand, it was not requiring much hard work from him because he was increasingly intellectualising, so he carried on, as he was keen for the session to go well, and chose to assume she was right. But as he relaxed into how easy the session had suddenly become, he started to feel sleepy.

Sometimes a session can be hard going and it will be derailed if the Clearer gives up on getting instructions across to the client. Cycles can be difficult to establish and the client may be in a bad way, going off on long tangents and never really grasping what it is that is being asked of them to start straightening this situation out. This requires tenacity and courage from a Clearer and sometimes they effectively give up on getting the instruction across to their client. In this case, they may end up with a pleasant enough chat or the client will just jump from one thing to another, but the session will not work. The Clearer has to be committed to helping the client, and to do this, the instruction must be clear and it must be communicated so that the client gets it and complies. It does not matter how long it takes to achieve this. This *is* the work. As soon as it is back on track, with the instruction clear, the energy snaps back and the muddled feeling that has likely built up clears. That muddled feeling is mind.

The third step: understanding what the client has communicated and letting them know

The third step in the clearing communication cycle consists of two actions performed by the Clearer: 1) understanding what the client has said and 2) letting the client know they have understood. This is straightforward but, once more, there are a surprising number of pitfalls to be avoided for it to be properly achieved.

If the client does not know they were heard and understood, even if they were, progress will slow down and finally stop. They are putting a lot of effort and goodwill into complying with the instructions and, if they start to be uncertain as to whether they are really being understood, or if the Clearer seems a bit offhand about the effort they are putting into what they are doing together, then the client will stop co-operating eventually. They may well carry on for a while because they want to have good relations, but sessions will deteriorate. It must be acknowledged precisely what the person said in complying with the particular instruction given.

The more experienced a Clearer is, the more this becomes clear because a non-understanding will feel wonky. In either case the Clearer will need to say to the client that they did not hear or did not understand. They will need to ask the client to repeat what they said or explain it more fully until the Clearer understands the compliance. The Clearer must then indicate to the client, clearly, that they have understood.

> I remember a time when I was really tired and distracted giving a session. I drifted off with a thought about something I was trying to handle around some building work I was having done. This was just for a couple of seconds, but I was really gone from the room. I was looking at my client but wasn't seeing her for those few beats. And when I snapped back, she was looking at me and had clearly said something of import. She was tearful and said, 'I never realised that before about my mum. I feel terrible.' And I realised I'd missed some potentially huge thing. I was mortified, and I hesitated. I hated to admit I hadn't heard it, but I knew I had to or we'd carry on and it would be a farce. So I said something like, 'I'm sorry, I didn't get that, would you repeat it please.' I think she was a bit surprised, as I'm usually pretty alert, but she said it again and I got it, and thank goodness I did. The session did wobble a bit at that point, and it took us probably a few minutes to secure that trust again, but it would have been a whole lot worse had I just let it go and pretended I'd heard her.

The Clearer should avoid saying the client's responses back to them or paraphrasing what they have said. This can be very tempting to do and seems so harmless or even actively helpful. It is a common way of proceeding in some talk therapies and advocated for perfectly coherent reasons within those frameworks. But it is better not to do it here. Repeating something back to a client, even if you are just checking out with them what they said, is risky. It is too easy to be wrong. Even one word out of place or an incorrect emphasis may signal to the client you have not understood them. The result of this could be having to make repairs to the relationship.

Sometimes a client communicates something unclearly and the Clearer may think they are being helpful in repeating it back, but more clearly. This is a mistake. Even if the Clearer is right, it has become the client's insight and if the Clearer repeats it for them in better shape, there is less chance of the client sourcing it from themselves and learning from it.

> Maxine was really struggling with some stuff around her purpose in life and trying to say what it was that gave her a sense of meaning. She was talking a lot about the things she'd enjoyed as a child, including pottery, and the pottery classes she had taken as an adult and the way she liked the feel in her hands and the expression with which she could work.
>
> Janet was following all of this and prompting Maxine as necessary. It was quite emotional in places as Maxine expressed pleasures she had never told anyone about before and Janet was very engaged. So at one point, when Maxine was trying to say something about her creativity with her hands and what that said about who she was, she thought she was helping Maxine and said, 'I understand what you're saying, you're a potter.' But Maxine looked at her, quite shocked: 'No, that's not what I mean at all. I don't care if I never do any pottery again in my life, that's not what I'm saying.' Janet realised she had been drawing her own conclusions and had put words into Maxine's mouth that were quite a distance from what she was actually trying to explore and explain.

Perhaps even more tantalising is when the Clearer thinks they can see a key point the client is missing about their case and is tempted to tell them. While in a small minority of cases it may help to do so, it is far safer not to say anything. First, the Clearer could easily be wrong and this will signal to the client that they are not understood at all. It is best, and probably more usually correct, to assume one is wrong about the causes of people's cases. Even if the Clearer is right, it is not OK to say it. If the Clearer has an insight about the client's case and tells them, it robs the client of their own process and the development of their own understanding about their situation. The Clearer may also be too far ahead of the client's own understanding and it will simply lead to confusion.

I made a mistake working with one client. He was having difficulties dealing with his ex-wife over access to their children and it seemed so obvious to me that he was blaming her for what were, in many instances, things he had mostly initiated himself. He told me how controlling and difficult she was, for instance, but when he spoke about his own behaviour and what he had expected of the marriage, I could see that he was very controlling himself.

We worked a lot with communicating to her as though she was present and there were years of bitterness stacked up. He occasionally expressed his regrets and talked about her being a good mother, but these were just moments in what was otherwise an anger-fuelled communication of blame. I realised he had to do this before he could move on, so we talked about it and he recognised that he was holding on to a lot of frustration that needed to be expressed. Some of the trouble, however, was that he was actually not practised at talking about how he actually experienced life, so it was all directed outwards. At the end of one session I suggested he look at a book that deals with communication in intimate relationships. I thought he would get something out of the information in there, and he thought this was a good idea. But during the week before our next session, I got an email from him. He thanked me for the recommendation but said the book was no good for him. He was already good at communicating; it was his ex-wife who needed to get better at it.

I realised the mistake I'd made. I had assumed his case was at least partly clear to him, but it wasn't at all. In the end, I think I was both right and wrong. He did need to get better at really communicating what was going on for him in relationships and he did improve at this. But I had also not taken seriously enough his real need to discharge his anger and pain. I had disrespected him in thinking I knew best and realised I had been humouring him. As soon as I dropped this, it felt like we really began to work together and he started to open up about how desperate he felt about the marriage failing and what it meant to him.

It is key for the client to know what they want to communicate and to get that across. Doing it for them will not help. It might seem infuriatingly obvious that they are hanging on the edge of a huge revelation and the Clearer might be itching to reveal it. They might be correct and it might change the client's life to know it, but it will take them much longer to get it and own it if the work is done for them. The Clearer might be in the right ballpark, but clients have their own way of saying things, and it is important to go with that.

Paraphrasing a compliance back to the client is too close to evaluating what they have communicated. The task of asking for a compliance is designed to improve the client's ability to relate and become clearer about what they think. Being right about what they need to say or are going to say or have said does not help and is not the point. They will learn nothing by anyone trying to repeat what they have said back to them, and they might lose something. If the Clearer is not sure about what the client said, they should ask them to repeat it, even at the risk of seeming to be stupid or not to have been listening. They will get clearer and maybe even learn something more, and the Clearer will also get clearer without having to second-guess them or risk making an error. If the fear is they might find it irritating to be asked to repeat it, then the reason should be explained. People who understand why something is being done are usually happy to continue.

The four steps of the clearing communication cycle are:

1. The Clearer gets a clear thought across to the client.

2. The client does what is asked of them.

3. The client responds and communicates the results of complying with the instruction or responding to the question.

4. The Clearer listens, understands and makes it clear that this has been done.

Using the clearing communication cycle in Mind Clearing

> Progress does not take place by the person just talking and telling stories. That won't do it. It has to be the result of responding to you and following your instruction. That is what untangles the knots of life, the hang-ups in the mind. It is beautiful.[14]

Following the clearing communication cycle makes for real progress because it puts into steps *explicit understanding between two people and makes it concrete*. This is the magic that makes for significant shifts and dissolves the mind.

There is no need to assess or diagnose the client. If the clearing communication cycle is applied well, the client will do all the assessment needed themselves. Some assessment of the client is, of course, unavoidable and necessary for deciding what to work on with them and how to do so. A person needs to be good at assessing in order to be good at Mind Clearing, but it is still not about diagnosing the client as a type; that is not what helps.

Within a Clearing session the focus is on completing clearing communication cycles and helping the person communicate what has been withheld and what all their aberrant behaviours are actually saying in distorted form. So content matters to the extent the person finds it hard to communicate it.

There are specific ways within Mind Clearing to approach problem areas, such as depression, trauma, boundary violations, current problems and relationship issues. Within those areas, the cycles must be kept clear as the engine of the help. The focus, however, remains on the individual and their ability to get themselves across, through and despite the content. This is an important shift in emphasis from many talk therapies, and goes hand in hand with the philosophical position that there is an individual with whom we can and must work.

Breaking the communication process into its component parts and seeing that each one is fulfilled is a vital helping aspect of Clearing. Though there are many subtleties involved in carrying it out with skill, what is going on at the core in this cycle is repeated until the client is able to communicate to others without the need of substitute ideas and behaviours. In finding compliances and learning to deliver them clearly to someone who really wants to know, the mind starts to dissolve because the reason for it being there begins to come apart.

The cycle points to and strengthens the individual. By having to locate the *one who can do the work of looking*, the client has to start looking in, in order to look out from their point of stability. Many people need careful instruction simply in how to look, but this is helped by the Clearer addressing the individual and keeping the cycles clean. In this way, Mind Clearing shifts the mass of mind by finding a point of leverage.

7
WORKING WITH ATTITUDES

Fixed attitudes are the building blocks of the mind. The main feature of any attitude is its *meaning* or *significance*. In fact, an attitude *is* the significance we have given to an event or memory. When we back off from another person and have an idea about ourselves and them, this itself is the act of taking up an attitude, which is a point of view. Where before there was just relationship, now we have given meaning to a situation, so it is *significant* in particular ways depending on our particular make-up. We label a piece of experience that is too much to face as it is. By labelling it we gain some idea of control over it.

Attitudes are a problem when they become fixed. As such, they make up the mind. Examples of attitudes might be 'people are good', 'people are bad', 'life sucks', 'I'm not good enough', 'I'm special', 'nobody loves me' and so forth. As soon as you identify with any idea, such as a core belief like 'I exist' or a more surface idea such as 'people can't be trusted to do the job properly', you filter what you allow to be true in life, in your particular story. That filter means you will resist anything not in line with the state of being you have taken on. So gradually more and more events get pushed into the subconscious mind because they do not fit with your dominant attitudes or points of view and you have more and more evidence supporting these as a result.

A person going around with the attitude 'people are bad' will be able to give all kinds of examples of this to confirm it. In their subconscious will be memories of events they resisted that serve as evidence that 'people are good'. Those events were resisted because they did not fit with the conscious half of the pair. The person can relate much more easily to the attitude that 'people are bad' because that is the accessible side of the opposite, it is conscious. The idea that 'people are good' will be difficult to grasp as a reality because the person cannot relate to the subconscious aspect of the mind.

Bob is going around with the attitude 'No one loves me,' so he has an attitude on his perception that acts as a filter. If someone comes along and offers him chocolates, this could be construed as evidence that some people, at least, do love him. It is not in line with his dominant view of life which precludes acts of kindness directed at him, so he partially, or maybe even totally, resists the experience and pushes it into his subconscious. At the time he might have refused the chocolates or taken them with suspicion, but he will probably soon have a somewhat hazy memory of the incident and perhaps none at all, as he has dismissed it as effectively untrue. He may even find a way to turn it into evidence that he is not really loved; it might have been that he was offered strawberry creams, which he does not like, an event which he twisted into the idea that the person deliberately gave him something he would not like in order to demonstrate their dislike with the subconscious thought, *she knows I don't like strawberry creams and she gave them to me anyway!*

The opposite to an attitude will always be there, mostly in the subconscious. But people can get stuck in a mind trap, flipping from one side of a pair of opposites to the other, and back, over and over. The bipolar condition is an extreme example of this, but many of us can get stuck in a less violent opposition. In making a decision a person can be driven by an underlying pair such as 'I want it/I don't want it', and flip from one to the other and not find a way out. Each time a decision is made, the person then flips back to the opposite which seems suddenly very attractive.

In the end, the opposites are meaningless because both sides of any attitude are untrue. The attitude, for instance, that 'I am capable' is only relative. I might be capable at building matchbox houses but not very capable when it comes to working out mathematical problems. These designations only have meaning in relation to other things; they have no absolute truth. Establishing the truth or otherwise of such beliefs might be of some use, and some therapies use this as a technique. But this will not change the underlying attitude; we will still be trapped in its duality.

Many methods have worked on getting people to stop acting on the negative of an attitude by replacing it with the positive. For instance, it sounds like good sense to stop going around with an attitude like 'everything is bad' and to learn a more positive outlook on life by adopting an 'everything is good' attitude. But the problem with that approach is that they are still caught in the mind trap of opposites. The person has merely swapped them over and has probably also put some new ideas on top of the old ones in the effort of doing so. The person is no closer to reality. Both attitudes, 'everything is good' and 'everything is bad', are still ideas. No idea is any closer to reality than any other idea. Some ideas are undoubtedly preferable to others in improving our functionality, but no idea is finally better than reality, and all fixed attitudes cause us difficulties in relating to others.

Anything or anyone associated in a person's mind with the opposite of an attitude with which they are identified will be regarded as the enemy. Even though, most of the time, we are not trying to do anything to anyone, if someone becomes associated with a resisted attitude, then they become the enemy.

Michael: I had this thing where I thought my boss was really my enemy. She would do things like schedule meetings on dates I couldn't make, or set a new project team up with me in a role I didn't like. Things like that. And it would set off in me this whole thing where she was out to get rid of me or undermine me. I got into such terrible states about it and would go on and on about it to my wife and friends. It was so automatic for me to think like that and see her (and other people in my life) as the enemy that I didn't bring it up in sessions for ages. It was just business as usual for me. But when I sorted out some other stuff around not trusting people and communicated all this material I'd never said, some things changed that I hadn't expected. I was generally a bit more able to let things go and I started noticing different things about my boss and not automatically assuming she was deliberately setting me up for a fall. In fact, I started to think she might not actually be thinking about me at all when she was doing these things. I wasn't particularly on her radar, except, I'm a bit sad to say, as someone to avoid because I'd get pissed at things. So I finally got round to looking at that in sessions and I saw that I was going round with an attitude that 'It's not fair' and feeling really angry about it. I worked on it with my Clearer and I finally got to a point where I could see how I was using this attitude to stay angry and not take responsibility for my life in some ways.

In the mind there is conflict,[1] but if you get the subjective reality of this for yourself, then you can become conscious that people are not out to get you. Getting clearer on reality cannot be entirely successful *until* the attitudes that are dictating how you see the world are rendered obsolete.

States

Along with attitudes, there are *states*. A state is an attitude plus the energetic, bodily, emotional part of the distortion that goes along with it. Our whole being will reflect and be imbued by the state that goes with the attitude. For example, depression is usually a state. It is a syndrome of negative attitudes combined with physical manifestations.

The attitudes in the mind are real, not just cognitive; they have an energetic and physical aspect. Depressed people do not just feel depressed, they *look* depressed. That is the state reflected in their whole being. This is why it does not work long term just to decide to think differently. We have to act to remove the attitude from the narrative that we call our personal identity; this must be done energetically as well as cognitively.

Frustratingly, it would take longer to reason our way out of an attitude than it does to get in it in the first place, and there is a danger that, in trying to do so, we will create new attitudes in the attempt to get rid of the old ones. Even if we can see our attitudes and how we operate from them, it is not possible simply to drop them because we have a strong investment in maintaining them. The investment will not be released unless the original communication is found and delivered and received. When that happens, there is no need to keep it going.

Attitude clearing

A person is free of their mind when they no longer have any *fixed* attitudes. Such a person is free to choose what attitude to take on or even choose not to take any attitude on.[2] To help people free themselves of attitudes, Berner developed a technique. Techniques are, he said, 'a method for accomplishing more smoothly, more rapidly and more definitively, that which eventually happens anyway'.[3] To dismantle attitudes, he took the clearing communication cycle and added steps for dismantling attitudes: *attitude clearing*.

Berner believed that, if he could get a person to see what problem an attitude was a false solution to, he could then get them to see what the attitude was actually communicating to others. In other words, he could get people to recognise what they were *really* saying through the attitude and get them to say it directly instead of through distorted behaviours.

Getting the message

For this process to work, people first have to see:

  - ◉ *that* they are taking on an attitude by their own free will

  - ◉ *why* they are taking it on

  - ◉ that they must get over that reason for having the attitude.

They must see that what they are doing is engaging in a false solution that, rather than helping, serves to perpetuate the problem. The real solution lies in finding and delivering the message. Attitude clearing takes people through these steps systematically.

In terms of why people identify with ideas in the first place and split away from themselves, Berner said:

> Therapeutically, you are not after that decision. You are after discharging the emotional charge that led up to the split so they can feel what they have not felt and express what they have not expressed. If they do that, it will automatically dissolve the split and the decision to not be themselves.[4]

In Patanjali, Berner found confirmation of his approach in the advice to ponder the opposites,[5] since duality is what structures the mind. Unless we do this, we will continue to identify with the attitudes and regard them as true.[6]

Ben's case illustrates how attitudes and beliefs can arise from a normal childhood, with loving parents and no outstanding trauma. It also shows how once the seed of a belief or attitude has been set, it develops, its logic becoming 'confirmed' by investments that seem useful.

As a baby, Ben communicated, as babies do, by making faces, using eye contact, moving his limbs, and crying. All the time he was learning how his signals brought responses. This worked well until his parents decided, as parents do, that he shouldn't always get attention on demand and it was time they stopped picking him up every single time he cried.

When he reacted with red-faced fury, his parents thought he must be in pain (perhaps he was) and they picked him up, so the signal-response equation was restored – until they strengthened their resolve and toughed out even his most strident bawling. It was, they decided, just a phase in his development that he would grow out of.

And they were right: his behaviour changed as his mind began the process of adjusting his perceptions to 'make sense of' his experience. Of course, this process was non-verbal up to that point, though if he could have put it into words, he might have said, 'Asking doesn't work.'

However, it was not as if his parents had suddenly withdrawn their love; they still responded to his signals for much of the time and remained attentive to his needs. Thus, Ben's growing up proceeded smoothly enough. He still lapsed into fury from time to time when he failed to get the attention he sought, except that now he gave up more quickly.

But when he fell quiet on such occasions, his parents thought he seemed miserable and withdrawn. So they began to 'coax him out of it' with extra attention, partly out of guilt for having ignored him in the first place. In other words, a form of indirect communication was developing. Direct asking had stopped working for Ben, but a non-verbal substitute, becoming withdrawn and miserable, was proving more effective anyway.

By the age of 4 years, his withdrawn states had become familiar. He was now 'the moody member of the family', prone to sulks, often for no obvious reason. But it was no great problem; his parents had learned how extra treats and cuddles worked wonders. He was, they thought, 'just moody by nature', simply needing more attention than his older sister.

However, by the onset of puberty, his sulks had evolved into door-slamming, I'm-not-speaking episodes, when he felt a certain level of frustration. He complained that his parents 'just didn't understand' him, which was true, for how could they if he didn't communicate directly?

By his late teens, Ben realised that sulking was childish and unattractive, so he learned to use charm to get what he wanted, again, an indirect communication. In fact, he became so adept at manipulating people that he landed a job in marketing where such skills were valued. On the face of it, Ben had 'grown up'. He was earning good money, was popular and, being handsome as well as charming, he was not short of girlfriends. But when he was 30 he fell in love, proposed marriage and was rejected. He fell into a depression and ended up coming for Clearing sessions.

The way he told it in his first session, Ben had enjoyed a happy childhood, loving parents, and success, until his girlfriend rejected him. Now he was hurt and angry, in particular because when pressed to give reasons for rejecting him, she explained that she found him 'fun to be with but too superficial and unforthcoming for a long-term relationship'. This was a description that echoed previous relationships. He felt misunderstood by women and at a loss to understand why they saw him that way.

But when, in his next session, he worked with the Clearer to communicate to significant others in his life as if they were present, he did seem unforthcoming to the Clearer. He was happy to tell others how he saw them, but unwilling to reveal much about himself. When the Clearer discussed it with him, he thought about it and thought it was explained by his being easily hurt, so he tended to clam up about personal matters rather than be open about how sensitive he was. For example, his last girlfriend used to ask him, 'What's the matter?' (because he still tended to go quiet when charm didn't work), and he would reply, 'Nothing', believing that if she really loved him, she would know how he felt without his having to tell her. 'Real soulmates', he explained, 'should know each other's needs and feelings intuitively without having to spell them out.'

As Ben began to explore the attitude that came into play when he was emotionally challenged, he suggested, 'It's no good asking for what I want' as a way to describe it, or 'Asking for what I want is dangerous,' or, another way to describe it, 'It's dangerous to show my feelings,' and 'Others should know how I feel without me having to tell them.' He thought each one said something about what was going on for him, but his final choice of attitude to work on was, 'I can't ask directly for what I want.' And when asked to nominate an opposite belief as step-two of attitude clearing, he chose, 'I'm wide open about what I want.'

When the time came to identify Ben's investments in holding his belief, he nominated: 'I avoid the risk of rejection' (if I don't ask, people can't say no).' Also, 'People have to work harder to please me if it's not clear what I want,' and 'By not asking for what I want, I avoid showing my vulnerability.'

The next stage was to find the message represented by his belief, and Ben identified this as: 'I want love and contact with you.' However, before he could communicate this, in particular to his mother, he needed to express his original fury at being denied such love and contact when it seemed to him that he was asking for it loud and clear.

When this final step was completed, Ben confirmed that, in future, and where appropriate, he would communicate directly rather than getting sidetracked by his old belief.

Pre-requisites for attitude clearing

In order to engage successfully with attitude clearing a person must:

- be able to engage in and complete communication cycles

- be free from immediate problems and distractions

- be able to look inside and communicate clearly and openly what comes up as a result

- be capable of originating a conscious thought.

This last point, being capable of originating a conscious thought, means the client must be able to have a thought by conscious choice. This is different from the automatic or story-based thinking and connections of the mind. For example, if a person is instructed to look at the pine tree outside the window and say, 'The pine tree is pink,' and they can do so, then they can originate a thought from themselves. If they do not comply with the instruction because they insist the pine tree is actually green, not pink, then they cannot get past the automaticity of their mind. The Clearer would usually already have a good idea of whether their client could do this from the work already done.

The mind automatically attaches meaning to what people are seeing and categorises it. If a client automatically attaches the meaning 'green' to the sight of the pine tree, then they may not be able to separate out the actual tree from the meaning 'green' in this instance. They must be able to choose to attach one meaning or another to something in life rather than automatically connect the thing with what they think it means. This is the capacity to appreciate the difference between the thing itself and the meaning we attach to things. The ability to choose to believe something, rather than be at the mercy of automatic ideas about the world, is what we are looking for in order to work with attitudes directly.

It might take some time for a person to be able and willing to do this. But it is important to be able to do so because this is the point where the individual is strong enough to deal with the mind. The more freedom the individual has, the more creativity and space there is. The more mind there is, the more fixed and repressed a person becomes.

For a Clearer, there is no point in dealing with the mind; that would be like trying to reason with a puppy.

> The individual must 1) be able to communicate; 2) be able to think a thought of his own; 3) must (sic.) be free from problems in his life; 4) dismantle the mind; and 5) take the original reason for the mind's existence and dissolve it to the point where it ceases to exist.[7]

There has to be a good, trusting relationship between Clearer and client for all of this to work. Most therapists and Clearers know this, but they may not appreciate the details of why this is. The reason is that we are all here to relate to others. For this very reason, however, we keep ourselves in a state of ignorance and inability. Deep down, this is because we do not want to hurt others. If we free ourselves from the false solutions of the mind, and come into our power as individuals able to choose what to think and do, we are afraid we will hurt others. For this reason, we keep ourselves constrained and small and stupid.

The remedy for this, as all religions teach, is to consciously take up a moral code[8] to check our behaviour. This prevents us from doing serious harm to others while we are in the process of becoming ourselves and releasing ourselves from the constraints of the mind. (For more on this, see the discussion on guilt and karma in Chapter 8; also see Chapter 5 for a discussion on the moral imperative.)

There are four steps or techniques to Berner's programme for clearing attitudes, as listed below and detailed in the sections that follow:

> Step 1: finding the attitude and then finding an opposite to the attitude
>
> Step 2: pondering the opposites
>
> Step 3: identifying the message, or the medium is the message
>
> Step 4: delivering the message

Step 1: finding the attitude and then finding an opposite to the attitude
FINDING THE ATTITUDE

The attitude worked on could be any of a number of attitudes the person is using as a false solution to a problem in relating. It must be an area the person is interested in, or they will judge that they are not making progress. What the Clearer is interested in working on is not the point, though they can be a useful guide on what areas might be fruitful.

The Clearer may need to explain and encourage the person to explore what sort of ideas and behaviours they are attached to, and need to act on in their daily life, that are holding them up. This might be something like, 'I'm not good enough,' 'Others can't be trusted,' 'I'm better than others,' 'Life is bad' and so forth.

The attitudes people identify are often more complex at the beginning, as the person starts out less clear. They might come up with something like 'Other people can never be trusted,' 'I'm only trying to help' or 'I do my best but it's not good enough.' It will work anyway and, as the person gets more clarity and knows what to look for, they tend to get more succinct. They may work through, for example, 'Life is bad' or 'Nothing works out for me' to the simplicity of an attitude such as 'bad'.

Another way of helping the client identify attitudes is to ask the person what they are dramatising in life. For example, a person might be dramatising that they cannot cope, or that life is hard, or that others are stupid or that they are always exhausted. They believe these statements to be true; after all, they have accumulated a lot of evidence to back them up. They might say, 'That's not an attitude, that's how it really is.'

This is not to deny that bad (or good) things happen to people. It is to say that, even though some bad things may have happened to John, for instance, it is only when he gets stuck in the attitude 'bad things always happen to me', or 'everything's bad' or 'no one loves me' that this becomes an ongoing problem for him and an area of stuckness. He will start acting this out and finding supporting evidence rather than just have occasional bad experiences. He will not define himself by these events.

> I've had people for sessions who seem very able in many ways and I've wondered whether to do attitude work with them. But I've learned it's often too early. A typical example of this was a woman who had a lot of understanding about her case and was very willing and fairly able in communicating. We did a few sessions and it became apparent to both of us that she had a very obvious attitude going of being better than others. We did a bit of work in looking at how it worked in her life and how it was running her but it quickly became clear that, although she had some appreciation that it was an attitude, this was really a theoretical understanding. She was actually too identified with it at the level of body and behaviour to work on it at that point. She was quite clear in herself that it was actually true: 'Well I am better than others,' she told me, 'Not absolutely everyone, but nearly everyone.'
>
> We did some more work around this and she communicated a lot of material to her parents. The attitude began to loosen up a bit as she saw around it and experienced greater appreciation of others.

A clue to something being an attitude is a person saying that something is *always* like this, for example, 'I'm always unlucky,' 'People are *always* on my back,' 'I *always* mess it up,' 'She *never* listens to me.' The fact is that sometimes one is unlucky, or people give us a hard time or we do something daft, but not *always*. 'Always' is a clue to what the person is dramatising in life. From there they can be helped to see what attitude they are tending to get stuck in. They might not be in that attitude all the time, but it comes up and gets in the way of their getting on with their lives. The attitudes they are in all the time will be more difficult to identify; they are as invisible to us initially as the air we breathe.

> 'It's always the same,' he said, 'I can never stay in a job long. They always get fed up of me and give me a hard time. I don't get it, me, but I've given up now. I do my own thing.' This was at the start of sessions with Matt. He wasn't my usual sort of client, but a good friend had

recommended sessions and he decided to try it, even though it was very unfamiliar territory. Matt arrived with all sorts of ongoing problems that we gradually unpicked and was deeply entrenched in a belief that others couldn't be trusted and also had what we identified as a 'fuck you' attitude that gave him no end of trouble. It took a lot of work to get through this part of his mind. I had wondered at one point about whether he'd make it, but Matt found huge value in the sessions and, although he'd sometimes have a 6-month break, or a year at one point, he found his life gradually and significantly improving. The sadness and heartache behind his 'fuck you' attitude was huge when we finally got to the message at its core. It changed his life to express it.

Attitudes are ways of being in life; they are what we think of as our personality traits. Sometimes people say them right out: 'I'm the kind of person who tells it like it is' or 'I'm a good guy.' There might be truth in these statements, but they are attitudes they are dramatising in life and about life. If they can get out of such an attitude easily enough, then it is not a fixed attitude, or not a deep one, but if they say, 'Well it's not an attitude, it's the truth, I *am* a good guy,' then we can be sure it is a fixed attitude.

Having an attitude is not a problem in itself. We can take on a point of view at will and it can be useful. We need a point of view sometimes to get things done: to complete a puzzle, to get across Paris with a large piece of luggage. The problem comes when they get stuck. When a fixed attitude that the person has an interest in working on is identified, then the next step in the programme can be taken.

FINDING AN OPPOSITE TO THE ATTITUDE

In order to ponder the opposites,[9] a person needs to find a working opposite to the attitude on which they want to work. Attitudes are always negative from the person's point of view. Even a 'life is wonderful' attitude is negative if a person is stuck in it. They know at some level it is not true but are using 'life is wonderful' as a neurotic manipulation of others. It is an attempt to communicate something else and it is not true in itself because it is an idea about life. Moreover, it is exhausting to maintain. So finding the opposite is always finding the positive, from that person's point of view, even if it looks technically like a negative view on life.

> I always need to entertain people in life and I know it's not really jolly. It is sometimes, but actually it's a real strain much of the time, but I've got to do it. I've got to be this 'fun' person because otherwise people will be bored by me, because really I think I'm terribly boring. So I decided to work on this attitude of, 'I've got to be happy or others won't love me.' It took me ages to come up with an opposite because I just couldn't get the idea of me really being anything more positive. Finally I got an opposite of, 'Everyone loves me happily and fully, whatever I do.' It was a bit long-winded but seemed to do the trick, at least the first time round. It was very difficult to imagine that opposite.

Finding an opposite is not done in order that a few affirmations can be performed to get the client out of a negative state and into a positive one. That is not what is going on here. There are a few reasons for finding an opposite to work on alongside the actual attitude. It is partly to help them practise getting into and out of an attitude by their conscious volition. Also, it is a good idea to work on the opposite of an attitude at the same time as the side in which they are fixed. That way, the whole of the attitude is being dealt with, like the whole of an iceberg, the bit we can see and the bit we cannot see.

Finally, using the opposite prevents the person from fixating on one attitude by deliberately focusing on it over and over. This could result in overload. It is better to have more freedom and movement in the technique so that the person does not get bogged down with all the associations or memories stacked up around one attitude. Berner summarises step 2 as, 'having him purposefully and knowingly get the idea of himself in the undesirable state, and in its opposite'.[10]

The opposite needs to be an opposite that resonates with the attitude. It has to *feel* like an opposite. This is the difference between the *conceptual* opposite and the *attitudinal* opposite. The opposite of 'others are bad' might technically be 'others are good' or 'others are not bad'. That might work, but if the person easily gets into that and does not really find it a challenge, it could work better to find a more extreme

MIND CLEARING

opposite, one that the person feels stretched in getting into; it might be something like, 'others are wonderful, beautiful and trustworthy and I love them all'. They must be exercising their ability to get into and out of attitudes and not for it to be too easy. The opposite must have the sense of being an opposite life attitude. For instance, finding the opposite to a 'poor me' attitude might come up with things such as 'lucky me' or 'I'm the luckiest person in the world'. That could work. But 'poor me' is a victim state, so a powerful opposite to it could also be something like 'I'm a victimiser' or 'I'm a bully'. If the person is stuck in seeing themselves as the oppressed, then they will certainly be manipulating others with this attitude but probably unaware of doing so. To see themselves as the active oppressor of others could be a powerful opposite, stretching their capacity to conceive of themselves in that attitude and strengthening the ability to choose to adopt one attitude and then another.

The attitude itself that you choose to work on is not neutral, it is the meaning part of a whole energetic distortion in which the person is. It is best to find an opposite that resonates with the distortion, and the process will be more powerful.

Step 2: pondering the opposites

Once the opposite is chosen, the person is given the instruction to *get the idea* of being in the chosen attitude with the instruction: 'Get the idea of you being in an ("I'm bad", "I'm not good enough", etc.) attitude'. First of all, the person is being told to perform a specific action, so this activates the clearing communication cycle and has them do something. As long as that action has been explained to them and they understand, then there is no doubt for the person about what it is they should do.

'GET THE IDEA'

In this instruction they are also explicitly being told to 'get the idea'. To 'get' something allows latitude to do it in any way they like. And what they are being told to do is get the *idea* of being in the specific attitude.

They do not have to get into the attitude or state itself in order to do this. For example, if they are working on 'everything is bad', they do not have to get that whole feeling that goes along with the idea of everything being bad. It might go along with a whole negative, depressed state of being. They might go into that state because it is so familiar to them that this is the easiest way of getting the idea of being in the attitude. But they are not actually being asked to do so. They are being asked to get the *idea* of them being in the attitude. With practice they will eventually be able to get the idea of being in the attitude without having to go into the state.

STATES

If the person gets into the associated state in order to get the idea, they are actually keying in to all the emotional and bodily responses that go along with the attitude they go into. This is all right, but then it will be much harder work because all the emotional and bodily states will be being dealt with at the same time as the attitude. We do not actually have to do that in order to gain freedom from the mind. The fixed attitude can be disconnected from the experience. The precise point of connection between the attitude and the state must be identified for this to happen. It takes a lot longer to make progress if the whole state is being cleared along with the attitude. That is not the point of this work. There are other techniques for clearing the emotions and body that are more effective.

But it does not finally matter in order for the technique to work. They can get into the state or not, but it is best and more economical if they can simply get into the idea of the attitude. This will need to be explained. Eventually they will be able to take on the attitude, simply as an idea, as a conscious act of will. You want them to be able to do this, so this is what you ask them to do.

One thing to avoid is using the word 'feeling'. When people try to get a feeling, it usually drags along body and emotion. We are dealing with the mind, and bringing the body into it complicates matters. They will probably bring body and emotion into it anyway with the state, and that is fine, but that is not what is being asked of them for this technique.

What we are setting out to do is deal with the significance we attach to events. The person needs to get the significance part of the attitude;

the attitude is mostly its significance. It might seem like an intellectual nicety, but this is not just an intellectual move. They have to perform an actual, internal action in order to get the idea of being in the attitude in order to comply with the instruction. Even if they understand this in principle, performing the action is another matter. Even the most able intellect may struggle to get the idea of being in the attitude if they are closely identified with it. This is because the identification is a *fact*. Facts are different from ideas, but getting the idea of being in an attitude is an action that functionally challenges the fixidity of the idea that the attitude is a fact because a person has to choose to get into it. So they will eventually notice it is not a necessary fact of life. To deal with ideas, we have to bring ourselves more into reality.

> Clearer: Get the idea of you being in an 'I'm useless' attitude.
>
> Client: Um...OK, yeah, got it.
>
> Clearer: Tell me how you went about getting that.
>
> Client: I remembered a time I felt useless. It was when I was about 15 and I was playing cricket with some other kids at the back of the house and I just couldn't hit the ball, so I gave up because I felt so useless.
>
> Clearer: Thank you. Get the idea of you being in an 'I'm the king of the world and can do anything' attitude.
>
> Client: (long pause) OK.
>
> Clearer: How did you get that?
>
> Client: It was difficult. First I tried to imagine it being true and I couldn't. I kept feeling useless. Then I remembered winning a race when I was about 10. I'd never won anything before and it was amazing.
>
> Clearer: Thank you.

This goes on for some time, going from the attitude to its opposite and back again. Each time the client thinks of a memory of feeling useless in order to get the idea of being in the attitude, then finds a way to get into the opposite. Then it changes:

Clearer: Get the idea of you being in an 'I'm useless' attitude.

Client: (considerable pause) OK, got it.

Clearer: How did you get that?

Client: Well, I couldn't come up with any more memories, but I realised I didn't need to because I just *feel* useless, so I just got that feeling.

Clearer: Thank you.

At this point he dropped a level of complication in getting the idea of being in the attitude and used the feeling of being in the state, which was very familiar to him.

'GET THE IDEA OF *YOU* BEING IN THE ATTITUDE'

The use of 'you' in the instruction points to the fact that it is 'they', the individual, who has to do the work. In every clearing communication cycle the person has to take an active part in completing it. They must do the work to receive the instruction, look inside *and* communicate what came up. Doing so makes new pathways of good communication and dissolves mind. Each time a clearing communication cycle is successfully completed, a little bit of the mind becomes redundant. A direct communication that is received by another satisfies the part of us that originally felt unmet. The hold that our distorted behaviours have on us is weakened by every direct and satisfying communication we make that improves our ability to do so next time.

When the person has indicated that they have done the work and got the idea of being in the attitude, they are asked to examine how they achieved this. Getting into an attitude is usually automatic and unconscious. We suddenly find we have gone from being more or less OK to being in an attitude. Someone says something or does something or we have a thought and we are right in the state and we do not know how we got there. Attitudes and their accompanying states are so familiar we do not think about it. When we are asked to describe how it happened, we usually have no idea. We might be able to narrow it down to something someone said. If we go into a victim state and attitude of 'no one loves me', we might just be able to identify the incident that triggered it.

> The Christmas cards got handed out at work and there wasn't one for me. My colleagues made a show of looking, but mine had been lost; perhaps it got wedged in the box because it did turn up later. But anyway, despite putting on a front of laughing along with everyone else at how I was clearly 'out of favour', inside, I plunged into the familiar 'no one loves me' state. I knew, rationally, that I hadn't really been missed out or, if I had been, it was just a mistake and not personal. But it was almost as though I wanted to be missed out, so I could nurse this 'no one loves me' thing. When I looked at it, it was difficult to see how I actually got into this state and even harder to see how I could get out of it.

In this step of dealing with fixed attitudes, the Clearer asks the person to look at how they went about getting the idea of being in that attitude. And, because this time they got the idea of being in the attitude deliberately, rather than through an automatic reaction, they can start to look at the way they are getting into it, but consciously this time. If the person thinks about it, they will start to see the mechanism by which they get into the attitude and this will start to break the automaticity. It is not enough to try to work out how we get into attitudes, we have to get the idea of doing it as an act of will in order to experience ourselves doing so, and know its use in doing it.

Typically, to begin with, getting the idea of being in the attitude is achieved through memory. If you give the instruction 'Get the idea of you being in an "I'm bad" attitude,' they might, for instance, search around for a bit and come up with a memory of a time they did something they felt bad about. It does not matter how they do it at first, it will change of its own accord. They must just find a way to do it using the imagination, the memory, the state they actually get into, or any other way they can get into it. The person can get it very fully or just a bit, but the point is they have to get the idea of being in the attitude.

> Brenda was working on a fixed attitude of 'I'm not enough'. To get the idea of being in that attitude she started out by finding memories of when she felt she

was not enough. At work her boss criticised some work she did on a project and this triggered the feeling of not being enough. She had lots of memories like this to draw on, and every time she was instructed to 'Get the idea of you being in an "I'm not enough" attitude,' she looked inside for a memory of a time when some event led to her feeling like she was not enough and went through incidents from the past and more recently.

After a while of doing this and struggling to come up with a new memory, she realised she did not have to get a memory to get the idea. The feeling of not being enough was so familiar that all she had to do was get the feeling and this came with the idea that she was not enough. Again, after a while, she listened to the instruction and realised more fully that she was being asked to get the *idea* of being in the attitude and did not have to go into the whole state and the associated feeling of heaviness. So she experimented and found she could get just the idea of her being in the attitude. This put her back in the realm of memory for a bit, but she soon started to see she could get the idea without needing feelings or memories. She initially imagined putting the idea on, like a hat, or using some other mechanical image to get the idea like imagining it as a grey fog in which she could be. But this too changed and, increasingly, Brenda found she could simply source the attitude and get the idea of being in it without mechanisms.

At that point she started to have insights about how and why she was going into the attitude. She started to notice how invested she was in going into it and how reluctant she was to let it go. When she got the idea of being in the attitude 'I'm not enough,' she realised she resented seeing it as just an attitude. She reported that, when she did this, she felt like there was a little voice in the background saying, 'But it's true, it's true, I'm not enough.' As well as this, she started to experience how angry she felt when she took on the attitude.

When the person has done their best to describe how they got into the attitude, it is also an important step to ask them if they have any comments to make about this process. Sometimes they might have an insight or something to say about the process that is of value to them as they get to understand how they are going around in these attitudes, so they are given the opportunity to communicate this before moving on. They may suddenly have understood that it is *they* alone who are getting the attitude. This is a significant insight and there needs to be space in the process for them to communicate and absorb it. Without that opportunity, the person will stack up with things they have noticed and not said and it will quickly become difficult to continue. In Brenda's case, she had a lot to say about how angry she felt around the attitude and how she felt a huge impulse to blame people for her feeling that she was not enough.

> I struggled to get into my opposite attitude. It was, 'I'm a wonderful, warm person, overflowing with goodwill'. It was like pulling teeth. I felt it was impossible to get the idea of me being that, I was so into thinking of myself as grey and cynical and I found I liked that image of myself because I felt superior in it. If I were warm and happy, I'd have to stop thinking of myself as better than other people. So the first few times I just got this rather tepid idea of myself as basically fairly nice. I remembered times when I'd felt nice about myself and others. But eventually it got easier and I went through a stage of being really moved by it and crying every time I was asked to get the idea of being in that attitude. But finally, I just got it and it was no big deal.

They may have to get some complicated picture of themselves as, for example, the goddess of abundance, overflowing with goodness and love and everyone wanting them. Or they might eventually find a memory of themselves feeling abundant or look into an imagined future for an image. Once again, they get this across to the Clearer who must understand and acknowledge the communication and complete that clearing communication cycle.

Then they go back to the original attitude, and, this time, how they get the idea of being in the attitude might have changed a bit. Then returning to the opposite might be a little bit easier or a bit harder. It goes back and forth like this, as many times as it takes for the person to be able to get into the attitude and its opposite, consciously, seeing how they are doing it.

Eventually the person will realise it is they who are getting the attitude. It was they who were doing it all along; it was not just 'happening' to them as a result of other people's actions, they were doing it. This will not be just an intellectual recognition but a full appreciation that it is only she or he who has been getting into that attitude and victimising themselves and, by extension, others.

Eventually there will be a change. Either the person will get tired because they have really been trying to make intellectual sense of the whole thing, trying to find answers from within the mind, or the person will get better at getting the attitude and realise they have been doing it all along; in this case they will de-identify increasingly from the attitude and its opposite.

If the former is happening, then the Clearer should go on to the next steps, even though the likelihood is that they will need to go back over the process again. There is little to be gained at that point in continuing to ponder the opposites as they are caught in an intellectual loop. Performing the next steps will help them by releasing some stuck communications. When the process is gone over again, there should be some more progress.

If it is the latter, and the person is de-identifying from the attitudes, then the Clearer should keep going for a bit as this gives the person the chance to make a more substantial breakthrough. This happens in stages.

> If he does break through, what will happen is this: he will try
> to get the idea and he will succeed, but he will have had to go
> through a mental process or an activity to do it. At this point he
> is blowing his mind. There will usually be a release of energy,
> often noticed in the form of heat in the body.[11]

Finally, the person will go to get the idea of being in the attitude and they will find they do it without using the mind. But there is still a *process* going on. The person is not able to get the attitude just from themselves. Nonetheless, there is much more freedom because the attitude is no longer happening automatically. If the person can go on to originate it purely from themselves, using the will alone, then there is no need to go on to the next steps; they have gained freedom from the mind in this respect.

Step 3: identifying the message, or
the medium is the message[12]

The mind is a series of problems and false solutions, a series of communication difficulties, relating difficulties, understanding difficulties, in which the person has come up with substitute methods of trying to get something across to others.[13]

Every attitude is an indirect communication. When a person is unable to get across what they wish to communicate, they will eventually give up trying to get it across directly and take up an attitude as a substitute for direct communication. That attitude and the behaviours associated with it is the communication, but it has become distorted.

Attitudes become fixed when they become indirect and, by definition, dysfunctional attempts to communicate. Because they do not work as communication, they get caught in loops and, usually, increasingly fixed.

> As a child, Zoe saw her parents arguing and was frightened. What she wanted to say was, 'I don't like this, I don't want to feel alone like this,' and she might have tried to say this. But her parents did not get it or she certainly felt they did not get it. Maybe they were too involved in what they were doing and she was afraid of giving the message because she thought they might not love her if she did. One way or another, the message never got delivered and remained hanging in the space between them.
>
> We never stop trying to get the message across at a subconscious level. It is in the very nature of a communication that it must be communicated, and until that is fulfilled, the message will keep on knocking at the door. But in this case, verbalising it did not work, so Zoe decided, subconsciously, to get it across in another way. In this case, she turned the communication into withdrawing her love from her parents whenever it looked like they were disgruntled. In later life she did the same thing with other people when they seemed angry. She had the story going on that 'If I withdraw, they'll notice that I don't want to be left on my own.'

From this point on she mostly stopped trying to verbalise the message and the medium became the message; it became the behaviour of withdrawal when anything triggered the relevant memory for her. Subconsciously she used her withdrawal to get her message across, and this behaviour became part of her personality.

At a subconscious level we are communicating our messages loud and clear, but people on the whole do not get these messages because the messages are indirect. Also, we are invested in people being wrong so, in a sense, we do not want them to get the message because we have gone victim with it. To keep others in the wrong, we have to keep reviving the idea of ourselves as the victim of their non-understanding.

The purpose of going through these steps is to unpack the attitude to the point where that message is uncovered and delivered so that it no longer serves to distract the person from the present. Some people may be able to identify the message without all this work, but most people need to take steps towards it and de-identify from the attitude to see it clearly enough to see what the message is. The Clearer will probably need to help them get a 360° picture of how they are using the attitude as part of this process of understanding.

The realisation that they are actually originating the attitude themselves is a major step. But intellectual understanding is not enough. The person might be able to see that they are not only creating an attitude by their own choice, such as 'people are bad', but that they are keeping themselves in it and hurting themselves and others with it. They are going victim and mistreating others from that state. This knowledge alone probably will not shift the attitude.

Brenda, with her attitude of 'I'm not enough', was manipulating others from that attitude. Going around in 'I'm not enough' affected her behaviour enormously. She had a habit of putting herself down through different mechanisms. For example, she did not pursue promotions and yet became resentful when others were promoted over her, despite the fact that they had actively worked for the advancement and she had not only not worked for it, but tended to underplay and sabotage her own contributions. She also used it to avoid taking responsibility for a lot of relationship interaction in her life. In her story about herself, if she was not enough, then she could not be criticised. This was because she had already judged herself to be not enough. Any criticism of her behaviour could be countered by her saying, or thinking, 'I told you I wasn't enough, so what do you expect if I don't live up to your expectations?' From within her attitude of 'not enough' she could treat people with disregard, forget to call them or not think to tell them some important thing. But if they complained, she had already warned them, so in her mind it was not her fault. Further still, it was actually their fault in her narrative because they should have known what she was like. As Brenda worked more and more on this attitude of 'I'm not enough', she discovered how she was using it to blame others for her life being the way it was. And the more she was able to see this and express it in sessions, the more she found it changing in subtle ways in her life. Sometimes she felt much more aware of just how angry and bitter she was. But other times she found herself feeling greater sympathy with people and she started to socialise with people more, particularly at work.

Attitudes are often complex patterns of behaviour that always set others up to be wrong, keep the person with the attitude in the right and justify their avoidance of responsibility. At base attitudes are also, always, self-defensive and founded on a message the person did not manage to get across. This almost always happens early in life and the message is probably to a parent or primary carer.

THE INVESTMENT

The person needs to fully appreciate the investment they have in maintaining the attitude, that is, how the attitude is serving them in life. Attitudes are always a way of keeping others wrong and the person right. The reality is, of course, very different from what we imagine is going on when we are locked into acting out an attitude. When we are acting from an attitude we feel perfectly justified in behaving as we do and it is difficult to see that we are the ones doing it. Attitudes are victim states.[14]

Brenda: Once I'd worked on it for a while, I started to see that the attitude of 'others don't understand me' that I go around in isn't really about other people not getting me. I'm actually using it to keep seeing other people as being in the wrong. I begin to see that I set people up to not get me. I don't explain myself very well and then I blame them for not understanding. But really, I've done it, I've made it virtually impossible for anyone, except a clairvoyant, to understand what I meant. But as long as I went around doing this, and thinking people didn't understand me, then I could think they were wrong and I was fundamentally OK and it was all their fault. The crunch point to this is that I don't have to take responsibility for my relationships because they are the ones messing it up.

Of course, being in an attitude does not *actually* keep anyone from being wrong, but it *appears* to do so. If a client cannot see their own agency at all in having an attitude, then it is probably too early to be doing attitude clearing. In any event, once someone has done all they can to see how they are using it, it is time to go on to the last step.

At this point, it is often possible for the person to begin to see some of that for which the attitude is a false solution. The person took on the attitude because they were trying to communicate something to someone about themselves. That never works; if it did, the person would not need the attitude and it would cease to be. The nature of a fixed attitude is that it does not work, and that is why it is fixed.

THE MESSAGE

In Mind Clearing we ask: "What is it you are trying to tell others about yourself by going around in this attitude?" The only messages people ever have that they want to communicate to others is about themselves. There is something they believe someone failed to understand about them. This isn't the person; this is his attitude. The person is elsewhere, in terms of conceptual separation rather than spatial separation. The person is actually, if you want to locate him, usually located right with the attitude. But it is a conceptual separation. In other words, when you have a personality, the personality is right where you are but it isn't you… This allows the accumulation of all the incomplete communications that are being made about you to other people and about other people to you, because you are receiving them through a particular attitude.[15]

It might take some work to get the message, and the instruction might have to be changed or explained, but eventually the person will come up with something.

The important thing is to find what is called the *reactive message*. Very often people come up with lots of messages. Some will be more relevant than others and make good sense, but they do not have a great deal of punch. That is partly why all these steps are in here – to help a person work through the attitude to a point where they are clear enough, and have enough space around it, to see what the reactive message is. It is also why attitude clearing is usually only done when a person has already improved at getting themselves across.

The attitude or state they are going around in has real energetic power. It is not just an idea; it has substance manifesting in behaviour and the person's way of being. It is the surface of a whole syndrome. While we are looking for the cognitive element of the syndrome, when the exact message is found that is keeping the behaviour going, it connects with that whole energetic structure that has impact and charge. It is *that* message for which we are looking. The connection between the attitude and the message needs to be identified and will resonate with the attitude or state. When that message is found, it is time to move on to step 4.

Brenda, having worked through her attitude of 'I'm not enough', finally got to a place where she de-identified from the 'I' enough to see around it. This, together with insights she had during the process, resulted in her seeing how she had been using it to control people. She could see what her investment was in keeping it going. As she examined how she went about in life when she was in the 'I'm not enough state', which was much of the time, she increasingly saw that what she wanted to say about it was directed mostly to her mother. This was an instinct; when she felt that she had the attitude and tried to express what she really wanted to say, she simply found an image of her mother coming more and more strongly into her thoughts and a feeling of distress and frustration around not getting herself across.

While she used the attitude much more broadly in life, it came down to feeling that her mother in particular thought she was not enough as she was. With the help of her Clearer, she set out to look for the message this attitude was expressing. This took a lot of work as it had been covered over by habitual behaviours for almost 50 years. But she eventually began to come up with a number of messages she was then able to express in the session. These included 'You don't love me,' 'I hate you' and 'You never gave me enough attention.' The Clearer wrote these down and they went to the final stage of the process.

Step 4: delivering the message

The next step is to take what the person is trying to tell others about themselves by being in the attitude, and get them to communicate it, out loud, directly to those others. The person might know that it is intended for particular others, such as their parents, but it might be aimed at all others.

For instance, the attitude 'I'm special' may be the one being acted out in life, but what the person is really saying is, 'I hate you, get away from me, you're not special, you're nothing,' but they are 'communicating' it through this attitude because they think if they keep it up, people will realise, somehow, how wrong they are, how right the person is and how much the person hates them. It is quite shocking how we keep these attitudes going in the face of repeated failures in getting the message across. We are so heavily invested in being right that we carry on regardless.

Even after doing all this work to know what the message is, the person will probably not stop acting out the attitude to try to get it across. They will probably have a bit more choice in the matter and not dramatise it quite so much but still be operated by it. That is the way they have been trying to get it across all their lives. They do not have another way to be. They cannot really imagine another way to be, so they are hardly going to stop now, even knowing all they know about how they are doing this to themselves and that it does not work. We have to go further than the 360° view of the attitude. The next step is getting better at getting the communication across.

> The thing is that I've done loads of work on myself. I've had years of therapy and done group work and meditation and I know why I do things and how I do them. It's actually been hugely frustrating because all that understanding doesn't really help. It helps me a bit, but I still feel like acting out and it's so depressing that so much of that stuff is still there. Mind Clearing was an eye-opener after all those years of working at these things. To start with, I thought maybe we were just going to do the same old thing again. My Clearer asked me about myself and I told her, and it was like, 'Here we go again.' But we didn't. There were bits of what I'd done before, but this time it went further. She kept on working with me until I understood something I'd never understood before, that is, I realised what I was saying with all this acting out, or *wanting* to act out. And she helped me get it across as well. She didn't stop when I'd just said it; she got me to *really* say it. I felt silly at first, it seemed like some kind of role play, but by the end I was standing up and shouting it out and I couldn't stop. I said it over and over. It felt so good to get it out of my system. It was coming from somewhere I'd never known before and tears were running down my face and snot running out of my nose and I didn't care. The words felt like they were coming from my navel and straight up out of my mouth in this visceral torrent. And when it was done, it was done. It was different. Like nothing I'd ever done before. It wasn't an insight, although I had insights when I was doing it, and it wasn't intellectual. It was just a relief and the truth, and the world stopped turning and I was here like never before. I'm a changed man.

The person will probably need help to communicate the message directly. They have spent their whole life trying to get it across indirectly. The message has been buried in the subconscious for years. They did not even know what it was. It is essential that the Clearer understand the message themselves; otherwise, they could just become yet another person who did not get it.

It is the *reactive message* that must be delivered together *with* that reactivity that is being carried with it. That is not to say it will necessarily be a huge emotional blowout. It might be, but it might be quiet. It must, in any case, be real and full and carry the charge and communication of the attitude, but this time it will be delivered direct, with no distortion.

The first things people come up with in trying to pinpoint the exact message will probably be connected to the main message, like Brenda's example above. The exact message is probably buried under layers of ideas that will have to be peeled back. Seeing what investment they have in keeping the attitude going will help them find the message. The investment and message are intimately connected. In a way they are the same thing.

Earlier, in step 2, pondering the attitudes, it was said that it is not necessary for the person to go into the attitude or state but just to get the idea of them being in the attitude or state. Here, however, it is different. The reactive message, the original message, connects precisely with the mind stuff, the energetic stuff of the mind:

> very often that point at the center of the whirlpool, where the meaning of the state, the idea content, the significance, is joined with...the mindstuff...you're going to have to get an emotional expression along with it... That's where the reactive message is, right at that touch point where they are identified the most.[16]

When the message meets the energetic structure of the mind, and is released when the reactive message is delivered directly to another live human being who receives it, then everything at that level of the mind lets go. The web of connections to that particular attitude just lets go and there is space where that was, and relief. This is a by-product of getting the reactive message.

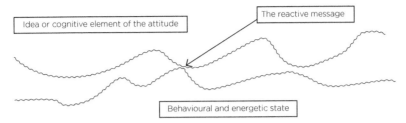

Figure 7.1 The point where the message meets
the energetic structure of the mind

It might take several rounds of pondering the opposites and finding the message before the underlying attitude is hit. But when it *is* hit and *delivered* with the full force of direct communication from the individual, it is quite different from any other message.

> Brenda identified a number of different messages. Other people were in there too, but the messages were primarily directed at her mother. She was encouraged to get those messages across to her mother as if she were in the room and could receive the communication, even though her mother had been dead for some years. She did this as well as she could and there was some relief in the process. She could feel some of the anger and bitterness draining out of her. But she and her Clearer discussed it and agreed that something was missing. Her communications were in the right ballpark but lacked the impact of the reactive message. So they worked together to explore what the attitude was really saying. The Clearer asked questions of Brenda, such as, 'What is it about you that your mother doesn't get?', 'What doesn't she know about you?', 'What have you not been saying to her?' and they worked on like this for some time.
>
> Although Brenda found it hard going, she increasingly felt the importance of getting the message just right and began to be more and more discerning about what she said. Every time she expressed the message a bit differently, she was able to score it on a scale of 1–10 of reality and accuracy. Then, finally, she said quietly, 'Don't leave me.' It didn't seem like much at first and the Clearer almost missed it because it was almost whispered, and Brenda seemed inclined to dismiss it as silly; she'd

laughed a bit as she said it. But it had a different ring to it, so the Clearer asked her to repeat it, louder this time. 'Don't leave me!' It sounded different again, real. So again, she was asked to repeat it, bigger this time, 'DON'T LEAVE ME!' Every time she said the words, they were clearer and louder and she sat up straighter and looked clearer, as though fog was clearing. Finally, Brenda, who typically spoke in a low, quiet voice, started screaming it to her mother, '**DON'T LEAVE ME!**', weeping. She was right there, behind the communication, feeling the truth of it and how much it mattered. The Clearer completely received the communication and this time it was different from all the other times of saying the message, and they both knew it. Something shifted in the whole of Brenda's being. She was relieved of a burden she had been carrying most of her life.

The person often does not get the whole message first time, or they may not deliver it fully. When the reactive message is delivered to the best of their ability at that time, the Clearer must then go on to the final stage and ask whether the person thinks they will continue to use it: 'Do you think you will still use this attitude to tell people "I hate you", "I love you" or whatever the message is?'

If there is any doubt in the person's mind about whether they will continue to use that attitude to get that particular message across, then it has not gone and the Clearer will return to step 2 and continue again from there. The attitude might have changed a bit. They could have taken a layer off it and it might then be appropriate to work on an attitude that is deeper.

If, in response to step 4, the person is completely clear that they will no longer use that attitude to get the message across, they can move on to work on another attitude. Even if they are sure they will not use it, it may still be there a bit. Either the person has not fully delivered it or it is not quite the right message. Time is the test of this. But if the reactive message is fully delivered in the moment, then the attitude will be blown out of the water and not come back.

Comments

Berner realised that the uncommunicated communication is what keeps the mind going, and he said:

> I have seen this many times and experienced it many times myself. It was my experience of that that made me realize that what existence is, is that uncommunicated communication.[17]

It is the stuff we have not directly communicated that becomes the mind and keeps us thinking of the world in a particular way.

> If you've found the right goal, the right barrier or attitude that was in the way, and it is the one the person is interested in working on, then if he keeps getting the attitude himself, of his own free choice until he really does have a subjective, direct, conscious experience that he is, in fact, the choice-maker, in the attitude's formation; and if you've found the message that he's trying to get across to other people; and if you improve his ability to get that message across directly so that he doesn't need this indirect method any longer, then the person will no longer choose to have this attitude. He will no longer be fixed in it or subject to it. His life will no longer be directed by it, nor will it interfere with him accomplishing his goals. That part of the mind has been cleared away and is no longer a barrier between him and others. That's what clearing means: to remove the barriers between oneself and others.[18]

It will probably take a number of rounds to get to the root of a particular attitude, but once it has been dealt with, it vanishes. With it go all the parts of experiences that were suspended in the mind, resisted because of that particular attitude. Depending on the scale of the attitude that has been dealt with, the person will feel free in all sorts of areas of their lives and ways of thinking. There will no longer be reactivity and resistance in those places.

There are different levels of the mind, and if a person can deal with their attitudes right to the inner core, then there will be no more trouble from the mind at all. It will no longer be a separate thing from the individual. The individual will have ideas and think, but those processes will be done by choice and not automaticity.

It might seem that this should be easy, that a long technique for getting people to speak from themselves and say what they have not said in life is not needed. It might be supposed that people can just be encouraged to go ahead and say it all. But experience suggests that most people cannot do that. The only thing that will help most of us is to actually get better at relating, measurably and demonstrably. And for this, the clearing communication cycle is what works. Talking can work by chance, but setting out to deliberately go through the steps takes chance out of the equation and makes help more likely and replicable. It takes skill and application, but it can be done. It requires the Clearer also to improve *their* relationship with the person in front of them. In this way, the work is a collaboration because the Clearer has to be genuinely involved.

The person has more or less given up on getting what they really want to say across in life. We can be sure of this. That is why they are using attitudes with distorted behaviours with which to communicate. So they will not say what they really want to say unless the relationship with other people is improved first. This is not sitting down and going through the motions of asking and listening. This is actual improvement.

That is what help is: the Clearer has to decide to help the person get better at relating, and to do that, they have to get better at relating to that person.

Patanjali describes ways in which we can discipline the mind and gradually reduce the influence of memories and attitudes through practice, and finally cancel the mind out. Perhaps the anti-memories he alludes to in Book I are something like the effect of attitude clearing.[19] In any case, he supports the view that tracing our attitudes and memories back to their source is the way to deal with them conclusively.[20]

> In Patanjali's system, it is not sufficient for one to uncover the historical genesis of one's current attachment or aversion. One must abandon the root of suffering (which is the past experience) in its subtle form.[21]

Once this is done, because of the nature of subtle forms as universal, all instances of aversion or attachment to that aspect of experience will go. The past events held in the mind will no longer be used to maintain attachment or aversion, forcing and attitudes.[22]

I came to my final Clearing intensive having had many sessions over the years. They had made a big difference in how I lived my life, so I knew the method worked. Yet a major problem remained: I sometimes got a pain in my throat so overwhelming that I couldn't speak or even breathe easily.

It happened when I had something difficult to say, and the only way through it was to break down and cry uncontrollably. Thereafter, if the person I wanted to speak to had stuck around, I could say what I wanted to say. Oddly, it also happened when people got together to sing. It could be a hymn, a choral society at a concert, or a knees-up in the pub; something about people putting aside their differences to join in song made me want to seize up: their faces were so beautiful. Again, weeping without restraint was the only thing that lifted the pain in my throat – which usually meant retiring to the bathroom and missing the best bits. So I'd booked this one last intensive over a long weekend to address it.

My Clearer was a down-to-earth woman, very practical with years of experience. We had worked well together previously so I trusted her abilities. She started by inviting me to focus on the pain in my throat, so I closed my eyes and did my best to relax and recall a time when it had happened.

I seemed to fall into a black hole and gradually found myself remembering what had happened when I was 16. I'd woken early in the morning with a stabbing pain in my abdomen, a pain that rose with every breath until I wept. My mother came into my bedroom to find out why I hadn't got up. She was smartly dressed, ready for work, in a hurry. 'What's the matter?' she asked, frowning. I tried to tell her about the pain but was incoherent. 'Oh, for heaven's sake,' she said. 'You have an exam today. You're trying to get out of it. That won't work with me. Get up and get going.'

Then she was gone, leaving me alone with the pain. I cried, moaned and vomited, unable to stand, before it lifted after about 6 hours. Then, I felt so drained and weak that I went back to bed. My mother was furious when she came home and found I'd failed to sit the exam. But I said nothing.

When I finished telling my Clearer this, she asked me to say aloud to my mother, as if she were present, what I couldn't say at the time. But I still couldn't; the pain in my throat stopped me – even after a bout of crying which normally released it. So now she asked me what attitude I was stuck in, in believing I couldn't speak. I found it boiled down to 'I have no voice.' Next, she got me to find the opposite of that attitude and, out of several possibilities, I settled for 'I'm free.'

But I was still so stuck in my voiceless state that I couldn't even get the idea 'I'm free.' So now my Clearer got me to describe the pain incident from beginning to end, again and again. But still it gripped me. Only when she asked me to speak to my father as if present did it begin to slacken, for my father had been crucially involved at the time and speaking to him brought back the rest of what had happened.

I remembered how the pain had come on, worse than ever, just as I was starting my university entrance exam. My best friend phoned my mother and asked her to come, but she was at work and refused. So my friend took me home. After hours of agony, I managed to get into the bath. Soon, I felt a kind of 'pop' in my abdomen. The pain stopped. I wept with relief. But I still missed my exams, sitting in the garden feeling weaker every day. On the tenth day, my father came home from work and found me unable to stand. He carried me to the car and took me to a doctor. Peritonitis had set in from a ruptured appendix; I was in hospital for the next 6 weeks.

Now that I'd told the full story, I was able to work on 'I have no voice', following my Clearer's instructions to go back and forth, back and forth – first getting the idea 'I have no voice' and then getting the idea 'I'm free', until I could identify with either attitude freely, simply as a mental exercise. Now my Clearer again asked me to say to my mother what I'd been unable to say when I was 16.

I closed my eyes. And my mother seemed to be floating in front of me, her face a mask of fear and anxiety. We seemed to be in space surrounded by stars. I saw her as trapped inside a structure – a sort of cage with bars – slowly spinning, lost and alone. I saw myself as a small child inside the cage with her as she tried to keep me safe and close to her. Then I saw myself as a grown woman, slipping out of the cage, leaving her alone. My heart broke and my voice returned – without pain or tears. I was free. 'Love me as I am,' I said. 'The way I love you.'

The pain in my throat has never returned.

8
GUILT AND KARMA

Karma, or guilt, is a major stumbling block to progress for many of us. If, with a good Clearer and determination, a person is able to go through all the steps of attitude clearing but still not crack it, or if they are stuck in negativity and blame that is not dealt with in the other processes of Mind Clearing work, then there is a good chance that at least some of what is stopping them progress is deep-seated guilt. If a person feels weighed down by guilt, often subconsciously, they will not allow themselves to progress. But a good deal can be done to help people with this.

Berner used the Sanskrit term *karma* instead of guilt. Guilt is often defined as no more than feeling bad about something one has done. It is not a three-dimensional idea. Karma is a more rounded theory of cause and effect and better suits what really goes on for us.

Patanjali says the unconscious mind is the 'transmigratory, evolving karmic baggage of a person'.[1] Karma and ideas are virtually the same thing. Ideas are the effects of karma in our subconscious and they produce more karma. This may be foreign to Western ideas of how things work but, unpacked, is perfectly understandable.

The cycle of karma, of cause and effect, is not a mysterious natural, or even divine, force but the direct result of our actions. We create the world we see through karma. The Christian concept of conscience has similarities to the idea of incorrect action and guilt.

In order to deal with the mind, a person needs to be reasonably free of guilt, that is, they will not get stuck in the attitude of being guilty. It is not to say they will not do things they think they should not have done, but they will not get fixed in an attitude about it.

Many people get stuck in their growth process because they will not allow themselves to be happy or get better. This is because they have done things that, in their own estimation, are wrong. They consequently believe, on some level, that they should be punished for what they have done. It is not some remote god or obscure law of nature that creates karma, it is us. We judge ourselves as being wrong and have an inner balance. Deep down we think we should be punished for the things we have done wrong. Conversely, we tend to think we should be rewarded for the good things we have done.

> You will see to it that you learn the lesson that you need to learn by suffering whatever you need to suffer until you've learned that lesson, at which point you will be free of that karma. Or if you've done good things, when you've lived it up and gotten all the good things that you feel you're supposed to get and you're back to equal, the good things stop.[2]

As soon as you have a mind, you also have karma or guilt. Having a mind is, by definition, doing harm to others and we feel guilty about it.[3] We believe we are bad because of the things we do to others. No one is actually an inherently bad person. There is no such thing. But we believe we are bad and develop fixed ideas about what kind of people we are. In this way, karma builds up as the effects of past actions result in new experiences and actions.[4]

We feel bad because, at base, we care about others deeply. But the guilt we feel about what we have done, or what we have failed to do, actually leads to us treating others more badly. When we do something we think we should not have done, we back off from others.

> You quit reaching out so much, and you just reach out in the ways that in the past you found didn't hurt other people. And so your personal power is throttled way back, held in and closed up. And of course that leads to tension. Your energy had no place to express itself. This leads to frustration, disappointment and lack of fulfilment in life. And you walk around with a guilty conscience.[5]

This situation is very uncomfortable, so we strategise in order to deal with our heavy conscience. We try to find a space to move around in it, or it would seem intolerable and we would just clamp down and stop doing anything. We feel bad, so the solution we generally hit upon is to try and reduce the 'badness' of what we have done.

Bob made a mess of Angela's cottage when he borrowed it, and he felt bad about it. He didn't clear out the fridge and left dirty bedding on the floor of the bedroom and left the bathroom with boot prints all over the floor and a grimy bathtub. He knew she had had to clear up his mess, but he could not bear to be direct about it; not even to say to Angela, 'I made a mess of your cottage, I did that and I'm sorry.' He could not face that because he believed he could not face the pain of his own culpability, partly because he has avoided this deep-seated pain for a long time and also because he had some attitudes and ideas around being punished. So instead of that, he tried to reduce the bad feeling about what he did to Angela by lessening what he did in his mind. He started changing the story a bit, saying to himself, 'Well, it was a mess anyway, the things were old, they were worn out, so no big deal if I messed it up some more. Yeah, I did it, but it wasn't so bad.' It went further than this, and he started thinking, 'Well, Angela's not that nice really; she hurt me that time when she said something about my house, so it's OK because she's not a great person anyway.'

People do this all the time. We could not treat people like this, and much worse, if we let in the reality that they are real, living people we are hurting. We go further than avoiding the responsibility for what we feel bad about and sometimes blame others for their actions.

Roger: Well, yes, I went behind his back and messed up his job, but it was because he snubbed me that time and made me look a fool in front of my boss, so it was his fault.

This is the mechanism that makes people critical of others. Our bad conscience makes us critical of others. It is the reverse of what we might think would happen. Guilt does not make us treat others better. It leads us on a path of treating people worse and worse as our conscience gets heavier and heavier with guilt. Guilt makes us stop seeing the real individual in others.

Ella felt bad about the way she snubbed John, so she backed off from him. She did this out of love, really. But it did not feel like love to John. He just felt upset she snubbed him and is so distant.

Getting over our guilty conscience can be achieved. The most obvious way is literally to confess what we have done. The Christian churches have this; it is one of the seven sacraments. Although it is not much used in the Protestant denominations, it is still considered a sacred sacrament to confess one's sins because it is such an important act. Of course, this is usually seen as confessing what the *Church* considers to be a person's sins. What is actually important is what our own individual conscience considers sinful.

It is no good confessing to something other people think is wrong if we do not think it was a bad thing. This just makes the situation worse.

> Jo was angry with her boyfriend, David, because he went out and had a good time with his friends on Wednesday night and did not call her to see how her day went or to tell her where he was. She believed it was a bad thing he did. He, on the other hand, thought it was no big deal. He felt bad when he realised she was upset, not least because it caused a rift between them that was uncomfortable. But he did not feel bad about going out and having a nice time with his friends. In his mind he had done nothing wrong; he simply did not get round to calling her and did not hear his phone because the pub was noisy. But Jo wanted him to admit it was a bad thing and she would not let it go until he confessed. So he agreed that it was a bad thing because he could not think of another way to resolve the dispute. But this just made the situation worse. Confessing to it, when he did not think it was a bad thing, created another problem between them because David then felt he had been unjustly dealt with by her.

For the purpose of getting over guilt, it is vital to speak the truth according to oneself alone. Confession gets us over what we feel guilty about because we own up to who did the bad thing. It was not just the thing we did or failed to do that we feel bad about, it was also not owning up to it. We hid it away and then we were untruthful about it. But confession often carries consequences in life. We were not honest in the first place because we thought we would be punished for it. This is what often happens to us as children, and we subconsciously think this will happen any time we confess that we did something. And sadly people will indeed hold us to account and punish us sometimes, even as adults, so it is not unreasonable to suppose this will happen. To be able to confess, despite the possibility of undesirable consequences, requires us to let go of our idea of controlling the consequences: 'To the degree you are attached to having things the way you want them to be, you will tend not to confess what you have done.'[6] The consequences of not doing so are huge. We become more and more distant from others and the situation for us deteriorates. So there must be no punishment attached to confession in a helping relationship. There might be some reparation to be done at some point that might be worked out, but the confession itself should just be a confession that is heard and accepted by another person fully, with no comeback. If there is comeback, the person will not open up. They have to feel they can say anything to their Clearer or they will not risk saying what they really want to say in life.[7]

Jonathan was not an immediately obvious candidate for karma clearing. An accountant, he came for sessions because he felt stuck with a belief that he didn't deserve success, and his stooped posture and apologetic manner seemed to reflect this. He'd heard that Mind Clearing addressed stuck beliefs and he was keen to lay this one to rest. I confirmed that we could work on it but first needed to do some preliminary work to lay the foundation.

As part of this preliminary work, I explained karma work and invited Jonathan to try it. But after only four rounds, he said, 'That's all I need. I don't have any other regrets that I haven't already dealt with.' When asked how he'd 'already dealt with' them, he said it was 'best to draw a line under regrets rather than letting them bug you' – and he'd done just that, particularly with regrets from long ago when he'd just qualified and done things he'd now regard as unethical. 'I have much higher standards nowadays,' he added.

'Give me an example of something unethical you did before you knew better,' I asked, and he told me something that would surely have got him into serious trouble if it had come out at the time. When I explained that bad karma from long ago was just as damaging as recent bad karma, he agreed to continue with the process.

Two sessions later, Jonathan was freely remembering actions from the days when he was, as he put it, 'sailing close to the wind'. And now, as he reviewed and faced those actions, he felt genuine regret towards those he'd treated unethically by his current standards, as well as recalled actions not connected with his work that he regretted 'from the old days'. By the end of three sessions, it had become apparent to Jonathan that his 'I don't deserve to be here' belief had arisen as much from a buried sense of guilt around his past behaviour as from a belief of earlier origin. We did go on to identify and tackle an associated belief, but the karma clearing had been an essential preliminary.

Confession, or what is called karma clearing, is very powerful and can unlock deep patterns of negativity. But there are some limits to the use of confession for getting over guilt. It is always a technique we have to exercise our wills to perform. Whenever the will is used, this is out of line with the true individual; it is forcing, so it is always in the realm of dualism. If a person keeps confessing what they *did* that they thought was wrong, they will eventually get stuck in this side. So, to avoid getting jammed up going in only one direction, this should be alternated with what they believe they *failed to do*. In much the same way as pondering the opposites in attitude clearing, this will keep the process open and prevent the person from getting fixed in one side or another.

Karma clearing was a shot in the dark for me. I had no real idea what it meant but just decided to trust Fiona who was a long-time friend and mentor. She was looking for clients for this new process and I was looking to make some progress in my daily life. I booked an intensive of ten 2-hour sessions over 10 days. I liked the idea of doing this work away from the responsibilities and constraints of my busy life – a sort of holiday, I thought, with lots of free time to relax and enjoy my surroundings.

On the train journey, I wondered occasionally about the word *karma*. Something about past lives, I thought; you had to pay in the next life for bad things you had done. Or was it the next several lives? I shrugged and returned to my book. I would find out soon enough.

I settled into my room, went for a walk and turned up on time for my first session. We sat opposite one another in straight-backed but comfortable chairs. Fiona fixed me with her blue gaze. When the session began I was expecting a preamble or maybe an explanation. Instead I got an instruction:

'Tell me something you have done that you should not have done in your own estimation,' Fiona said. She had explained a little about what we were doing and the instructions, but I found it very upfront and was a bit flummoxed, so she repeated the instruction.

I sat back in my chair feeling confused. What kind of things could she mean? Things I've done now, or ages ago or before I was born or what? So I asked her to explain.

'It doesn't matter,' she said, 'It just needs to be something you have done that you should not have done in your own estimation.'

So I sat and pondered. 'Well, I don't know where to start. I mean I ate too much cake on the train and I definitely shouldn't have done that because now I feel a bit sick. Is that the kind of thing you mean?'

'Is that something you should not have done in your own estimation?'

'Um...yes,' I said, hoping that was the right response.

'Thank you,' Fiona said. 'Tell me something you failed to do which you should have done in your own estimation.'

My heart sank. This was no fun at all, it was hard work. I thought about it for a moment.

'I guess I failed to be kind to my grandmother.'

'What did you fail to do exactly?'

'I failed,' I said, gulping, suddenly distraught. 'She looked after me at her house when my mother went back to work when I was 6 weeks old. When I went to school she moved in to our house, so she was there at lunchtime and when I came home.'

Fiona had her eyes fixed on me; it was kind but there was no escape: 'So what exactly did you fail to do?'

'She got dementia and started to do weird things. Nobody explained what was going on. I was horrible to her. I got angry and shouted at her.'

'And what did you fail to do?'

I thought I'd answered, and was just about to remonstrate, but then I replayed my responses and realised, to my slight discomfort, that I still hadn't answered the question directly. So I went back to thinking of my grandmother and why I felt so horrible. I went cold all over when I remembered. 'I failed to give her the right cutlery every time I laid the table day after day. I always gave her the sugar spoon when I should have given her a soup spoon. She always noticed.'

'Thank you,' said Fiona.

We started again.

'Tell me something you have done that you should not have done in your own estimation.' *Well, I guess I can't use the cake incident again*, I thought. 'I'm not too sure about "in your own estimation". What does that mean?'

'It means you know for yourself that you shouldn't have done something, rather than somebody else deciding you shouldn't have done it. You are looking for your own inner standard.'

I thought about that for a while and she gave me the instruction again. 'I threw a can of peaches at my grandmother.' I felt sick with horror when I thought about what I had done. Why did I remember that? I was 13, for God's sake!

'So, you should not have done that in your own estimation?'

'Yes,' I said, quite sure this time.

'Thank you.'

'Tell me something you failed to do that you should have done in your own estimation.'

'I failed to say I was sorry before she died.'

'She?' asked Fiona.

'My grandmother,' I said, and began weeping, feeling overcome with guilt at how I had treated her.

'Thank you.'

'Is there something that you would like to say now to your grandmother?'

'Now?' I was perplexed. How could I do that?

'You could speak to her now, as if she were right here, in this moment.'

'How could she hear what I might have to say? She died years ago.'

'If you get it across properly, it will make a difference.'

The strange thing was, I believed her.

'What would you like to say to her?' asked Fiona.

My eyes filled with tears and I stared at the floor. 'I'm sorry,' I whispered.

'Speak to her. Take a moment and get a sense of her. Try closing your eyes; sometimes that helps. Then speak to her directly as though she were with us right now and could hear you.'

I took my time and closed my eyes. She had always had a sort of powdery, Yardley's kind of smell and pale, papery skin. The funny thing was I could smell it. I mean really smell it.

'Nan', I said tentatively, 'Nan?' Something seemed to break inside me and it all poured out – grief and rage and shock. 'I didn't know, I didn't know. Nobody told me. They didn't tell me. How was I supposed to know?'

'What do you want to say to her about that?' said Fiona.

The 'I'm sorry, forgive me' came out of me as if wrenched from down in my toes, followed shortly by 'Thank you for looking after me.' I took a long, shaky breath.

'Thank you,' said Fiona. 'Did you get it across to your grandmother?'

'Yes, I did.'

'Good, we'll continue with that tomorrow. Do you have any comments about this session?'

I couldn't believe how quickly the time had passed. I felt wrung out and stunned.

Karma clearing is particularly indicated where someone is stuck in a negative, critical state, as so many of us are. It is an aspect of the victim state. This technique will open up some space and people will feel a lot better for having confessed the things they did they think they should not have done, as well as the things they failed to do they think they should have done.

Karma clearing is also indicated where a person has persistent bad luck that does not seem in line with the rest of their lives.

Paul came for sessions because he saw himself as unusually unlucky and had begun to suspect he might be playing some part in his own misfortunes. Reviewing his life in his first session, he certainly seemed to have suffered a more than average share of bad luck, from physical accidents to losing money, to having his house burgled and vandalised, and losing his job when his employers went broke or sold their businesses.

He communicated well; no self-defeating beliefs or attitudes were apparent, and he seemed to organise his life efficiently. In other words, nothing pointed to Paul contributing to his own bad luck. So I thought karma clearing might be indicated and explained it. If he was somehow sabotaging his life, this could be because he was unconsciously punishing himself for things he had done that he felt bad about.

But Paul had reservations: he didn't like the term 'karma' because, to him, 'karma' implied a belief in reincarnation he didn't share. However, he agreed to go ahead when I explained that it accommodated clients who believed they'd had previous lives, without implying that such beliefs were necessary, and our focus would be on the life he knew he'd lived.

I alternated the instructions: 'Tell me something you've done that you shouldn't have done in your own estimation,' and 'Tell me something you've failed to do that you should have done in your own estimation.'

After perhaps 15 rounds, he said, 'I shouldn't have stolen some apples from my headmaster's orchard at boarding school when I was 10,' followed by, 'I failed to share those stolen apples with the others in my dormitory.' But he'd said the 'failed to' part in a way that didn't ring true, so I said, 'Clarify to me why it was wrong for you to steal the apples but would have been right to share them with others.'

He thought for a while, then said, 'I'm beginning to get bogged down with this "in your own estimation" part. I mean, I only thought stealing the apples was wrong because everyone knows stealing is wrong. But I don't really think I was wrong. The apples were windfalls, being eaten by wasps, and we boys were given so little fruit back then that it's a wonder we didn't get scurvy. So, in my own estimation, I was right to steal them but wrong to eat them all myself.'

From then on, the session took off as he re-evaluated memory after memory in the light of his own estimation. In particular, he remembered times when he'd behaved badly, 'Because', as he put it, 'other people behaved that way, so I did too' – for example, when he joined others in bullying weaker boys at school.

Towards the end of session two, he found himself feeling devastated by his failure to help his brother when he was in financial trouble, and we broke off karma clearing temporarily while he expressed his deep regret to his brother as if he were present.

Paul found the work valuable not only because he felt as if a weight had been lifted from his mind, but also because each time he homed in on his own inner standard, he gained a clearer sense of who he was. He saw how letting other people's standards be his yardstick had masked his own standards. That, in turn, meant he didn't trust his own judgement and therefore had sometimes placed himself riskily in other people hands, particularly in money matters.

In the worse cases, if a person is given the instruction 'Tell me something you did you think you shouldn't have done,' they will say, 'Nothing, I haven't done anything to anyone.' They have persuaded themselves that everything is the fault of others; they never did anything bad to anyone. It will take persistence to get someone in this condition to look in the first place and to come up with anything at all. They are so steeped in guilt they cannot face looking at what they have done to others and have directed it all out at the world in criticism that is really self-criticism and at base, guilt. They prefer to move right on from that inner stuff and look at the fault they are projecting onto others. So a Clearer will have to be persistent with someone like this, and it may be too difficult at that point. The person may be better off discharging all the anger and frustration they are carrying around. They will not be able to see their part in anything until a good part of this anger is expressed.

Eventually, though, if karma clearing is pursued, the person will come up with something. It will probably be quite vague and general to start with. They might say, 'Well, I suppose I've sometimes been a bit mean to people.' This is a start. When they have come up with a few things like this, they can be asked for specific examples of being mean and they might struggle with that but finally come up with, 'Well, I've sometimes been a bit mean to my mother.' From there, they can be encouraged to give a concrete instance of when they were mean to their mother. It will probably come along with a lot of blame towards others and lots of justifications, which should be ignored. They will come up with specifics. Eventually, they might say something along the lines of, 'Well, I told her she was stupid when she bought the wrong attachment for the vacuum cleaner. That was mean. I feel bad about that.' And they might then start to say, 'But it was pretty stupid. I've had to put up with her stupidity all my life, and it drives me crazy.' This second bit is quite normal but unhelpful. If there is a lot of it, it may be necessary to go back and get them more discharged around their anger. They should be encouraged to say all that stuff they have been bottling up. In karma clearing we just want the thing about which they feel bad, not the justifications. The justifications just pile on more things to feel bad about later. They undo the karma clearing.

When the person has communicated something they did they think they should not have done in their own estimation, then they can be asked to consider what, again in their own estimation, was the effect of what they did. They might say, 'How should I know what the effect on her was?' So it will be necessary to keep going and be patient, and finally they will be able to say it: 'It upset her. Yes, she was upset about it.' They can finally confess what they did and what effect it had.

Karma clearing is powerful. The person has been feeling bad about this thing they did for years, maybe most of their life. They never told anyone before, and now they have. The person was critical, bitter and eaten up inside with guilt and anger. Now they have looked at the reality of what they did and said it. It does not matter what anyone else did when it comes to karma clearing. The thing hanging us up is what we know *we* did wrong.

With karma clearing, people can come back to life. When a person can confess what they feel they have done wrong or failed to do, and see their part in what has been going on in their lives, then there is not so much need to be bitter and critical of others. They are freed up to treat others better. They can relax all the tension that has built up around their guilt and withholding. It can have a profound effect on their physical health and luck in life.

> This is a very powerful, simple approach to resolving the unchanging and critical case, that kind of person who won't let himself improve. Such people batter their heads against the most complex and clever techniques, but they won't get better because they, in their hearts, don't feel they deserve it. For the stubborn type of person who feels he never did anything to anybody, it takes a very clever [Clearer] to get him started. Once started and he's got the idea, he'll say, 'Hey, this is the greatest technique that I ever came across. I slept soundly for the first time in my life.' Then almost anybody can work with him, in any technique, after he has confessed for a while.[8]

The results of our past actions in our present lives are all a form of self-imposed penance.[9] Karma is very little different from attitudes as they are all the fruits of action done in ignorance. Dealing with karma is working on the fixed attitudes in a different way.

9
DOS AND DON'TS OF MIND CLEARING

Things always to do in Mind Clearing
Always work with the client's agreement

In the initial interview it is vital to check that the client is there because this is what they want, rather than because they are doing what someone else wants them to do. Once this is clear, then it is essential that Clearer and client can work together in sessions. It is easy to have a sense of whether a person is with you as you work together. Signs that they are not with you are that they may be resistant to doing what is suggested, or go off track or become critical. If the client is not working with you, this could be for a number of reasons. It might be that you are not working in the area in which they are interested, or the work might be too hard or too easy for them. It could be transference that has come up, or a perceived or actual non-understanding. Whatever the reason, it is up to the Clearer to find out why the client has stopped working with them. Finding it out will raise the level of communication.

Always get the information about the client from the client

Do not decide what is wrong with the client and work from that. Put aside information from other people about the client as far as possible. It would be foolish to ignore important facts about someone, but the Clearer can ask about these things. The information must come primarily from the client.

Always maintain the clearing communication cycle

The clearing communication cycle[1] is what works and is how people develop in their ability to communicate. As a direct result of getting better at getting themselves across to another individual, the mind drops away as it is no longer needed. If cycles are not maintained, the session will not be effective and the person will go away dissatisfied. The Clearer will also be dissatisfied.

Always take care of the physical environment

The only point of a session is to help the person get better at presenting themselves. Anything that significantly distracts from this should be taken out of the equation. The Clearer has the responsibility to make sure the physical environment works for the purpose of giving sessions. The environment should not be a distraction.

Always co-operate with the individual and ignore the reactivity of the mind

Ignore any reactivity of the mind and relate only with the individual. The reactivity is the mind. This can be difficult, especially if the client is acting out in a big way or continually angles for social contact, but this must be ignored. Genuine insights should never be ignored, but distractions should be.

Always keep your attention on the client

If the attention of the Clearer wanders, then the affinity with the client is reduced. Something might be missed and the client will feel less understood.

Always mean what you say

The Clearer must make sure that anything they say in a session is true for them. They need to keep the session real, so everything they say must come from them and they must mean it. If the Clearer does not mean what they say, the session will become what so many conversations in life are: fake. The person will know it and they will see that this is no different from the rest of life, and they will have no faith in the Clearer or the process.

The Clearer does not, and should not, reveal information about themselves except on rare occasions; knowing when to do so is something that can only really be learned through experience. But they should give honest answers to questions and mean what they say.

Even if a client asks something confronting such as, 'Do you find me attractive?' the Clearer must be honest. Maybe they do find the client attractive, in which case they should say so and then continue with the session.

Admit mistakes and go on

Mistakes happen and must be acknowledged, and then the session continues. It is a mistake to try to cover up mistakes, and the client probably noticed anyway. Do not make a fuss or overdo it; just say what happened and that it was a mistake, and move on.

Things never to do in Mind Clearing
Do not diagnose the client and
get fixed in that diagnosis

It is tempting to diagnose a person and to go in and try to work out how to fix them, but this is something that must never be done in Mind Clearing. It is likely the Clearer cannot help but notice ways in which the client is caught up. This is a form of diagnosis and to be expected of good Clearers; it can be important for knowing what tools to use with that person. But as soon as this becomes fixed as a *diagnosis* it becomes a distancing strategy and the Clearer is no longer really open to what is true for that person. They might be correct in what they observe, but they are no longer really engaging. In this respect they are in fact incorrect. It is far more effective to get information from the client at the time and help them do the work.

The person might be all over the place, but unless they are helped to sort through what they are actually presenting so they present better and get clearer on things for themselves, then sitting and talking will not help them. The client has to get better at making their own judgements and decisions. It will not help for it to be done for them. The help does not happen by fixing people.

Practical help might be like that. If a person goes to a doctor with a broken arm and the doctor can fix it, then that is the help to be got from the doctor. Mind Clearing is not dealing in that kind of help. Help with the mind consists in assisting the person in getting better at looking inside, seeing what is going on and communicating it. When a person starts improving their skill at looking inside, what is really going on is technically the opposite of looking inward. The person is actually looking *outwards* from their centre. They are looking out *at* their mind, thoughts, body, emotions, at other people, *from* themselves. It strengthens the individual and people become clearer about who and where they are. To do that, it is vital to help the person develop their judgement and work with that.

Never try to teach covertly

If the Clearer thinks the client would benefit from knowing something they seem ignorant of, then specific teaching is OK. But this should never be attempted implicitly, through the techniques of the session. This is covertly trying to get something across. It is not dealing honestly with the client. It is a form of distorted communication.

Do not play games with a client

Playing games with a client is similar to teaching covertly. The Clearer should never try to set the client up to come up with the 'right' answer through questions or any other way of trying to get them to see something they think is important. This is manipulation. It is indirect communication and should not be done.

Never evaluate or invalidate your client

Deciding what is wrong with clients is an evaluation and an invalidation. It goes back to always getting the information from the client. It is vital to work with the individual, not work with ideas about them.

Never call attention to yourself during the session

The session is for and about the client, not the Clearer. The Clearer drawing attention to themselves in the session should be avoided as far as possible. There are so many ways the Clearer can draw attention to themselves in the session. For instance, it may be tempting to mention a situation similar to that about which the client is talking. It can be friendly and may possibly be helpful sometimes, but it is in fact the

Clearer drawing attention to themselves. Other ways are moving about, fidgeting, yawning, looking around, even some forms of dress.

Never go on with a session in the presence of a known withhold

If someone indicates there is something they have not said or will not say, the Clearer must not go on with the session until the client has communicated it. They want to communicate it or they would not have mentioned it, so the Clearer should get it out of them through ethical and kind means, and then continue.

Never make comments or give advice

Making comments or giving advice come under evaluating, invalidating and drawing attention to yourself. The Clearer's comments might be correct and their advice might be good, but this must not be done. Attention must be kept on the client; the Clearer must work with them at developing and expressing their own judgements and communicating them. If it is clear that teaching them something may benefit them, then this should be introduced explicitly and should be brief.

10
THE MIND CLEARING PROJECT

Mind Clearing is a fully developed practice for dealing with the mind, but only a few core techniques have been discussed in any detail here. These include the clearing communication cycle, attitude clearing and karma clearing. The technique of communicating to others as though they were present is also mentioned, though not looked at specifically. There is no space to go into anything else here. But more importantly, there is a limit to the value of reading about techniques without experiencing them in practice.

So there is a great deal more to Mind Clearing than what is in these pages. Lawrence Noyes, in particular, has developed extensive training material, papers, lectures and manuals to guide practitioners in dealing with many problem areas with which people present. The core principles remain the same throughout, built into specific steps for different types of issue.

The approach is always person-centred, working from presenting problem areas chosen by the client with the aim of clearing these and revealing the responsible initiating adult at the core. It is diagnostic insofar as it is recognised that the mind has a universal structure and that in consequence, problems fundamentally come down to the original reason we have a mind in the first place. For the same reason, problem areas are common to many people and can often be approached in similar ways with a variety of clients. But each individual is addressed directly as unique throughout; we all have important differences. It is person-centred because it is based on the premise that there is a person at the centre; not one that needs to be constructed, but one already there, already whole and who is the driver of all self-examination and progress.

All the approaches to any problem area are based around the clearing communication cycle and on increasing the client's ability to present themselves directly, through choice, without the automaticity of the mind, such that fixed attitudes stop running them. With the basic principles presented in this book, difficulties at every level can be dealt with.

Mind Clearing is not a cure-all

Mind Clearing is not a universal fix. Berner started out looking for a cure-all technique. In a sense he found it, but not where he was originally looking. First, he gradually understood that dealing with the mind to the extent that all difficulties are gone for good cannot be completed with any technique. All techniques require the use of discipline and the will; in other words, force. But force is out of step with who we really are, it is a form of resistance to reality. Wilful techniques can get us only so far, they cannot reach the heart of our distortions. For that, we have to surrender.

Second, as he mapped more and more clearly what we human beings actually are, he recognised the different elements that go into making up the suffering of the human condition. The mind is only the outermost layer of that, the first one to tackle.

Third, he distinguished ever more clearly that each element must be worked with differently. Any form of talking help will mostly deal with the mind. The other layers obscuring our original centre, are better dealt with in other ways.

The Mind Clearing project

Mind Clearing is a beautifully crafted tool for help, nonetheless. With it we can deal with a considerable amount of the cognitive layer of the human condition. It goes far beyond an intellectual changing round of ideas. The mind is the meaning we ascribe to otherwise neutral things and events. But any reality those ideas have is intrinsically linked to our material experience of reality, so dealing only in the intellect will change nothing. The distinction between mind and body, for example, so powerful in Western thought and medicine since at least the seventeenth century, can be useful for achieving change by examining elements in turn, but it is ultimately based on a false dichotomy. Mind and body cannot be separated.

Finding and delivering the message that is keeping a series of fixed attitudes and meanings locked in place unlocks patterns that key straight into the body and emotions, and resonates with the whole person. The more precisely the message is identified and the more fulsomely delivered, the greater the resonation with the individual and the deeper the release from structures of cognition, as well as body tensions and emotional holding.

The body can and does change as a result of this work. Long-held tensions associated with withheld communications release, along with the communications that are finally fulfilled and finished. Cognition, or the mind, is keeping part of the edifice of the human condition locked in place. Freedom from the tyranny of the mind is a very real freedom.

Results to expect from Mind Clearing

With Mind Clearing we can expect to become a great deal freer from mind chatter and subconscious motivations. Much of that chatter, as well as the subliminal thinking that keeps us in the past rather than present, consists of the unfinished communications and layers of ideas stacking up in the mind and taking us further and further from the now. As we fulfil those communications we allow events to become the past and we arrive more and more in the here and now. There is less for the mind to chatter about. As we act more and more from a clear place of who we are, we are more here, more original, more creative and more engaged. We will find we have fewer or no current problems nagging us, as we are able to deal with these as they arise or turn them into projects rather than problems. Saying what we would previously have withheld becomes a matter of real choice. Maybe we choose not to do so at times as the wisest course of action. But the new thing is that we know what we think and *could* communicate those thoughts if we chose. Consequently, stress levels are lower, thought processes clearer and people more empowered to meet difficulties openly and constructively. Fundamental to this, the past will no longer be a place of no-go areas and a cause of present reactivity; relationships will be easier, more authentic and fulfilling, and there will be freedom from guilt and stuck ways of being. Some victim states may be gone for good and those that remain are less fixed, so we are freer to choose to let them go and find other ways to be.

In helping professions we are also always looking for stability in any progress made. The stability of progress in Mind Clearing is in direct proportion to the gains made in the ability to communicate directly. The work done in Mind Clearing sessions all works through a number of key elements coming together within the relationship between Clearer and client:

- The clearing communication cycle emphasises the attention that goes in the direction from Clearer to client. In being seen, the individual is called on to respond. Being seen makes it correspondingly easier for the client to find themselves within the mind and differentiate themselves from that muddle.

- It asks the client to go inside, with specific tasks. To do this, the client must perform an action to locate the stable point of who they are. From that point, the client can increasingly differentiate and make decisions.

- The performance of an action embeds the learning into the whole person; it is made real and pathways are changed, and new ones are made.

- As the response is communicated, the truth of what is said is tested in real relationship and discernment is developed.

- As the response is communicated, the person gets themselves across more and more directly to another person.

- As the response is communicated, the thoughts withheld are presented, defused and can go into the past and no longer contribute to the mass of mind.

- As the response is communicated, the client increasingly looks out from a clearer, stable point of who they are to the person in front of them.

- As the response is received and acknowledged, the unfinished communications, as well as the withheld ideas and thoughts, find a resting place with another person, one who wants to understand and makes it clear when they have done so. Those withheld thoughts and ideas are done with.

- When a key message is uncovered and delivered, one that is keeping strings of fixed attitudes in place, then whole chunks of mind and muddle cease to be relevant and are deactivated.

- Me and you are more than two. One person taking on the responsibility to help the other become better at communicating, engaging with the other in that project, is more than the sum of its parts.

This is what works. The Clearer adds their abilities in relating to that of the client and they work together towards greater understanding. This material gain, or a part of it, is taken forward into ordinary life. The individual comes to the fore, freer from the automatic thinking of the mind to the extent they have communicated and presented themselves and been received.

Life may look much the same in many respects as it did before; the people in that person's life may well not change, the job may be the same and family life carries on, but life will be changed. The inner world, the amount of mind stuff between the person and others, will be reduced; the mind will be cleared.

Here are a few things that people have said about Mind Clearing:

Having been a therapist myself for over 20 years and having had traditional talk therapy on and off myself, I have been amazed at the deeper, lasting effects that Mind Clearing has provided to me. I have experienced for myself personally, and with those that I have worked with, dramatic life-changing results. My teacher often said the mind is a substitute for real relating. I realised in myself and my clients how much more time is spent in the mind, working on the relationship, rather than just being present in the relationship and truly seeing the person. What we are really trying to do in life is to have connection with one another. Mind Clearing has given me and my clients a tool and the ability to assist with this deep desire to connect, rather than be in my mind and feel isolated and disconnected.

It has been like peeling away the layers of an onion that is opened up, sometimes one thin layer at a time; sometimes bigger chunks. In Mind Clearing, working with my clients or having it run on myself, having the courage to face the layers built up from past misunderstandings and traumas together and not doing it alone. Mind Clearing works on the premise that this is nothing to be "fixed"; we are perfect in every way yet, what we work on instead is the misunderstandings, created in the mind. I have experienced this in myself and with working with my clients.

Mind Clearing has given me the tools for self-enquiry, closure and freedom from the pain of traumatic incidents that I have carried in my soul for over 40 years. I have been able to gain freedom from old behavioural patterns that no longer serve me or the others in my life and a continual ability to show up authentically with those around me.

It has impacted my relationships with the people in my life who are most dear to me and brought me a sense of inner peace and deeper connections. I cannot recommend enough this powerful process for any mental, emotional or spiritual place of self-discovery and what we most yearn for, connecting in relationships.

– LT, California, USA

In all my Mind Clearing sessions I have come away feeling my mind is literally clearer. Clearer in the sense that I feel lighter and freer to just be me. It is like letting go of clutter. The unspoken, the unfinished, the inappropriate decisions or conclusions...that is, the miasma of old stuff that clouds present-day reality is getting released. I have found myself feeling more and more relaxed in situations where I would normally have been shy or self-conscious, and some previously difficult relationships are improving. The questions and instructions encourage me to look deeper than I could on my own. As I rummage in my mind bits of memory surface that once I say them, I realise how much they governed my thoughts and feelings without realising...and suddenly I think, *How ridiculous that is!* Then I experience a huge relief as I automatically let go of it.

– FJ, London, UK

Mind Clearing was immediately helpful to me in getting over an emotionally difficult time in my life. Since then, it has enabled me to see how the fixed ideas I have about myself and others cause me to react emotionally to what people say before I am even conscious I am doing it. Through dismantling these erroneous beliefs one by one during sessions, I feel like I am gradually reclaiming my self from my mind. Since starting Mind Clearing I have noticed that my relationships are going better and that I feel much less self-conscious and anxious and in life. Slowly but surely, I am taking responsibility for the way that I am, and I fear that finally, at the age of 32, I may be growing up. Damn you, Mind Clearing!

– SK, Nairobi, Kenya

The process of Mind Clearing for me has been by far one of the most significant and useful bodies of work that I have encountered during my seemingly arduous search for what makes me tick and do life in the particular and frequently frustrating way that I do. These processes have enabled me to finally become aware of, or get free from, certain behaviors, attitudes and attachments I have been trying to get at for years. And I mean years. It has taken me, in a lot of instances, from being 'at the effect of' to being 'at choice'. For me, this is nothing short of monumental.

Mind Clearing is like going on an expedition through the interior of your mind...never knowing what exactly you might find along the way, realising whether it's a land mine or a diamond field, each is its own sacred gift.

– CQ, Florida, USA

I started having Mind Clearing sessions about 3 years ago on a regular basis. At first, the sessions helped me to unburden myself of unresolved issues that were echoing in my mind; then, as we went deeper, I became aware of my attitude of blaming others and not taking responsibility.

For the first time in my life, I feel heard; and while I am searching within, with the Clearer's guidance, I am blasting out confusion, patterns and buried emotions that keep me down. Mind Clearing is empowering me to become myself and acknowledge my place in the world.

I am better able to communicate who I am and what I want, and I have much better relationships with others as a result. For me, Mind Clearing is the way forward to a more conscious, worthwhile way of being and living.

– DR, London, UK

I have had years of psychotherapy and trained for a while in person-centred psychotherapy too. There were some benefits, but I struggle to say that the therapy was worthwhile and my life was still not going well; in some areas, it was a disaster. I came across Mind Clearing years before but only started to have sessions about 3 years ago. For me, the difference was clear and immediate. Several things stood out. First, I felt it was really collaborative for the first time. There was nothing being enacted upon me and I was being called upon to be really there and accountable. Second, we worked on what really mattered to me in a focused, structured way that was satisfying and useful. I could immediately see value in improved relationships and a lessening of the sense of 'problem' I had had since I was a child. I also felt seen and got in a way that was subtly new; or maybe not so subtle. I felt actually helped and, in experiencing this, realised how deeply I had previously felt that help wasn't really possible. The bottom line is that, although it isn't always easy, it does work. The more I understand about it, the more impressed I am by Berner's insights and the techniques he put together. I can thoroughly recommend Mind Clearing to anyone who wants their life to go better on any level.

– AW, Norwich, UK

Many people see the goal of their work in Mind Clearing as being to reach a point where they are free enough from their fixed ways of being that their lives go better. They do not necessarily have an interest in taking the work further; life is good and they want to go out and enjoy it. The success in doing this is a very real result and one can stop there.

That was not the end as Berner understood it. For him, a well-functioning life, free from the fixidity of the mind, was just the start of the journey, the groundwork for a whole new level of understanding. He worked, right up to the end of his life, to take his own development further. Those other steps are not what everyone wants. Perhaps only a few people really want that; when they gain freedom from their minds and appreciate how good life can be, that is more than enough. But Berner's other methods reflect some of his further research.

The body and Emotion Clearing

Much of Berner's work has to do with the mind and uses the intellect and communication to make progress. Like most Western therapeutic practices it tends to prioritise thinking and speaking. However, he did appreciate the importance of other elements of the human experience and understood the relationships between them.

The body stores partially resisted traumas, non-understandings and non-communications in its structure that, over time and if they are not released, manifest as distortion and sickness. In fact, meaning structures came about because of our wish to distance ourselves from felt discomfort. So the body's tension is intimately related to the mind. Because of this, it is possible to free some of the mind through the body, as well as the other way around.

In our development, as soon as there is any kind of emotional upset with another person, it is felt as a physical sensation. As a result, the body tenses as the unwanted sensation is resisted. We may only tense infinitesimally, maybe only in a few muscle fibres, but unless that small part is experienced and received, the area of tension will remain in the body, often at a subconscious level.[1] So now, although the tense area may only be very small, the breathing has changed, the centre of gravity has shifted, usually slightly upwards, and there is a small distortion in the emotional field that is reflected in the body.

Patanjali also noted that disrupted breathing is a sign of poor health and a barrier to progress as it is a distraction.[2] A change in the breathing pattern may at first be a tiny area of weakness, but it has an effect on everything else including how a person moves. The particular characteristics of the distortion are related to the particular idea that formed in the mind in relation to the event that was resisted. The body distortion and related idea resonate together.

Around that initial hitch in the breath and the resulting tension, other tensions accumulate. This will happen quickly or slowly, and to greater or lesser degrees according to the person, but every time there is another event that was resisted, the tension will build up around that original weak point and become more and more of a marked trait, a noticeable area of tension or an actual distortion in the body. With experience, we can see the 'personality' reflected in how a person moves and breathes. The mind and body, thus, cannot really be seen as separate, though we make that distinction in order to deal with them most economically.

The body is affected by outside influences as well as internal ones. There are inherited tendencies, genetic changes and environmental factors, both social and physical, that all affect the body too and so have an effect on the mind. We are subject to ageing, diseases and accidents. In the bigger picture there may be some meaning in these influences, but most of us will never understand the world at that depth. So we might well not be able to sort the body out entirely, but a lot of the stress and tensions held in the body are within our control.

We can bring consciousness to what is held and resisted at a physical and emotional level. Meditations that focus on the body, such as vipassana, bring consciousness to the body. Very often, in the process of doing this or any similar practice, a person will experience considerable pain and discomfort. This is because we bring awareness to areas that are unconscious and resisted.

Through being willing to experience the resistance at a body level, understanding will arise, automatically, about what has been held out and why. The body can change, sometimes dramatically, as a result, and areas of mind can fall away.[3]

Emotion Clearing came out of Berner's research into how to deal with the emotions, and indeed components of attitudes, fixed at a body level that are difficult to access through Mind Clearing alone. This was because he found that when the mind has been dealt with to a reasonable extent, then the body and held emotions typically represents the next challenge for people. During the period in which he was considering how to deal with emotions, he came across Janov's *Primal Scream*[4] therapy, which had also been connected, early on, with Dianetics.[5]

Berner immediately understood that Janov had hit upon an answer to many of his own questions. However, although people would commonly experience great relief, at some point they would become stuck, sometimes feeling worse as they became fixed in a position and a cycle of expressing the same thing over and over. Seeing value in the principle of feeling the emotions in the body and expressing them, he incorporated a similar technique into his own work but added to it in order to prevent people from getting stuck. Putting in the communication of a specific message, such as he had developed in Mind Clearing, broke these fixed cycles and enabled people to release the caught emotions and not keep them cycling. Thus, Berner turned Emotion Clearing into a workable way of dealing with the body and emotions, and added an important tool to his portfolio.[6]

The Enlightenment Intensive[7]

As he was developing Mind Clearing in the 1960s, Berner noticed that some people progressed more quickly than others. Looking into this carefully, he saw that this was not necessarily related to the density of mind each person had, though that was a factor. What he noted was that those who progressed more quickly had a sense of who they were as separate from the mind. They were able to understand the project and work on the mind as a particular thing, separate from themselves and working from a point of relative stability. People who did not have this stable sense of who they were, implicit or otherwise, were more closely identified with the content of their minds and consequently took longer to de-identify from it.

Berner, always invigorated by a challenge, wondered what it would take to bring this group of people to a point of de-identification from their mind so they could progress more quickly. He knew about peak experiences, or moments of enlightenment. He had had several of these himself, had observed others in that state and, moreover, there is a large body of literature on the subject. Peak experiences are partly defined by the recognition people have of the unchanging nature of who they really are in contrast to the ever-changing state of the mind and world. So Berner thought that if people could have a peak experience before embarking on Mind Clearing, they would have a head start. But the big difficulty with peak experiences is that we cannot *make* them happen. Yet, the circumstances in which they take place do tend to have certain common characteristics. So Berner set out to identify and reproduce the most conducive environment he could in order to give people the best chance of experiencing this direct knowing so they could make swifter progress in their self-development. This approach was very much in step with the times, as instant 'this' and instant 'that' was almost a mantra of the 1960s, and, coupled with meditation and enlightenment, it spoke clearly to the times.

At that point, around 1966, Berner was engaged in learning about Zen Buddhism, which recognises and promotes the value of these enlightenment moments in a structured environment. Zen is a Japanese branch of Buddhism within which the *sesshin* is an intense period of meditation undertaken by monks to boost their practice and push for an enlightenment experience. To this end, they can sit for hours and days contemplating an unanswerable question, or *koan*. Famously, this might be 'What is the sound of one hand clapping?' or 'Who am I?' The unanswerable question is designed to bypass the thinking processes and open the meditator to what is behind thoughts and experience reality directly.

But Berner understood his audience; he knew the stories of Westerners joining sesshins in Japanese monasteries and struggling with the discipline, both mentally and physically. He recognised that the traditional model might not be the best way for his students to gain the desired insight. But it was fresh in his mind when, one day, meditating alone in the Californian desert, he saw how he could combine one of the long-established practices of Zen with the one-on-one communication work he had already developed and found so effective in Mind Clearing and allied methods. Elements of both could be brought together in a process that suited the time and place.

The Enlightenment Intensive, which is based on the structure of the sesshin but includes partnered communication, was quickly refined into a workshop format that has remained largely unchanged for 50 years. It was successful from the start and is still popular worldwide. Berner trained many people in leading the workshops, and the movement has developed over the years and influenced thousands. Noyes has also refined the training and workshop and continues to train people in running them.

Like Mind Clearing, the Enlightenment Intensive also finally pointed the way to something else for Berner. It was, even more than Mind Clearing, a very wilful practice. While it clearly brought, and continues to bring, people to a much closer understanding of themselves and life, he increasingly understood that the discipline was out of step with the insights he and others had. When he met Swami Kripalu, he moved beyond this as well.

Surrender Meditation[8]

Soon after Berner met Swami Kripalu, he asked his teacher if he could be initiated into Surrender Meditation[9] and Kripalu consented. This was the most advanced practice he offered and Swami Kripalu was sceptical about the ability of most people, including many of his own students, to maintain the practice correctly.[10] Nevertheless, when a student asked to be initiated, Kripalu preferred to comply and did so with Berner, or Yogeshwar Muni, for by then he had been given his renunciate or sannyasin name. From this time on, Berner made Surrender Meditation his main practice and taught it to his students.

The ultimate purpose of surrender in the Indian traditions is enlightenment, but few people reach this. Many, however, practise surrender and find enormous value and insight from doing so. The Hindu traditions are not the only ones to regard surrender as the highest discipline. Most, if not all, of the mystical hearts of all religions offer this teaching in some form. For example, Shinto, the native Japanese religion, has at its heart the practice of surrender to the divine, called *furube* (shaking) or *reido* (soul work).[11] Christianity's Holy Spirit 'possessed' Christ's disciples after his death manifested in their speaking in tongues and is called upon to cleanse.[12] Sufi 'dancing' is connected with this surrender to divine energy. Chi gong offers a spontaneous, usually secular practice. There are many more instances where surrender can be found instituted into a religion or abstracted into health techniques such as the Chinese *Buqi*[13] or the Japanese practice of *Katsugen Undo*.[14]

It might be supposed that, because surrender is a non-doing rather than a doing practice, it should be the first and easiest discipline to learn and the fastest and simplest way to deal with life's difficulties. But that would be to misunderstand the situation in which we are. We cannot bypass neurotic structures so easily. They must be systematically worked through before surrender is possible, let alone desirable.

There is a reason why the mystics left surrender for last and why Swami Kripalu was reluctant to initiate his students. Surrender is the *disciplined* surrender of self. The ego must be sufficiently subdued to not take over the process of surrender and use it for its own purposes.

Do-it-yourself Mind Clearing

We need help to deal with the mind at a level of depth because the mind began in relationship and must be addressed in that arena. Alone we are likely to be deceived by the mind at some stage. The clearing communication cycle addresses what we need for significant progress. However, there is a good deal we can do on our own with an understanding of the principles of Mind Clearing coupled with some personal discipline. This takes a good deal of commitment but can be valuable, especially when allied with Mind Clearing sessions or with a mindfulness meditation practice. What follows are some examples of the kind of issue that might be tackled with do-it-yourself Mind Clearing.

Pondering the opposites

As we start to become more aware of the structures of our minds and the fixed attitudes we can get locked into, then it may be possible to do some of the work in unfixing them through solo attitude work. When we are in the middle of a state of mind,[15] then it is especially difficult to see it as an aspect of the mind. The nature of a state, defined by the attitude associated with it, is that it seems true to us when we are in it. So, for instance, if I am triggered by an event to go into my attitude of *others don't get me*, then my whole being resonates with that state. I believe it and act from it. However, the more work we do to identify and unfix the attitudes, the more likely it is that we will start to become aware of such attitudes and states in the moment. At one and the same time, then, I might be in a state of *others don't get me* which feels utterly true and real, while also recognising that this is in fact an attitude into which I have slipped. At such times, it may be possible to take some time to practise a bit of attitude clearing alone, with the idea of stepping aside from the state. Below are two examples of doing just this.

> John: Am I a good Samaritan, or one of those who would pass on the other side? I'm not into organised religion, but that question used to pop up frequently anyway. I'd done good things, but hadn't I done more bad things? And weren't the good things I'd done disqualified because it had suited me to do them, making me a closet psychopath, ultimately completely selfish? I didn't quite think I was one; nevertheless, when I was training to practise psychotherapy and came across tests for psychopathy, I couldn't resist ticking the boxes to calculate my own rating. I didn't qualify, but I continued to think about it.
>
> The question took root way back. We three children all knew our mother had an infallible instinct for good or bad in people – an instinct she once employed to justify banning a new friend from setting foot in the house

because she'd instantly placed him on the dark side of the line. She'd placed me slightly more subtly. 'The males of this family alternate through the generations,' she said. 'They go good-bad-good-bad and so on. Well, your paternal grandfather was a bad man.'

By the time I was practising regularly, the question was not exactly an everyday issue, but it was still there – enough to arise out of the blue when I went for a walk one day. And without consciously setting out to do so, I found myself pondering the opposites: remembering times when I'd done good things, then times when I'd done bad things, back and forth, back and forth, back and forth; and also making up good Samaritan scenarios to experiment with good and bad responses.

But what I found was how arbitrary separating good actions from bad actions proved to be! I knew intellectually this was often (always?) the case, and that philosophers could debate the rights and wrongs of some things forever. Now the reality of it was tangible: deciding what was good or bad really was up to me.

I persisted with the process, walking along the river, the sun on my back, good to bad, good to bad... Then suddenly, the whole notion of whether I was good or bad struck me as so ridiculous that I fell about laughing (good thing we live in a secluded spot). Not only was the assessment of my actions as being either good or bad up to me, how I *acted* on such assessment was also up to me. And, with that realisation, the whole notion of me being intrinsically either good or bad evaporated.

I'm not even somewhere between the two. I'm neither – not even on the scale. So where does that leave me in practical day-to-day living? It leaves me with total responsibility for deciding how to act and how I feel about myself as a result.

We can do a lot of work on our own. Here is another example:

Lorna: I was feeling pretty terrible. Nothing seemed to feel right. I was plagued with regrets about the past and anxiety about the future. What seemed to make it worse was that I was staying in a perfect place. I could look out of my bedroom window down to a great lake, glowing with autumn colour. The haunting calls of loons echoed across the water in the early hours and the sky was a crisp blue. I was loved and looked after and had only beauty in front of me and friends at my side; yet everything, *everything*, looked bleak and lost and bad.

And one time I woke at 4 a.m., my heart pounding, feeling worse than ever, disappointment nagging at me, numb to the moonlight on the water, and I sat up and thought that I must deal with this. If this state of 'everything is bad' was not going to tarnish my every waking hour, and sleeping hour, given my vivid dreams, then I would have to tackle it, there and then. So I sat and contemplated the opposites, just 'everything's good' and 'everything's bad'. I didn't get the idea of these states through memories, just an idea or sometimes a feeling of good and then bad, good, then bad. Bad was easy; it was so familiar, a grey, heavy feeling. Good was harder, not so near to me, and I struggled to get the idea of being in a 'good' attitude. But I managed. And I didn't think I'd achieved anything, but eventually I fell asleep.

Next morning, I awoke to a different world. It wasn't good and it wasn't bad. It was itself and I could enjoy it. It was as though a grey film had been removed from everything and I was free to enjoy it, or not, in an ordinary way. A wonderfully ordinary way. And ever since then my lifelong relationship with that state, 'everything is bad', has been different. It hasn't gone, but I know it's not me.

Karma clearing

Guilt or karma is something that can very usefully be looked at alone. It is something we have hidden largely from ourselves. Hiding it from others is there, but hiding it from ourselves is the real trick; we tie ourselves in knots trying to wriggle out of the bad feeling of having done something that goes against our inner standard. So the power of sitting with a paper and pen and writing down the things we think we have done that we should not have done, and the things we have failed to do, is a major task. It is a task that is surprisingly hard to keep to but it can bring enormous relief. What karma clearing requires is that we fully recognise what we have done about which we feel bad. Once we have done this alone and allowed ourselves to experience that 'badness', usually accompanied by bodily sensations, then we will be freer. If we can then tell someone else, even better.

> Rachel: At the end of my Clearing session, my Clearer suggested that I carry on the process of karma clearing and explained how to do it. I thought it would be easy, especially as I had some time alone in a hotel, where no one knew me, before my flight back. I had the idea that I could just sit down and devote an otherwise empty evening to something positive and get it over with. But when I sat down with my pen and paper I recognised what I was up against: me! I had half thought that, in the session with my Clearer, a huge part of the difficulty in coming up with things I'd done that I felt bad about was that I didn't want to tell her and felt ashamed because of what she might think of me. But I found out that I didn't even want to tell myself. The words were there, hovering just out of reach to begin with, but I had to force myself to write them down. I wrote a few minor things, but I knew there was more. So I tried harder and wrote something about cheating on a boyfriend in college. It was difficult, as I felt pretty horrible about it and kept trying to justify it, even to myself alone in that room. And even when I'd written it, I knew it was only a partial truth. It was so difficult to write it all down, confess what I'd done to myself and put it on the page so I could read it in black and white. It was a strange experience actually, to see that I was in such conflict with myself. And I experienced huge sadness as I finally wrote those things down – all the things I felt bad about and hadn't said. I couldn't do it for very long in the end, probably just 20 minutes. But the result was that I felt sober and more real.

'Communication to other'

The mind is made up of failed communications. Another practice we can get some success with alone is to speak to others out loud as if they were present. Again, we probably need to have had some success with this in sessions to see success alone and, as with karma clearing, to do it for long is difficult. But we can gain considerable relief. This is especially so if we have a good sense of connection with others or with a sense of the divine.

It is important here to say what we have not said *out loud*. We need to imagine the person as present with us and receptive to what we have to say, whatever it is. Then say it; say what you really want to say, what has not been said, what has been held back and suppressed. The extent to which we can do this fully is the extent to which we will be clear of those unfinished communications. This is known as 'communication to other'.

> Molly: I tried communication to other alone a few times and it helped me get a bit of distance from situations that I might not otherwise have got. One time in particular, I was alone in the house and realised that a difficult situation at work was going round and round in my head and I was angry with a couple of the people involved. So I started talking out loud to them. I'd had some practice at this in sessions, so I relaxed and decided not to censor what I said, but just to say it. After a couple of false starts, I surprised myself with the passion that came out of me. It certainly helped the situation and I felt more able to meet the situation in the work environment and deal with those people.

Casual connections

Another area we can work on alone is casual connections in the mind.[16] With mindfulness, the automatic connections the mind makes between ideas it classifies as similar can be broken. This will gain a certain amount of freedom from automatic thinking and correspondingly clarify the mind. More complex connections can also be disarmed on one's own with adequate discipline and time by becoming conscious of the connections. By doing this, it might be useful to communicate one's findings to someone open to hearing them, as the deeper one gets with the mind, the more there is likely to be emotional charge related to those connections. However, the automaticity of the connections can be undone alone.

One way to experiment with this is to work with something that keeps going round in the head, perhaps a song or a repetitive thought pattern. Use it as a meditation and go over it step by step. Do not expect anything in particular and be open to what is there. Follow areas that feel sticky and charged. Maybe you will find you are resistant to looking into a little area of it, so open to that area and keep opening. Follow the connections and there is every chance you will find a key connection. It may just pop up and the cause of the repetition will be made conscious and you will discover your choice.

> Jane: I tried this with music. I often have a song or tune stuck in my mind, so I tried dealing with it as a casual connection to see if it was true. I had had a bit of a requiem going round and round for what felt like days, so I decided to stop and look at it. I was on a walk on my own at the time, suddenly irritated by this repetitive sound in my head distracting me from the spring countryside. So I lay down in the meadow, a little away from the path, closed my eyes, and really listened to the music. I went over and over it, 'hearing' each note. And I found it! It wasn't a big thing, but I became aware of a little hitch in my internal sound system where the end of one bit of the music came and immediately the whole thing started over. I don't think it was actually how the requiem went, but in my head, it just kept going round in this loop. I'd read the bit in the manual where Berner talks about this sort of thing, and I didn't have the same experience he describes. I didn't notice if one note at the end was the same as at the beginning, or anything like that, but as I listened to the end and how it moved back to the start, the connection disintegrated. And that was that. I had this feeling of choice. I could choose to hear the music or not, and I chose not to.

People clearing

Sometimes people go round and round in our minds. Something is sticky about our relationship with these people. We are angry with them, or feel bad about something, and we think about them. We can do something about this. Dealing with people on our own requires concentration. Communicating out loud can work, but so can holding them in our consciousness and allowing ourselves to experience them. We have held out or resisted something about them, so this is not necessarily comfortable or easy to do. The things we are resisting are often resisted at a deep level, so keeping our attention on them can be hard work. But when it is done, even to a degree, then the relationship with that person will probably be eased. Here is an example:

> Melanie: I had a brief flirtation with Richard on a residential workshop and I knew I was a bit fixated on him. I didn't want to have a relationship with him, but I felt a mixture of embarrassment and anger and betrayal around him and didn't like to think of him, so I did my best to put him out of my mind. I did fairly well with this, especially as our paths didn't cross much. But when I knew he was going to be at a conference I was going to, I felt increasingly anxious about it.
>
> The night before I knew I would meet him, I lay in bed, unable to sleep with worry about it. So I decided to act. I brought an image of him to mind and relaxed. I consciously breathed easily and let my limbs release into the mattress as I held the image of Richard at the front of my mind. I found it really difficult. All these feelings of shame and anger came up and my mind wanted to slide off the image and go somewhere more comfortable. But I carried on and it was like burning off the feelings. I kept simply deciding to experience whatever I was feeling and relaxing. I had to keep telling myself that it was only me who was going to know about the stuff that came up. That helped.
>
> At the time I didn't feel any better. In fact, in some ways I felt worse and, after quite a while, decided it was a waste of time, and I must have gone to sleep. But the next day, when I arrived at the conference, I met Richard quite early on and it was great. I could tell immediately that I didn't feel anything of what I'd felt before. It was completely OK. I actually noticed for the first time that Richard seemed to be feeling some awkwardness around me. I felt perfectly friendly but also pretty much uninterested.

11
MIND CLEARING AND MINDFULNESS

There has been a seismic shift in recent years within the industry of psychological health. Mindfulness meditation has been recognised as a powerful tool for helping people manage their minds and gain relief from distressing and distracting psychological symptoms. It is so ubiquitous now that it made the cover of *Time* magazine in 2014.

The quiet revolutionaries, such as Jon Kabat-Zinn, who has been a major voice for this approach for decades, have won a somewhat surprising victory, as mindfulness is being adopted by increasing numbers of more mainstream professionals and put at the heart of well-being projects and programmes in Europe and America. There is no longer much argument about *whether* it works; research funding is increasingly being devoted to figuring out *why* and *how* it works.

Mindfulness is, for many, an end in itself. It is posited that the fruits of greater awareness will naturally emerge from the increasing prevalence of practice. It is being brought into therapy programmes, education, industry and so on, packaged for the variations in audience. The reported effects are so positive that only good can conceivably come of it. It is real help and there seem to be no drawbacks.

This last chapter is not about its value, for that is undisputed and applauded, but about where we go from here. Mind Clearing offers a very real next step and the tools for mindfulness mastery.

Mindfulness is based on a model of the human being and fulfilment fundamentally at odds with the biomedical model and many forms of psychotherapy. So while it is useful as a stand-alone technique, there is something of an unanswered question as to how it can become more integrated into the fabric of health and well-being provision without losing something essential or changing its host. Both or either can, of course, be considered to be positive outcomes depending on where one stands.

Becoming more mindful and aware, we discover we are not quite who or what we thought we were. Observing our inner landscape with equilibrium allows us to notice our minds operating. We not only discover that the mind and emotions are a shifting cloud-scape but, in order to engage in any kind of mindfulness, the inner observer of these clouds must be located. The observer consequently comes more to centre stage and the clouds are perceived as smaller than we might have thought.

The observer comes into focus as being closer to the source of fulfilment, more real and ultimately more familiar, than the patterns in the clouds. For those who have tasted the benefits of mindfulness, the model it rests on, which includes the basic premise that 'you are not your mind', is not just a theoretical possibility among others of equal validity. It is an experienced reality. But mindfulness meditation on its own will not deal with the mind unless you have a lifetime or more to spend. This is not what most of us want. It also takes support and is why meditation, in its original contexts, has often been taught in dedicated communities. There is a teacher who has been through the various stages of meditation themselves. There is support, guidance, a common understanding and goal, plus some degree of focused communication. Not only this, but the community will generally exist within a wider context that supports and celebrates the work of those who have taken up the practice as their life's work.

In a modern, secular society, the practitioner may be part of a like-minded community, increasingly an online and geographically scattered one, but the wider, dominant social context is unlikely to be grounded in a supportive model of who we are.

Mindfulness as a path is also made more difficult because modern people are not often familiar with the performance of inner discipline; there are fewer and fewer arenas in which this is taught. What we in the modern world, East and West, tend to be more familiar and comfortable with are practices that have more to do with communication, engagement, goals and results, rather than rigours and austerities for their own sake and progress that ultimately relies on grace.

Through being more mindful, we do find better places within ourselves than the ones we started in; we can gain greater freedom in our responses to the world. But it usually only changes the surface of our minds. Basic mindfulness meditations were only ever meant to take us to the foothills of real change. And, indeed, the claims being made for it are realistic in this respect. It helps people in many ways but does not pretend to be a complete cure; it is a management technique with benefits.

Progress through mindfulness slows over time, and those who want to develop the observer in themselves will need help. As the surface stills, we discover more intransigent layers of conflict within ourselves and with others. These are areas of our subconscious where the light of awareness barely glimmers. The deeper patterns are more difficult to open up and transform. We need information and assistance to deal with them and continue to progress.

For those people who experience this change in perspective, the question may arise about what to do next. Business as usual that focuses largely on the shifting clouds of the mind will no longer be enough, as other possibilities have been tasted.

Plenty of psychotherapists know this and many are seeking ways to incorporate mindfulness into their work. But it is not straightforward to marry regular one-to-one help with mindfulness meditation in a truly integrated approach. Mindfulness is a solitary path, however packed the meditation hall or numerous the books may be.

We also know that talking to another person helps too and speaks to modern needs and views of self-realisation. But the talking so often finds the focus returning more to the clouds of the mind than the observer. So there is often a gap between meditation as a formal exercise for taming the mind and the business of helping people through communication interventions.

Mind Clearing and mindfulness

Berner's insights lay in bringing together the principles and practice of what actually helps with a deep appreciation of the dimensions of who we are and why we suffer. Mind Clearing is practical and secular but open and realistic about the different dimensions in which we operate. It takes up the baton where mindfulness techniques find the end of their reach. It takes the insight, long known in psychotherapy, that the relationship between client and Clearer or therapist is where deep progress takes place and marries this with the crisp reality of the now, which we discover when we embrace mindfulness.

It is certainly beneficial to learn equilibrium in the face of difficult memories and ideas, and this is what mindfulness teaches as a technique. It is mostly a time-bound negotiation between the past and present. But why stop there when we can take it to another level?

Mind Clearing is mindfulness mastery. It is revolutionary to bring those difficult memories and ideas right into the present and finish them. When this is done, the individual gains actual and permanent freedom from that piece of the past. Thus, they are more present as of fact, rather than wilful choice. It is about finding the doors to right here and right now in the ordinary, easily missed work of sitting with another person and being who you are with them.

The effects of Mind Clearing are therapeutic, but it is not therapy. It does not set out to organise the psyche but to obviate the individual's need for the mind. Berner's comprehensive models offer the mindfulness movement the possibility of completion according to its own rules. Not only does his model of the mind contribute to current thinking and explain why mindfulness is important for mental health, it also offers a logical, practically worked-out programme for taking it further. It does so in a way that maintains and validates the secular use of meditation for health. It can accommodate the biomedical model and hold its own.

The approach is essentially political because it is grounded in the dynamic of person-to-person relating. Its technology is understandable, testable and repeatable. It is the nuts and bolts of relationship.

AFTERWORD

This book has a personal significance for me on several levels. First, it addresses some of the questions I had started asking in the 1960s. I was in my mid-twenties and had gained an impression that life ran a hidden agenda I was not party to, an impression enhanced when I came across people who apparently *were* in the know – people such as a sage, well known at the time, called Krishnamurti,[1] whom I once sat next to over lunch at his boarding school, Brockwood Park[2] in Hampshire (we talked about farming). That afternoon, I asked one of the school's pupils what it was like to be educated at a place where 'K', as most people called him, gave live talks and the curriculum was based on his principles. 'Frustrating', he replied, 'because every time he talks, I'm on the edge of my chair thinking *I'm about to get it*. But I never have got it – and in 2 weeks I graduate and go back to America, so I probably never will.' I thought I knew what he meant.

Yet it did not seem as if sages like Krishnamurti actually *meant* to hide that agenda. In fact, as I listened to recordings of his talks, it seemed that he was often more frustrated than his listeners by their inability to *get it*; it was as if he spoke in a code that I, and evidently most of his listeners, hadn't yet deciphered.

Four years of psychoanalysis made me marginally more self-aware but did not teach me that elusive 'code'. So, in 1979, I sold my farm and set up a residential venue for groups, called Grimstone Manor.[3] I aimed to base it on Esalen,[4] a centre in California that I had recently visited. It was a wildly grandiose plan, but I had a hidden agenda of my own: I would earn my living doing something useful, indulge my addiction for restoring old buildings – and invite wise teachers from all over the world to run workshops. I would take part in some of the workshops myself and one day one of these sages would surely reveal the nature of that other 'hidden agenda' in words I understood.

Bookings started to roll in, from tai chi through Native American workshops on sexuality, to Buddhist retreats and groups run by

Gestalt therapists. And when I was joined by an ex-journalist called Jean Campbell to run the domestic side of things (Jean later became my wife), Grimstone really took off; we even had several genuine Esalen sages running workshops for us. Ram Dass[5] was perhaps the best known of them, and when it was my turn for a private interview with him, I planned to ask him how to go about cracking that code. But first I had a pressing question: 'In your Monday talk', I told him, 'you said *this* [I forget the detail], but on Wednesday you said *that*. How do you account for contradicting yourself like that?' 'It's because I'm inconsistent,' he replied. And on cracking that code? 'Meditate alone for an hour every day, Tony.' (No, I didn't.)

In 1984 along came a man called Jake Chapman,[6] a Professor in Physics and Systems Analysis with the Open University.[7] He wanted to bring about 40 people to Grimstone. But as far as we knew, he was unknown as a group leader. (So was he any good?) However, he dangled two carrots: 1) he wanted to book Grimstone for two whole weeks, and 2) it sounded as if his workshop would be aimed specifically at investigating that hidden agenda. It was, he explained, no good listening to sages to gain access to it (he called it the *Truth*): one must conduct the search for oneself under conditions designed to maximise the chances of success. Such retreats were called Enlightenment Intensives (EIs), and whilst they gave no guarantee of finding this Truth, many of those taking part in them had found it – or at least a slice of it. I agreed to his terms on the condition that I took part.

It would be nice if I could say that during that EI in the summer of 1985, I at last cracked the code and all was revealed, but I am afraid that did not happen. However, enough *was* revealed for me to understand that the hidden agenda indeed existed – that it was vast, and that, with luck and persistence, I might catch glimpses of it from time to time. But of more significance to me ultimately, I got an inkling that the Truth is not really hidden, except by the ersatz reality our minds create as our solution to life's challenges.

When I heard that there was a one-to-one practice called Mind Clearing based on the same principles as Jake's retreat, I found a practitioner and signed up for sessions and, in due course, trained as a practitioner myself, as well as training to run EI retreats.

So running Grimstone had now served one of its main purposes. It had also introduced me to many different approaches and some wonderful and unusual people, particularly some of the group leaders, like Jake, who remain close friends today. Now, 30 years later, the Grimstone story takes a fresh twist for me. Three of my daughters – Sally, Claire and Alice – had all helped Jean and I run the place and they, too, became interested in EIs and Mind Clearing; so much so for Alice that she trained as a practitioner herself. And, having already written a successful book about Shiatsu,[8] she has now written this book about Mind Clearing. And I am absolutely delighted; the practice changed my own life for the better and I believe it richly deserves the wider exposure this long overdue book will give it.

Tony Whieldon
Perth, Canada
June 2015

NOTES

1. Eliot, G (1994) *Middlemarch*. Wordsworth Editions Limited, Hertfordshire, p.390.
2. Berner, C (2010; first published 1984) *Communication Mastery: A Manual for Clearers Vol III Mind Clearing*, p.8.

INTRODUCTION

1. That life is suffering is the first Noble Truth of Buddhism.
2. From a 2013 unpublished paper by Lawrence Noyes, 'What Is Clearing?', part of the Lawrence Noyes Year II Mind Clearing Training.

CHAPTER 1

1. See Norcross, JC, Vandenbos, GR, and Freedheim, DK (2011) *History of Psychotherapy: Continuity and Change* (2nd edition). American Psychological Association, Washington DC. Also see Engel, J (2009) *American Therapy: The Rise of Psychotherapy in the United States*. Gotham, New York.
2. The counterculture is particularly associated with the 'cultural revolution' of the 1960s which, it has been argued, was really a 'long decade', beginning in the mid-1950s and petering out in the mid-1970s.
3. See Cushman, P (1995) *Constructing the Self, Constructing America: A Cultural History of Psychotherapy*. Addison-Wesley, Reading, Massachusetts.
4. 'Noumenon' is a term used by the philosopher, Kant, as distinct from 'phenomenon', which is the world as we know it, the stuff we can see and feel. Noumenon is that which we cannot experience through our senses.
5. See de Michelis, E (2004) *A History of Modern Yoga, Patanjali and Western Esotericism*. Continuum Academic, London.
6. Mesmerism was developed by Anton Mesmer (1734–1815), an Austrian physician who developed the idea of animal magnetism. This was later known as hypnotism. He initially used magnets, placed on the body to regulate body fluids which, when out of balance, caused disease. In time, he stopped using magnets and preferred a version of laying on of hands for healing. Mesmerism was hugely popular in France and championed in America, in particular by Charles Poyen.
7. The Emmanuel Movement was started by the Reverend Elwood Worcester (1862–1940). It was a programme designed to bring science and religion together for mental and physical health and combined free medical examinations, lectures and one-to-one psychotherapy. It was hugely popular for a short time until the medical profession appreciated that it could ill afford to let it become more so. Yet, it had an influence on professional psychotherapy as a result of its successes and publications.

8.   This has been reprinted many times over the years and is readily available.

9.   Such as Fritz Perls, who founded Gestalt therapy. He was initially interested in Hubbard's work but equally swiftly put off it by the man himself.

10. This in-house method of self-examination is called *auditing*. It is difficult to find criticism of this. Though former members are often highly critical of the organisation as a whole, many were often drawn to it originally by the value they experienced in auditing and are happy to acknowledge this.

11. Such as Corydon, B (1996; first published 1987) *Hubbard: Messiah or Madman?* Barricade Books, Fort Lee, New Jersey; Reitman, J (2011) *Inside Scientology: America's Most Secretive Religion*. Houghton Mifflin Harcourt, New York; and Ross, MW (1998) Effects of Membership in Scientology on Personality: An Exploratory Study. *Journal for the Scientific Study of Religion* 27(4): 630–636.

12. See Atack, J, 'Possible origins for Dianetics and Scientology.' Available at http://home.snafu.de/tilman/j/origins6.html, accessed on 13 February 2015.

13. *Dharma* is a Sanskrit term meaning, roughly, universal principles. A dharma session consists of teachings on the basic laws and principles.

14. Swami Kriplalu or Kripalvananda was a master of Kundalini Yoga.

15. Swami Kripalvananda visited the United States between 1977 and 1981 and stayed mostly at the Kripalu Yoga Ashram in Pennsylvania and also in California. As his health began to fail in 1981, he returned to India where he died later that year.

16. The *Yoga Sutras* of Patanjali can be found in numerous translations. The one used here is: Ranganathan, S (2008) *Patanjali's Yoga Sutra*. Penguin Books, New Delhi, India.

17. Berner found that the mind cannot be finally dissolved through techniques such as Mind Clearing alone. In the end, in his opinion, surrendering to the divine, or love, or the highest one can conceive is the only way to finally find freedom from the mind and other contingent aspects of the human being.

18. For more on these, see Chapters 7 and 8.

19. See, for instance, Caplan, E (1998) *American Culture and the Birth of Psychotherapy*. University of California Press, Berkeley, p.151.

20. That is, the countries in Europe from which the immigrants came, from around the seventeenth century onwards.

21. Ibid.

22. Wolitzky, DL (2011) Psychoanalytic Theories of Psychotherapy. In Norcross, JC, Vandenbos, GR, and Freedheim, DK (eds) *History of Psychotherapy: Continuity and Change* (2nd edition). American Psychological Association, Washington DC, p.83.

23. For more on this, see Chapter 5 on why we should deal with the mind as a moral imperative.

CHAPTER 2

1.   He was not the only one to seek a better solution. For instance, Albert Ellis (1913–2007), one of the fathers of cognitive behavioural therapy, noted that

patients typically say to him, 'yes, I see exactly what bothered me now and why I was bothered by it; but I nevertheless still am bothered. Now, what can I do about that?' Quote from Dobson, K, and David, D (2001) Historical and Philosophical Bases of the Cognitive-Behavioral Therapies. In Dobson, K (ed) *Handbook of Cognitive Behavioral Therapies* (2nd edition). Guildford Press, New York, p.13.

2. Wolitzky, DL (2011) Psychoanalytic Theories of Psychotherapy. In Norcross, JC, Vandenbos, GR, and Freedheim, DK (eds) *History of Psychotherapy: Continuity and Change* (2nd edition). American Psychological Association, Washington DC, p.70.

3. The mind-cure movement was a loose band of people of different backgrounds who sought to put forward the view that mental health factors played an essential role in all diseases. Some took this so far as to suggest that all physical ills are the result of mental factors.

4. Pavlov is famous for his experiments with conditioning behaviour in dogs, but the work was taken up by behaviourists who argued that human psychological problems are also learned and we can, in consequence, learn new behaviours to deal with our difficulties.

5. Cognitive behavioural therapy came, in part, out of behaviourism.

6. Psychological projection is the idea that those aspects of ourselves which we supress and deny are attributed to others. So if a person denies their anger, for instance, they will project that anger and see it as a feature of the behaviour of others. Transference is the psychological transference of feelings about a parent or significant early figure in a person's life onto the therapist who serves to stand in for that person.

7. Cognitive behavioural therapy is a form of counselling or psychotherapy that sets out to deal with both the problematic ideas a person has as well as associated problematic behaviours.

8. Psychosynthesis is a psychotherapeutic model, transpersonal and humanistic, developed by Roberto Assagioli (1888–1974).

9. For more on attitude clearing, see Chapter 7.

10. Unconditional positive regard involves an approach to the client that is supportive and systematic. Rogers asserted that this was the most important element of psychotherapy. With this supportive regard from the therapist, the client is able to access their own powers of understanding and healing for themselves with no further intervention or method.

11. See communication cycles, Chapter 6.

12. Berner, C (2009; first published 1984) *The Basics of Clearing: Clearing Manual Vol II*, p.20.

13. For how the mind comes into being, see Chapter 3.

14. From Chuang Tzu, 'The Dexterous Butcher'. Available at www.bopsecrets.org/gateway/passages/chuang-tzu.htm, accessed on 15 May 2015.

15. The Way is a Japanese and Chinese notion of the true, spiritual path towards unity. Anything practised as Way has a quality of flow and no-mind.

16. Berner, C (2010; first published 1984) *Communication Mastery: A Manual for Clearers Vol III Mind Clearing*, p.18.

17. This can be appreciated through mindfulness meditation (see Chapter 11).

CHAPTER 3

1. See Ranganathan, S (2008) *Patanjali's Yoga Sutra*. Penguin Books, New Delhi, India.

2. Berner, C (2014; first published 1984) *Communication Mastery: A Manual for Clearers Vol I The Mind*, p.29.

3. See Ranganathan, op. cit., p.277: 'Because people are generally ignorant about several issues – that they have *vasana-s,* the rules of Nature, the fact that their mind is an entity of Nature, and the fact that *they are distinct from their mind* – they repeatedly have rude awakenings to psychic impulses, forces and events that appear to arise without their consent or control.'

4. For more on the Enlightenment Intensive, see Chapter 10.

5. Ranganathan, op. cit., p.288.

6. Berner developed his Enlightenment Intensive (EI) workshops because he saw that people who had a sense of who they were, that is, as individuals distinct from their minds, tended to progress more quickly in other work. The EI was designed to give people the chance to glimpse who they were as individuals apart from their minds or personalities and de-identify from the mind, even if only for a moment. He developed the EI to help people experience this directly.

7. Nature is understood by Patanjali to be everything that is not the person or individual. That includes the mind and all its aspects, such as personality or ego. It also includes the world. He regards animals as being individuals, so aspects of what we might think of as the natural world are not strictly nature as he see it.

8. Ranganathan, op. cit., p.272.

9. For instance, see Deuteronomy 30:19. God gives people the choice between life and death, and we must choose life to be with God.

10. Ranganathan, op. cit., pp.96–97.

11. See Chapter 4.

12. Ranganathan, op. cit., p.98.

13. In some Buddhist schools, samsara (ordinary life) is actually identical with nirvana (Heaven). The difference is in our perception. So to separate out the sacred and profane, physical and metaphysical, is to be trapped in the mind's dualistic thinking.

14. There is actually some debate about whether people are born with some mind. If one has sympathy for transmigration of souls, or reincarnation, then it is inevitable that we are in fact born with minds. But this is not a necessary belief. Berner's model is true for the development of human beings whether one believes we actually started a long time before our current incarnations or began with this life we are living now.

15. The Garden of Eden in The Bible (Genesis 2).

16. The enlightened state is of course not accepted even as a possibility in some approaches. Since it is a condition outside the dualistic condition, it cannot be described through language and is, by definition, unknowable in the usual state of consciousness. The account of the mind given here does not depend on the enlightened state being possible, yet the pre-self-conscious state of unity is sometimes likened to the enlightened state.

17. Berner, C (2009; edited by Lawrence Noyes) *Emotion Mastery, A Manual for Clearers*, p.84.

18. Berner, C (2014; first published 1984) *Communication Mastery: A Manual for Clearers Vol I The Mind*, p.37.

19. Matthew 18:3 states: 'Truly I tell you, unless you change and become like little children, you will never enter the kingdom of heaven.'

20. See Genesis 1:9.

21. See Genesis 3.

22. Projection, as it is used in psychoanalysis and psychotherapy, is a theory developed by Freud. He posited that anything we do not accept about ourselves is something we particularly notice in others or the world in general. So, for instance, if we deny our anger, we will very likely be very sensitive to anger in others and may be critical of them for being angry. He noted that we split off from those things we cannot accept in ourselves and *project* them onto others. In Mind Clearing, the mind is in fact a projection of what we have resisted which we project onto the world.

23. Berner, C (2010; first published 1984) *Communication Mastery: A Manual for Clearers Vol III Mind Clearing*, p.98.

24. Berner, C (2009; first published 1984) *The Basics of Clearing: Clearing Manual Vol II*, p.33

25. For more information on this technique, known as *communication to other*, see Chapter 10.

26. Berner, C (2014; first published 1984) *Communication Mastery: A Manual for Clearers Vol I The Mind*, p.36.

27. See Ranganathan, op. cit., p.144.

28. Ibid., pp.130–136.

29. 'The other is not "who" you are, it is a different unique individual, so its attribute of "who it is" is not the same as yours. Its attributes of existence, unity, and ability to act, however, are the same as yours, so you are in a state of the sameness of your knowledge of these three attributes with the corresponding three attributes of you. In other words, you are conscious of your knowledge of these three of the other's attributes. In this case, your state of consciousness includes your knowledge of that other as a unitary existence that acts, but not your knowledge of who that other is.' From Berner, C, *The Enlightenment Intensive Masters Manual*. Available at www.charlesberner.org, accessed July 2013.

CHAPTER 4

1. Berner, C (2010; first published 1984) *Communication Mastery: A Manual for Clearers Vol III Mind Clearing*, p.133.
2. Ranganathan, S (2008) *Patanjali's Yoga Sutra*. Penguin Books, New Delhi, India.
3. Ibid., p.275.
4. Ibid., p.181.
5. Ibid., p.143.
6. Ibid., p.186.
7. This map, a little different in detail from what is shown here, is from Noyes, L (2014) Berner, *The Mind*, p.90 (unpublished).
8. For more on this, see Chapter 5.
9. For more on this, see Chapter 4.
10. For more on the personality, see Chapter 4.
11. Psychoanalysis has made a great deal of use of free association in which the patient associates from one thing to another. Freud thought that this was accessing the unconscious, which could then be examined. It has some workability but is very inefficient as a method of helping people deal with their minds.
12. For more on do-it-yourself Mind Clearing, see Chapter 10.
13. Berner, C (2014; first published 1984) *Communication Mastery: A Manual for Clearers Vol I The Mind*, p.54.
14. Ibid., p.47.
15. Ibid., p.58.
16. Ibid., p.61.
17. Ibid., p.45.
18. Ranganathan, op. cit., p.143.
19. Berner, op. cit., p.83.
20. Ibid., p.89.
21. Ranganathan, op. cit., p.249.
22. Ibid., p.310.
23. Berner preferred the prefix 'un-' to 'non-' as it was for him a stronger opposite. Though in formal logic the opposite of X is non-X, he felt that un-X was a more thorough negation, so that is the opposite given here.
24. He is not alone in this; see, for instance, Dethlefsen, T, and Dahlke, R (2002) *The Healing Power of Illness: Understanding What Your Symptoms Are Telling You*. Vega Books, London.
25. Irving, J (2012) *In One Person*. Vintage Canada, Toronto.
26. Ranganathan, op. cit., p.278.
27. Ibid., p.83.
28. Ibid., pp.83–84.
29. This is not unlike Christ's parable in Matthew 7:24–27: 'Therefore everyone who hears these words of mine and puts them into practice is like a wise man

who built his house on the rock. **25** The rain came down, the streams rose, and the winds blew and beat against that house; yet it did not fall, because it had its foundation on the rock. **26** But everyone who hears these words of mine and does not put them into practice is like a foolish man who built his house on sand. **27** The rain came down, the streams rose, and the winds blew and beat against that house, and it fell with a great crash.'

30.   Ranganathan, op. cit., p.141.

31.   Ibid., pp.142–143.

32.   Ibid., p.256.

33.   Ibid., p.270.

34.   Ibid., p.270.

35.   See Ibid., p.141, for more on the ego in Indian philosophy.

36.   Ibid, p.277.

37.   Ibid, p.291.

38.   A direct experience of who you are is what the Enlightenment Intensive workshops were designed to give the best opportunity of having.

39.   I use 'subconscious' here rather than 'unconscious' to emphasise that nothing is ever finally unconscious but lies below the level of consciousness *at the moment*.

40.   Ranganathan, op. cit., p.221.

CHAPTER 5

1.   Ranganathan, S (2008) *Patanjali's Yoga Sutra*. Penguin Books, New Delhi, India, p.87.

2.   Ibid., p.272.

3.   Ibid.

4.   Ibid., pp.105, 289.

5.   Ibid., p.205: 'That which covers the light [the knowing self] is destroyed [by controlling the mind].'

6.   Ibid., p.280.

7.   Ranganathan, op. cit., p.99.

8.   Berner, C (2010; first published 1984) *Communication Mastery: A Manual for Clearers Vol III Mind Clearing*, p.16.

9.   The Protestant Reformation was sparked in Europe, partly by the excesses of the Roman Catholic Church, but also on theological questions such as whether we can and should pursue our personal salvation through correct living, as protesters suggested, or whether this was effectively out of our hands by God's omniscience, or predestination.

10.   See Chapter 8 for a discussion about karma.

11.   Ranganathan, op. cit., pp.142–143.

12.   Ranganathan, op. cit., p.166.

13.   Ranganathan, op. cit., p.174.

14.   Ranganathan, op. cit., p.304.

CHAPTER 6

1. Ranganathan, S (2008) *Patanjali's Yoga Sutra.* Penguin Books, New Delhi, India, p.155.
2. For information on the victim complex, see Chapter 4.
3. Berner, C (2009; first published 1984) *The Basics of Clearing: Clearing Manual Vol II*, p.39.
4. Ibid., p.40.
5. Ibid., p.49.
6. Ibid., p.92.
7. Ranganathan, op. cit., p.81.
8. Berner, op. cit., p.49.
9. Berner, op. cit., p.53.
10. See Chapter 4.
11. See discussion on series, Chapter 4.
12. Berner, op. cit., p.101.
13. Berner, op. cit., p.57.
14. Berner, op. cit., p.63.

CHAPTER 7

1. See Chapter 4 for a discussion on the nature of conflict.
2. This may be akin to the description Patanjali gives of the state we can attain, beyond engrossments but which is not yet enlightenment. See Ranganathan (2008) *Patanjali's Yoga Sutra.* Penguin Books, New Delhi, India, pp.118–119.
3. Berner, C (2010; first published 1984) *Communication Mastery: A Manual for Clearers Vol III Mind Clearing*, p.42.
4. Berner, C (2009; edited by Lawrence Noyes) *Emotion Mastery, A Manual for Clearers*, p.85.
5. Ranganathan, op. cit., p.183.
6. Ranganathan, op. cit., p.77.
7. Berner, C (2010; first published 1984) *Communication Mastery: A Manual for Clearers Vol III Mind Clearing*, p.15.
8. See Chapter 5.
9. See Chapters 7 and 10.
10. Berner, op. cit., p.44.
11. Berner, op. cit., p.57.
12. This is a phrase coined by Marshall McLuhan.
13. Berner, op. cit., p.109.
14. For a discussion on victim states, see Chapter 4.
15. Berner, op. cit., p.46.
16. Berner, op. cit., p.84.
17. Berner, op. cit., p.78.
18. Berner, op. cit., p.22.
19. Ranganathan, op. cit., p.128.

20. Ranganathan, op. cit., p.221.
21. Ranganathan, op. cit., p.145.
22. See also Ranganathan, op. cit., p.247.

CHAPTER 8

1. Ranganathan, S (2008) *Patanjali's Yoga Sutra*. Penguin Books, New Delhi, India, p.92.
2. Berner, C (2009; first published 1984) *The Basics of Clearing: Clearing Manual Vol II*, p.188.
3. According to Patanjali, it is the individual will of the person that brings us into sin. See Ranganathan, op. cit., p.288.
4. Ranganathan, op. cit., p.147.
5. Berner, op. cit., p.190.
6. Berner, op. cit., p.192.
7. Mind Clearing, along with most other professions, has a code of ethics which requires coaches to disclose information given in sessions if there is a danger to the client or to others in contact with the client.
8. Berner, op. cit., p.199.
9. Ranganathan, op. cit., p.149.

CHAPTER 9

1. See Chapter 6 for a discussion on the clearing communication cycle.

CHAPTER 10

1. If you practise vipassana meditation, you will start to become aware of this. Vipassana is a Buddhist meditation in which the practitioner focuses on the body and mind. It is said that the Buddha himself practised this kind of meditation.
2. Ranganathan, S (2008) *Patanjali's Yoga Sutra*. Penguin Books, New Delhi, India, p.107.
3. Ranganathan, op. cit., p.133.
4. Janov, A (1970) *Primal Scream*. Putnam, New York. (There have been several editions of this book since 1970.)
5. Engel, J (2009) *American Therapy: The Rise of Psychotherapy in the United States*. Gotham, New York, p.180.
6. For more information about Emotion Clearing, it is recommended to look for Mind Clearing practitioners locally as many have also trained in this work.
7. For a full account of the Enlightenment Intensive, see Noyes, L (1998) *The Enlightenment Intensive: Dyad Communication as a Tool for Self-Realization*. North Atlantic Books, Berkeley, California; also see Chapman, J (1988) 'Tell Me Who You Are.' Available at www.enlightenment-intensives.org.uk/TellMeWhoYouAre%28part1%29.pdf, accessed on 18 May 2015.
8. See Muni, Y (2005) 'Natural Yoga.' Available at www.charlesberner.org/Design/Natural_Meditation_2004.pdf, accessed on 31 December 2014.

9. Also called Natural Meditation.

10. See Levitt, AJ (ed) (2004) *Pilgrim of Love: The Life and Teachings of Swami Kripalu.* Monkfish Book Publishing, Rhinebeck, New York.

11. Kishi, A, and Whieldon, A (2011) *Sei-ki: Life in Resonance – The Secret Art of Shiatsu.* Singing Dragon, London, p.28.

12. For instances of speaking in tongues in the Bible, see Acts 2:4.

13. See www.buqi.net/en/systems/buqi.htm, accessed on 11 September 2015.

14. Developed from Shinto by Haruchika Noguchi and the Seitai Society of Japan.

15. For more on states, see Chapter 7.

16. For more on the levels of the mind, see Chapter 4.

AFTERWORD

1. Jiddu Krishnamurti was a writer and speaker on spiritual and philosophical matters. Taken up at a young age by a theosophist, Annie Besant, and groomed to become a great teacher, he left the Theosophical Society and later gained a large international following.

2. Brockwood Park School is a co-educational boarding school in the UK founded by Krishnamurti in 1969.

3. The centre in Devon is now a private home once more.

4. The Esalen Institute (Big Sur, California, USA) is well known for its alternative workshops. It has been the birthplace and haven for many forms of self-help and therapy since the 1960s.

5. Ram Dass, born Richard Alpert, was a Harvard academic who worked with Timothy Leary on the infamous 'acid tests' in the 1960s. In the 1960s he went to India and has since devoted his life to spiritual development and teaching.

6. Professor Jake Chapman, Demos Associate and former Professor of Energy Systems at the Open University, UK.

7. Founded in 1969, the Open University is a distance-learning, nationwide university based in the UK.

8. Kishi, A, and Whieldon, A (2011) *Sei-ki: Life in Resonance – The Secret Art of Shiatsu.* Singing Dragon, London.

INDEX

Page references to Notes are indicated by
the letter 'n'

blame 184, 186

body 39, 44, 83, 87, 90, 211

    and communication 113, 114, 119

    emotions 16, 35, 76, 77, 91, 162, 204

        Emotion Clearing 210–12

    identification with 84, 85, 86

    mind/body approach 19, 21, 204, 211

    sensations 46, 77, 78, 80, 211

    temperature 168

    tensions/discomfort 54, 79, 204, 211

    trauma locked into 79–80

brain 90

breathing, disrupted 211

Brockwood Park, Hampshire 227, 238n

'buddhi' aspect of mind 94

Buddhism 108, 213, 214, 230n, 233n

Buqi (Chinese health practice) 215

Calvinism 24

Campbell, Jean 228

Caplan, E 231n

casual connections 220–1

casual experiences 66, 67, 68, 72

change 80, 85

    as moral imperative 108–11

Chapman, Jake 228, 238n

chi gong 215

choice/freedom of choice 31, 42, 44, 105,
    107

    in meditation 38–9

    structure and content of mind 74, 83

Christianity 61, 109, 184, 187, 215

    Protestant Reformation 108, 236n

    see also Judaeo-Christian tradition

Chuang Tzu 232n

circles 71–3

clearing communication cycle 118–22,
    205

    formula 122

    four steps 144

    maintaining 197–8

    making concrete 121

    and Mind Clearing 119, 145–6

    see also communication; instruction,
        giving

cognitive therapy/cognitive behavioural
    therapy (CBT) 19, 30, 232n

colonialism 109

communication

    ability to communicate, raising 34

    basic cycles 117–18

    and body 119

    breaking down 117

    conscious 33

    direct, mind as substitute for 33, 48–51

    distorted perceptions (of others) 51

    and dualistic mind structure 61

    failed 48, 60, 115, 174, 219

    indirect, attitude as 169

    by infants 152

    and language 113, 114

    mediated 114–15

    message recognition 34

    mind controlling relating 51–2

    and progress in therapy 32–3

    pure 113–14

    pushing away and pulling closer 52

    responsibility for 115–16

    and thought 112, 113, 114

    turning one's back on the world 49–50,
        51

    and understanding 112

    see also clearing communication cycle;
        thinking/thought

community, vs individual 25

conceptualisation of ideas 28–9

confession 187, 189

conflict 19, 49, 150

    inner 13, 63

    nature of 62–4

connected experiences 66–77

    attitude connections 77

    Berner on 69, 71, 72, 73, 75

    case study 67–8

    casual 66, 67, 68, 72

    circles 71–3

    cotton wool narrative 75–6

    mental machines 73–5

    mind structures 67

    multiple connections 75–7

    music narrative 75–6

transfer 113, 114
unwanted thoughts 74
see also communication
thought *see* thinking/thought
time and un-time 85
Ting the butcher (Chinese story) 33
tiredness 87
tolerance building 29
transference 30, 31, 197, 232n
transmigration of souls 233n
transpersonal psychotherapies 20
trauma
   dramatisation of 78–9
   emotional experiences 77–9, 81
   and memory 93
   non-understanding 78, 79
   physical experiences 79–81, 83
   reaction to 63
   storage of 210

unconditional positive regard 31, 232n
unconscious, the 24, 30, 44–5, 51, 78, 184
understanding 32, 112, 145
un-groundedness 87
uniqueness 42
United States
   as metaphorical space 24
   psychotherapy 24
   twentieth-century 18
unity, vs duality 61
un-mass 86–7
un-space 86, 87
un-time 85

vagueness in communication 124
Vandenbos, GR 230n
victim state 34, 100–1
vipassana meditation 211, 237n

will 42, 104–7, 109, 189
   Patanjali on 104–5
wisdom 107
withdrawal from the world 49–50, 51, 101
withholding 60, 118, 135, 136, 196, 201
Wolitzky, DL 231n, 232n
Worcester, Elwood 230n

yoga 62, 108, 111
   see also Kundalini Yoga
Yoga Sutras (Patanjali) 22, 93, 111, 231n

Zen Buddhism 213, 214